MW00423383

Hard Press

SNAKE AND SWORD

*Contents*BY

THE SEARING OF A SOUL

PART III.

THE SAVING OF A SOUL

6

PART I.

THE WELDING OF A SOUL.

CHAPTER I.

The snake and the soul.

When Colonel Matthew Devon de Warrenne, V.C., D.S.O., of the Queen's Own (118th) Bombay Lancers, pinned his Victoria Cross to the bosom of his dying wife's night-dress, in token of his recognition that she was the braver of the twain, he was not himself.

He was beside himself with grief.

Afterwards he adjured the sole witness of this impulsive and emotional act, Major John Decies, never to mention his "damned theatrical folly" to any living soul, and to excuse him on the score of an ancient sword-cut on the head and two bad sun-strokes.

For the one thing in heaven above, on the earth beneath, or in the waters under the earth, that Colonel de Warrenne feared, was breach of good form and stereotyped convention.

And the one thing he loved was the dying woman.

This last statement applies also to Major John Decies, of the Indian Medical Service, Civil Surgeon of Bimariabad, and may even be expanded, for the one thing he ever *had* loved was the dying woman....

Colonel Matthew Devon de Warrenne did the deed that won him his Victoria Cross, in the open, in the hot sunlight and in hot blood, sword in hand and with hot blood on the sword-hand—fighting for his life.

His wife did the deed that moved him to transfer the Cross to her, in darkness, in cold blood, in loneliness, sickness and silence—fighting for the life of her unborn child against an unseen foe.

Colonel de Warrenne's type of brave deed has been performed thousands of times and wherever brave men have fought.

His wife's deed of endurance, presence of mind, self-control and cool courage is rarer, if not unique.

To appreciate this fully, it must be known that she had a horror of snakes, so terrible as to amount to an obsession, a mental deformity, due, doubtless, to the fact that her father (Colonel Mortimer Seymour Stukeley) died of snake-bite before her mother's eyes, a few hours before she herself was born.

8

Bearing this in mind, judge of the conduct that led Colonel de Warrenne, distraught, to award her his Cross "For Valour".

One oppressive June evening, Lenore de Warrenne returned from church (where she had, as usual, prayed fervently that her soon-expected first-born might be a daughter), and entered her dressing-room. Here her Ayah divested her of hat, dress, and boots, and helped her into the more easeful tea-gown and satin slippers.

"Bootlair wanting ishweets for dinner-table from go-down,[1] please, Mem-Sahib," observed Ayah, the change of garb accomplished.

"The butler wants sweets, does he? Give me my keys, then," replied Mrs. de Warrenne, and, rising with a sigh, she left the dressing-room and proceeded, *via* the dining-room (where she procured some small silver bowls, sweet-dishes, and trays), to the go-down or store-room, situate at the back of the bungalow and adjoining the "dispense-khana"—the room in which assemble the materials and ministrants of meals from the extra-mural "bowachi-khana" or kitchen. Unlocking the door of the go-down, Mrs. de Warrenne entered the small shelf-encircled room, and, stepping on to a low stool proceeded to fill the sweet-trays from divers jars, tins and boxes, with guava-cheese, crystallized ginger, *kulwa*, preserved mango and certain of the more sophisticated sweetmeats of the West.

It was after sunset and the *hamal* had not yet lit the lamps, so that this pantry, a dark room at mid-day, was far from light at that time. But for the fact that she knew exactly where everything was, and could put her hand on what she wanted, she would not have entered without a light.

For some minutes the unfortunate lady stood on the stool.

Having completed her task she stepped down backwards and, as her foot touched the ground, she knew *that she had trodden upon a snake.*

Even as she stood poised, one foot on the ground, the other on the stool, both hands gripping the high shelf, she felt the reptile whipping, writhing, jerking, lashing, flogging at her ankle and instep, coiling round her leg.... And in the fraction of a second the thought flashed through her mind: "If its head is under my foot, or too close to my foot for its fangs to reach me, I am safe while I remain as I am. If its head is free I am doomed—and matters cannot be any the worse for my keeping as I am."

And she kept as she was, with one foot on the stool, out of reach, and one foot on the snake.

And screamed?

No, called quietly and coolly for the butler, remembering that she had sent Nurse Beaton out, that her husband was at polo, that there were none but native servants in the house, and that if she raised an alarm they would take it, and with single heart consider each the safety of Number One.

"Boy!" she called calmly, though the room swam round her and a deadly faintness began to paralyse her limbs and loosen her hold upon the shelf—"Boy! Come here."

Antonio Ferdinand Xavier D'Souza, Goanese butler, heard and came.

"Mem-Sahib?" quoth he, at the door of the go-down.

"Bring a lamp quickly," said Lenore de Warrenne in a level voice.

The worthy Antonio, fat, spectacled, bald and wheezy, hurried away and peremptorily bade the *hamal*[2], son of a jungle-pig, to light and bring a lamp quickly.

The *hamal*, respectfully pointing out to the Bootlair Sahib that the daylight was yet strong and lusty enough to shame and smother any lamp, complied with deliberation and care, polishing the chimney, trimming the wick, pouring in oil and generally making a satisfactory and commendable job of it.

Lenore de Warrenne, sick, faint, sinking, waited ... waited ... waited ... gripping the shelf and fighting against her over-mastering weakness for the life of the unborn child that, even in that awful moment, she prayed might be a daughter.

After many cruelly long centuries, and as she swayed to fall, the good Antonio entered with the lamp. Her will triumphed over her falling body.

"Boy, I am standing on a snake!" said she coolly. "Put the lamp—"

But Antonio did not stay to "put" the lamp; incontinent he dropped it on the floor and fled yelling "Sap! Sap!" and that the Mem-Sahib was bitten, dying, dead—certainly dead; dead for hours.

And the brave soul in the little room waited ... waited ... waited ... gripping the shelf, and thinking of the coming daughter, and wondering whether she must die by snake-bite or fire—unborn—with her unhappy mother. For the fallen lamp had burst, the oil had caught fire, and the fire gave no light by which she could see what was beneath her foot—head, body, or tail of the lashing, squirming snake—as the flame flickered, rose and fell, burnt blue, swayed, roared in the draught of the door—did anything but give a light by which she could see as she bent over awkwardly, still gripping the shelf, one foot on the stool, further prevented from seeing by her loose draperies.

10

Soon she realized that in any case she could not see her foot without changing her position—a thing she would *not* do while there was hope—and strength to hold on. For hope there was, inasmuch as *she had not yet felt the stroke of the reptile's fangs.*

Again she reasoned calmly, though strength was ebbing fast; she must remain as she was till death by fire or suffocation was the alternative to flight—flight which was synonymous with death, for, as her other foot came down and she stepped off the snake, in that instant it would strike—if it had not struck already.

Meantime—to call steadily and coolly again.

This time she called to the *hamal*, a Bhil, engaged out of compassion, and likely, as a son of the jungle's sons, to be of more courage than the stall-fed butler in presence of dangerous beast or reptile.

"*Hamal*: I want you," she called coolly.

"Mem-Sahib?" came the reply from the lamp-room near by, and the man approached.

"That stupid butler has dropped a lamp and run away. Bring a pail of water quickly and call to the *malli*[3] to bring a pail of earth as you get it. Hasten!—and there is baksheesh," said Mrs. de Warrenne quietly in the vernacular.

Tap and pail were by the door of the back verandah. In a minute the *hamal* entered and flung a pail of water on the burning pool of oil, reducing the mass of blue lambent flames considerably.

"Now *hamal*," said the fainting woman, the more immediate danger confronted, "bring another lamp very quickly and put it on the shelf. Quick! don't stop to fill or to clean it."

Was the pricking, shooting pain the repeated stabbing of the snake's fangs or was it "pins and needles"? Was this deadly faintness death indeed, or was it only weakness?

In what seemed but a few more years the man reappeared carrying a lighted lamp, the which he placed upon a shelf.

"Listen," said Mrs. de Warrenne, "and have no fear, brave Bhil. I have *caught* a snake. Get a knife quickly and cut off its head while I hold it."

The man glancing up, appeared to suppose that his mistress held the snake on the shelf, hurried away, and rushed back with the cook's big kitchen-knife gripped dagger-wise in his right hand.

11

"Do you see the snake?" she managed to whisper. "Under my foot! Quick! It is moving ... moving ... moving *out*."

With a wild Bhil cry the man flung himself down upon his hereditary dread foe and slashed with the knife.

Mrs. de Warrenne heard it scratch along the floor, grate on a nail, and crush through the snake.

"Are!! Dead, Mem-Sahib!! Dead!! See, I have cut off its head! Are!!!! Wah!! The brave mistress!——"

As she collapsed, Mrs. de Warrenne saw the twitching body of a large cobra with its head severed close to its neck. Its head had just protruded from under her foot and she had saved the unborn life for which she had fought so bravely by just keeping still.... She had won her brief decoration with the Cross by—keeping still. (Her husband had won his permanent right to it by extreme activity.) ... Had she moved she would have been struck instantly, for the reptile was, by her, uninjured, merely nipped between instep and floor.

Having realized this, Lenore de Warrenne fainted and then passed from fit to fit, and her child—a boy—was born that night. Hundreds of times during the next few days the same terrible cry rang from the sick-room through the hushed bungalow: "It is under my foot! It is moving ... moving ... moving ... *out!*"

* * * * *

"If I had to make a prophecy concerning this young fella," observed the broken-hearted Major John Decies, I.M.S., Civil Surgeon of Bimariabad, as he watched old Nurse Beaton performing the baby's elaborate ablutions and toilet, "I should say that he will *not* grow up fond of snakes—not if there is anything in the 'pre-natal influence' theory."

12

PART II.

THE SEARING OF A SOUL.

CHAPTER II.

THE SWORD AND THE SNAKE.

Colonel Matthew Devon De Warrenne, commanding the Queen's Own (118th) Bombay Lancers, was in good time, in his best review-order uniform, and in a terrible state of mind.

He strode from end to end of the long verandah of his bungalow with clank of steel, creak of leather, and groan of travailing soul. As the top of his scarlet, blue and gold turban touched the lamp that hung a good seven feet above his spurred heels he swore viciously.

Almost for the first time in his hard-lived, selfish life he had been thwarted, flouted, cruelly and evilly entreated, and the worst of it was that his enemy was—not a man whom he could take by the throat, but—Fate.

Fate had dealt him a cruel blow, and he felt as he would have done had he, impotent, seen one steal the great charger that champed and pawed there at the door, and replace it by a potter's donkey. Nay, worse—for he had *loved* Lenore, his wife, and Fate had stolen her away and replaced her by a squealing brat.

Within a year of his marriage his wife was dead and buried, and his son alive and—howling. He could hear him (curse him!).

The Colonel glanced at his watch, producing it from some mysterious recess beneath his belted golden sash and within his pale blue tunic.

Not yet time to ride to the regimental parade-ground and lead his famous corps to its place on the brigade parade-ground for the New Year Review and march-past.

As he held the watch at the length of its chain and stared, half-comprehending, his hand—the hand of the finest swordsman in the Indian Army—shook.

Lenore gone: a puling, yelping whelp in her place.... A tall, severe-looking elderly woman entered the verandah by a distant door and approached the savage, miserable soldier. Nurse Beaton.

"*Will* you give your son a name, Sir?" she said, and it was evident in voice and manner that the question had been asked before and had received an unsatisfactory, if not unprintable; reply. Every line of feature and form seemed to express indignant resentment. She had nursed and foster-mothered the child's mother, and—unlike the man—had found the baby the chiefest consolation of her cruel grief, and already loved it not only for its idolized mother's sake, but with the devotion of a childless child-lover.

14

"The christening is fixed for to-day, Sir, as I have kept reminding you, Sir," she added.

She had never liked the Colonel—nor considered him "good enough" for her tender, dainty darling, "nearly three times her age and no better than he ought to be".

"Name?" snarled Colonel Matthew Devon de Warrenne. "Name the little beast? Call him what you like, and then drown him." The tight-lipped face of the elderly nurse flushed angrily, but before she could make the indignant reply that her hurt and scandalized look presaged, the Colonel added:—

"No, look here, call him *Damocles*, and done with it. The Sword hangs over him too, I suppose, and he'll die by it, as all his ancestors have done. Yes—"

"It's not a nice name, Sir, to my thinking," interrupted the woman, "not for an only name—and for an only child. Let it be a second or third name, Sir, if you want to give him such an outlandish one."

She fingered her new black dress nervously with twitching hands and the tight lips trembled.

"He's to be named Damocles and nothing else," replied the Master, and, as she turned away with a look of positive hate, he added sardonically:—

"And then you can call him 'Dam' for short, you know, Nurse."

Nurse Beaton bridled, clenched her hands, and stiffened visibly. Had the man been her social equal or any other than her master, her pent-up wrath and indignation would have broken forth in a torrent of scathing abuse.

"Never would I call the poor motherless lamb *Dam*, Sir," she answered with restraint.

"Then call him *Dummy!* Good morning, Nurse," snapped the Colonel.

As she turned to go, with a bitter sigh, she asked in the hopeless tone of one who knows the waste of words:—

"You will not repent—I mean relent—and come to the christening of your only son this afternoon, Sir?"

"Good morning, Nurse," observed Colonel Matthew Devon de Warrenne, and resumed his hurried pacing of the verandah.

* * * * *

It is not enough that a man love his wife dearly and hold her the sweetest, fairest, and best of women—he should tell her so, morning and night.

There is a proverb (the unwisdom of many and the poor wit of one) that says *Actions speak louder than Words*. Whether this is the most untrustworthy of an untrustworthy class of generalizations is debateable.

Anyhow, let no husband or lover believe it. Vain are the deeds of dumb devotion, the unwearying forethought, the tender care, the gifts of price, and the priceless gifts of attentive, watchful guard and guide, the labours of Love—all vain. Silent is the speech of Action.

But resonant loud is the speech of Words and profitable their investment in the Mutual Alliance Bank.

"*Love me, love my Dog?*" Yes—and look to the dog for a dog's reward.

"*Do not show me that you love me—tell me so.*" Far too true and pregnant ever to become a proverb.

Colonel de Warrenne had omitted to tell his wife so—after she had accepted him—- and she had died thinking herself loveless, unloved, and stating the fact.

This was the bitterest drop in the bitter cup of the big, dumb, well-meaning man.

And now she would never know....

She had thought herself unloved, and, nerve-shattered by her terrible experience with the snake, had made no fight for life when the unwanted boy was born. For the sake of a girl she would have striven to live—but a boy, a boy can fend for himself (and takes after his father)....

Almost as soon as Lenore Seymour Stukeley had landed in India (on a visit with her sister Yvette to friends at Bimariabad), delighted, bewildered, depolarized, Colonel Matthew Devon de Warrenne had burst with a blaze of glory into her hitherto secluded, narrow life—a great pale-blue, white-and-gold wonder, clanking and jingling, resplendent, bemedalled, ruling men, charging at the head of thundering squadrons—a half-god (and to Yvette he had seemed a whole-god).

He had told her that he loved her, told her once, and had been accepted.

Once! Only once told her that he loved her, that she was beautiful, that he was hers to command to the uttermost. Only once! What could *she* know of the changed life, the absolute renunciation of pleasant bachelor vices, the pulling up short, and all those actions that speak more softly than words?

16

What could she know of the strength and depth of the love that could keep such a man as the Colonel from the bar, the bridge-table, the race-course and the Paphian dame? Of the love that made him walk warily lest he offend one for whom his quarter of a century, and more, of barrack and bachelor-bungalow life, made him feel so utterly unfit and unworthy? What could she know of all that he had given up and delighted to give up—now that he truly loved a true woman? The hard-living, hard-hearted, hard-spoken man had become a gentle frequenter of his wife's tea-parties, her companion at church, her constant attendant—never leaving the bungalow, save for duty, without her.

To those who knew him it was a World's Marvel; to her, who knew him not, it was nothing at all—normal, natural. And being a man who spoke only when he must, who dreaded the expression of any emotion, and who foolishly thought that actions speak louder than words, he had omitted to tell her daily—or even weekly or monthly—that he loved her; and she had died pitying herself and reproaching him.

Fate's old, old game of Cross Purposes. Major John Decies, reserved, high-minded gentleman, loving Lenore de Warrenne (and longing to tell her so daily), with the one lifelong love of a steadfast nature; Yvette Stukeley, reserved, high-minded gentlewoman, loving Colonel de Warrenne, and longing to escape from Bimariabad before his wedding to her sister, and doing so at the earliest possible date thereafter: each woman losing the man who would have been her ideal husband, each man losing the woman who would have been his ideal wife.

Yvette Stukeley returned to her uncle and guardian, General Sir Gerald Seymour Stukeley, K.C.B., K.C.S.I., at Monksmead, nursing a broken heart, and longed for the day when Colonel de Warrenne's child might be sent home to her care.

Major John Decies abode at Bimariabad, also nursing a broken heart (though he scarcely realized the fact), watched over the son of Lenore de Warrenne, and greatly feared for him.

The Major was an original student of theories and facts of Heredity and Pre-natal Influence. Further he was not wholly hopeful as to the effect of all the *post*-natal influences likely to be brought to bear upon a child who grew up in the bungalow, and the dislike of Colonel Matthew Devon de Warrenne.

Upon the infant Damocles, Nurse Beaton, rugged, snow-capped volcano, lavished the tender love of a mother; and in him Major John Decies, deep-running still water, took the interest of a father. The which was the better for the infant Damocles in that his real father had no interest to take and no love to lavish. He frankly disliked the child—the outward and visible sign, the daily reminder of the cruel loss he so deeply felt and fiercely resented.

Yet, strangely enough, he would not send the child home. Relations who could receive it he had none, and he declined to be beholden to its great-uncle, General Sir

Gerald Seymour Stukeley, and its aunt Yvette Stukeley, in spite of the warmest invitations from the one and earnest entreaties from the other.

Nurse Beaton fed, tended, clothed and nursed the baby by day; a worshipping ayah wheeled him abroad, and, by night, slept beside his cot; a devoted sepoy-orderly from the regiment guarded his cavalcade, and, when permitted, proudly bore him in his arms.

Major John Decies visited him frequently, watched and waited, waited and watched, and, though not a youth, "thought long, long thoughts".

He also frequently laid his views and theories on paternal duties before Colonel de Warrenne, until pointedly asked by that officer whether he had no duties of his own which might claim his valuable time.

Years rolled by, after the incorrigible habit of years, and the infant Damocles grew and developed into a remarkably sturdy, healthy, intelligent boy, as cheerful, fearless, impudent, and irrepressible as the heart of the Major could desire—and with a much larger vocabulary than any one could desire, for a baby.

On the fifth anniversary of his birthday he received a matutinal call from Major Decies, who was returning from his daily visit to the Civil Hospital.

The Major bore a birthday present and a very anxious, undecided mind.

"Good morrow, gentle Damocles," he remarked, entering the big verandah adown which the chubby boy pranced gleefully to meet his beloved friend, shouting a welcome, and brandishing a sword designed, and largely constructed, by himself from a cleaning-rod, a tobacco-tin lid, a piece of wood, card-board and wire.

"Thalaam, Major Thahib," he said, flinging himself bodily upon that gentleman. "I thaw cook cut a fowl's froat vis morning. It squorked boofly."

"Did it? Alas, that I missed those pleasing-er-squorks," replied the Major, and added: "This is thy natal day, my son. Thou art a man of five."

"I'm a debble. I'm a *norful* little debble," corrected Damocles, cheerfully and with conviction.

"Incidentally. But you are five also," persisted the senior man.

"It's my birfday to-day," observed the junior.

"I just said so."

18

"*That* you didn't, Major Thahib. This is a thword. Father's charger's got an over-weach. Jumping. He says it's a dam-nuithanth."

"Oh, that's a sword, is it? And 'Fire' has got an over-reach. And it's a qualified nuisance, is it?"

"Yeth, and the mare is coughing and her *thythe* is a blathted fool for letting her catch cold."

"The mare has a cold and the *syce*[4] is a qualified fool, is he? H'm! I think it's high time you had a look in at little old England, my son, what? And who made you this elegant rapier? Ochterlonie Sahib or—who?" (Lieutenant Lord Ochterlonie was the Adjutant of the Queen's Greys, a friend of Colonel de Warrenne, an ex-admirer of his late wife, and a great pal of his son.)

"'Tithn't a waper. It'th my thword. I made it mythelf."

"Who helped?"

"Nobody. At leatht, Khodadad Khan, Orderly, knocked the holes in the tin like I showed him—or elthe got the Farrier Thargeant to do it, and thaid *he* had."

"Yes—but who told you how to make it like this? Where did you see a hand-part like this? It isn't like Daddy's sword, nor Khodadad Khan's *tulwar*. Where did you copy it?"

"I didn't copy it.... I shot ten rats wiv a bow-and-arrow last night. At leatht—I don't think I shot ten. Nor one. I don't think I didn't, pwaps."

"But hang it all, the thing's an Italian rapier, by Gad. Some one *must* have shown you how to make the thing, or you've got a picture. It's a *pukka*[5] mediaeval rapier."

"No it'th not. It'th my thword. I made it.... Have a jolly fight"—and the boy struck an extraordinarily correct fencing attitude—left hand raised in balance, sword poised, legs and feet well placed, the whole pose easy, natural, graceful.

Curiously enough, the sword was held horizontal instead of pointing upward, a fact which at once struck the observant and practised eye of Major John Decies, sometime champion fencer.

"Who's been teaching you fencing?" he asked.

"What ith 'fenthing'? Let'th have a fight," replied the boy.

"Stick me here, Dam," invited the Major, seating himself and indicating the position of the heart. "Bet you can't."

The boy lunged, straight, true, gracefully, straightening all his limbs except his right leg, rigidly, strongly, and the "sword" bent upward from the spot on which the man's finger had just rested.

"Gad! Who *has* taught you to lunge? I shall have a bruise there, and perhaps—live. Who's behind all this, young fella? Who taught you to stand so, and to lunge? Ochterlonie Sahib or Daddy?"

"Nobody. What is 'lunge'? Will you buy me a little baby-camel to play with and teach tricks? Perhaps it would sit up and beg. Do camelth lay eggth? Chucko does. Millions and lakhs. You get a thword, too, and we'll fight every day. Yeth. All day long——"

"Good morning, Sir," said Nurse Beaton, bustling into the verandah from the nursery. "He's as mad as ever on swords and fighting, you see. It's a soldier he'll be, the lamb. He's taken to making that black orderly pull out his sword when he's in uniform. Makes him wave and jab it about. Gives me the creeps—with his black face and white eyes and all. You won't *encourage* the child at it, will you, Sir? And his poor Mother the gentlest soul that ever stepped. Swords! Where he gets his notions *I* can't think (though I know where he gets his language, poor lamb!). Look at *that* thing, Sir! For all the world like the dressed-up folk have on the stage or in pictures."

"You haven't let him see any books, I suppose, Nurse?" asked the Major.

"No, Sir. Never a book has the poor lamb seen, except those you've brought. I've always been in terror of his seeing a picture of a you-know-what, ever since you told me what the effect *might* be. Nor he hasn't so much as heard the name of it, so far as I know."

"Well, he'll see one to-day. I've brought it with me—must see it sooner or later. Might see a live one anywhere—in spite of all your care.... But about this sword—-where *could* he have got the idea? It's unlike any sword he ever set eyes on. Besides if he ever *did* see an Italian rapier—and there's scarcely such a thing in India—he'd not get the chance to use it as a copy. Fancy his having the desire and the power to, anyhow!"

"I give it up, Sir," said Nurse Beaton.

"I give it upper," added the Major, taking the object of their wonder from the child.

And there was cause for wonder indeed.

A hole had been punched through the centre of the lid of a tobacco tin and a number of others round the edge. Through the centre hole the steel rod had been passed so that the tin made a "guard". To the other holes wires had been fastened by bending, and their ends gathered, twisted, and bound with string to the top of the handle (of bored corks) to form an ornamental basket-hilt.

But the most remarkable thing of all was that, before doing this, the juvenile designer had passed the rod through a piece of bored stick so that the latter formed a *cross-piece* (neatly bound) within the tin guard—the distinctive feature of the ancient and modern Italian rapiers!

Round this cross-piece the first two fingers of the boy's right hand were crooked as he held the sword—and this is the one and only correct way of holding the Italian weapon, as the Major was well aware!

"I give it most utterly-uppermost," he murmured. "It's positively uncanny. No *uninitiated* adult of the utmost intelligence ever held an Italian-pattern foil correctly yet—nor until he had been pretty carefully shown. Who the devil put him up to the design in the first place, and the method of holding, in the second? Explain yourself, you two-anna[6] marvel," he demanded of the child. "It's *jadu*—black magic."

"Ayah lothted a wupee latht night," he replied.

"Lost a rupee, did she? Lucky young thing. Wish I had one to lose. Who showed you how to hold that sword? Why do you crook your fingers round the cross-piece like that?"

"Chucko laid me an egg latht night," observed Damocles. "He laid it with my name on it—so that cook couldn't steal it."

"No doubt. Look here, where can I get a sword like yours? Where can I copy it? Who makes them? Who knows about them?"

"*I* don't know, Major Thahib. Gunnoo sells 'Fire's' gram to the *methrani* for her curry and chuppatties."

"But how do you know swords are like this? *That* thing isn't a *pukka* sword."

"Well, it'th like Thir Theymour Thtukeley's in my dweam."

"What dream?"

"The one I'm alwayth dweaming. They have got long hair like Nurse in the night, and they fight and fight like anything. Norful good fighters! And they wear funny kit. And their thwords are like vis. *Eggz*ackly. Gunnoo gave me a ride on 'Fire,' and he'th a dam-liar. He thaid he forgot to put the warm *jhool* on him when Daddy was going to fwash him for being a dam-fool. I thaid I'd tell Daddy how he alwayth thleepth in it himthelf, unleth he gave me a ride on 'Fire'. 'Fire' gave a *norful* buck and bucked me off. At leatht I think he didn't."

Major Decies' face was curiously intent—as of some midnight worker in research who sees a bright near glimpse of the gold his alchemy has so long sought to materialize in the alembic of fact.

"Come back to sober truth, young youth. What about the dream? Who are they, and what do they say and do?"

"Thir Theymour Thtukeley Thahib tellth Thir Matthew Thahib about the hilt-thwust. (What *is* 'hilt-thwust'?) And Lubin, the thervant, ith a *white* thervant. Why ith he white if he ith a Thahib's 'boy'?"

"Good Gad!" murmured the Major. "I'm favoured of the gods. Tell me all about it, Sonny. Then I'll undo this parcel for you," he coaxed.

"Oh, I don't wemember. They buck a lot by the tents and then Thir Theymour Thtukeley goes and fights Thir Matthew and kills him, and it'th awful lovely, but they dreth up like kids at a party in big collars and silly kit."

"Yes, I know," murmured the Major. "Tell me what they say when they buck to each other by the tents, and when they talk about the 'hilt-thrust,' old chap."

"Oh, I don't wemember. I'll listen next time I dweam it, and tell you. Chucko's egg was all brown—not white like those cook brings from the bazaar. He's a dam-thief. Open the parcel, Major Thabib. What's in it?"

"A picture-book for you, Sonny. All sorts of jolly beasts that you'll *shikar* some day. You'll tell me some more about the dream to-morrow, won't you?"

"Yeth. I'll wemember and fink, and tell you what I have finked."

Turning to Nurse Beaton, the Major whispered:—

"Don't worry him about this dream at all. Leave it to me. It's wonderful. Take him on your lap, Nurse, and—er—be *ready*. It's a very life-like picture, and I'm going to spring it on him without any remark—but I'm more than a little anxious, I admit. Still, it's *got* to come, as I say, and better a picture first, with ourselves present. If the picture don't affect him I'll show him a real one. May be all right of course, but I don't know. I came across a somewhat similar case once before—and it was *not* all right. Not by any means," and he disclosed the brilliantly coloured Animal Picture Book and knelt beside the expectant boy.

On the first page was an incredibly leonine lion, who appeared to have solved with much satisfaction the problem of aerial flight, so far was he from the mountain whence he had sprung and above the back of the antelope towards which he had propelled himself. One could almost hear him roar. There was menace and fate in eye and tooth and claw, yea, in the very kink of the prehensile-seeming tail wherewith he apparently steered his course in mid-air. To gaze upon his impressive and determined countenance was to sympathize most fully with the sore-tried Prophet of old (known to Damocles as Dannle-in-the-lines-den) for ever more.

The boy was wholly charmed, stroked the glowing ferocity and observed that he was a *pukka Bahadur*.[7]

On the next page, burning bright, was a tiger, if possible one degree more terrible than the lion. His "fearful cemetery" appeared to be full, judging by its burgeoned bulge and the shocking state of depletion exhibited by the buffalo on which he fed with barely inaudible snarls and grunts of satisfaction. Blood dripped from his capacious and over-furnished mouth.

"Booful," murmured Damocles. "I shall go shooting tigerth to-mowwow. Shoot vem in ve mouth, down ve froat, so as not to spoil ve wool."

Turning over the page, the Major disclosed a most grievous grizzly bear, grizzly and bearish beyond conception, heraldic, regardant, expectant, not collared, fanged and clawed proper, rampant, erect, requiring no supporters.

"You could thtab him wiv a thword if you were quick, while he was doing that," opined Damocles, charmed, enraptured, delighted. One by one, other savage, fearsome beasts were disclosed to the increasingly delighted boy until, without warning, the Major suddenly turned a page and disclosed a brilliant and hungry-looking snake.

With a piercing shriek the boy leapt convulsively from Nurse Beaton's arms, rushed blindly into the wall and endeavoured to butt and bore his way through it with his head, screaming like a wounded horse. As the man and woman sprang to him he shrieked, "It'th under my foot! It'th moving, moving, moving *out*" and fell to the ground in a fit.

Major John Decies arose from his bachelor dinner-table that evening, lit his "planter" cheroot, and strolled into the verandah that looked across a desert to a mountain range.

Dropping into a long low chair, he raised his feet on to the long leg-rest extensions of its arms, and, as he settled down and waited for coffee, wondered why no such chairs are known in the West; why the trunks of the palms looked less flat in the moonlight than in the daylight (in which, from that spot, they always looked exactly as though cut out of cardboard); why Providence had not arranged for perpetual full-moon;

why the world looked such a place of peaceful, glorious beauty by moonlight, the bare cruel mountains like diaphanous clouds of tenderest soothing mist, the Judge's hideous bungalow like a fairy palace, his own parched compound like a plot of Paradise, when all was so abominable by day; and, as ever—why his darling, Lenore Stukeley, had had to marry de Warrenne and die in the full flower and promise of her beautiful womanhood.

Having finished his coffee and lighted his pipe (*vice* the over-dry friable cheroot, flung into the garden) the Major then turned his mind to serious and consecutive thought on the subject of her son, his beloved little pal, Dammy de Warrenne.

Poor little beggar! What an eternity it had seemed before he had got him to sleep. How the child had suffered. Mad! Absolutely stark, staring, raving *mad* with sheer terror.... Had he acted rightly in showing him the picture? He had meant well, anyhow. Cruel phrase, that. How cuttingly his friend de Warrenne had observed, "You mean well, doubtless," on more than one occasion. He could make it the most stinging of insults.... Surely he had acted rightly.... Poor little beggar—but he was bound to see a picture or a real live specimen, sooner or later. Perhaps when there was no help at hand.... Would he be like it always? *Might* grow out of it as he grew older and stronger. What would have happened if he had encountered a live snake? Lost his reason permanently, perhaps.... What would happen when he *did* see one, as sooner or later, he certainly must?

What would be the best plan? To attempt gradually to inure him—or to guard him absolutely from contact with picture, stuffed specimen, model, toy, and the real thing, wild or captive, as one would guard him against a fell disease?

Could he be inured? Could one "break it to him gently" bye and bye, by first drawing a wiggly line and then giving it a head? One might sketch a suggestion of a snake, make a sort of dissimilar clay model, improve it, show him a cast skin, stuff it, make a more life-like picture, gradually lead up to a well-stuffed one and then a live one. Might work up to having a good big picture of one on the nursery wall; one in a glass case; keep a harmless live one and show it him daily. Teach him by experience that there's nothing supernatural about a snake—just a nasty reptile that wants exterminating like other dangerous creatures—something to *shikar* with a gun. Nothing at all supernatural....

But this was "super"-natural, abnormal, a terrible devastating agony of madness, inherited, incurable probably; part of mind and body and soul. Inherited, and integrally of him as were the colour of his eyes, his intelligence, his physique.... Heredity ... pre-natal influence ... breed....

Anyhow, nothing must be attempted yet awhile. Let the poor little chap get older and stronger, in mind and body, first. Brave as a little bull-dog in other directions! Absolutely devoid of fear otherwise, and with a natural bent for fighting and adventure. Climb anywhere, especially up the hind leg of a camel or a horse, fondle any strange dog, clamour to be put on any strange horse, go into any deep water, cheek anybody, bear any ordinary pain with a grin, thrill to any story of desperate deeds—a fine, brave, manly, hardy little chap, and with art extraordinary physique for strength and endurance.

Whatever was to be attempted later, he must be watched, day and night, now. No unattended excursions into the compound, no uncensored picture-books, no juggling snake-charmers.... Yet it *must* come, sooner or later.

Would it ruin his life?

Anyhow, he must never return to India when he grew up, or go to any snake-producing country, unless he could be cured.

Would it make him that awful thing—a coward?

Would it grow and wax till it dominated his mind—drive him mad?

Would succeeding attacks, following encounters with picture or reality, progressively increase in severity?

Her boy in an asylum?

No. He was exaggerating an almost expected consequence that might never be repeated—especially if the child were most carefully and gradually reintroduced to the present terror. Later though—much later on.

Meanwhile, wait and hope: hope and wait....

CHAPTER III.

THE SNAKE APPEARS.

The European child who grows up in India, if only to the age of six or seven years, grows under a severe moral, physical, and mental handicap.

However wise, devoted, and conscientious its parents may be, the evil is great, and remains one of the many heavy costs (or punishments) of Empire.

When the child has no mother and an indifferent father, life's handicap is even more severe.

By his sixth birthday (the regiment being still in Bimariabad owing to the prevalence of drought, famine, and cholera elsewhere) Damocles de Warrenne, knowing the Urdu language and *argot* perfectly, knew, in theory also, more of evil, in some directions, than did his own father.

If the child who grows up absolutely straight-forward, honest, above-board and pure in thought, word, and deed, in England, deserves commendation, what does the child deserve who does so in India?

Understanding every word they spoke to one another, the training he got from native servants was one of undiluted evil and a series of object-lessons in deceit, petty villainy, chicanery, oppression, lying, dishonesty, and all immorality. And yet—thanks to his equal understanding of the words and deeds of Nurse Beaton, Major Decies, Lieutenant Ochterlonie, his father, the Officers of the Regiment, and the Europeans of the station—he had a clear, if unconscious, understanding that what was customary for native servants was neither customary nor possible for Sahibs....

But he knew too much....

He knew what percentage of his or her pay each servant had to hand to the "butler-sahib" monthly—or lose his or her place through false accusation.

He knew why the ayah was graciously exempted from financial toll by this autocrat. He knew roughly what proportion of the cook's daily bill represented the actual cost of his daily purchases. He knew what the door-peon got for consenting to take in the card of the Indian aspirant for an interview with Colonel de Warrenne.

He knew the terms of the arrangements between the head-syce and the grain-dealer, the lucerne-grass seller, the *ghas-wallah*[8] who brought the hay (whereby reduced quantities were accepted in return for illegal gratifications). He knew of retail re-sales of these reduced supplies.

He knew of the purchase of oil, rice, condiments, fire-wood and other commodities from the cook, of the theft (by arrangement) of the poultry and eggs, of the surreptitious milking of the cow, and of the simple plan of milking her—under Nurse Beaton's eye—into a narrow-necked vessel already half full of water.

He knew that the ayah's husband sold the Colonel's soda-water, paraffin, matches, candles, tobacco, cheroots, fruit, sugar, *etc.*, at a little portable shop round the corner of the road, and of the terms on which the *hamal* and the butler supplied these commodities to the ayah for transfer to her good man.

He knew too much of the philosophy, manners, habits, and morals of the dog-boy, of concealed cases of the most infectious diseases in the compound, of the sub-letting and over-crowding of the servants' quarters, of incredible quarrels, intrigues, jealousies, revenges, base villainies and wrongs, superstitions and beliefs.

He would hear the hatching of a plot—an hour's arrangement and wrangle—whereby, through far-sighted activity, perjury, malpractice and infinite ingenuity, the ringleader would gain a *pice* and the follower a *pie* (a farthing and a third of a farthing respectively).

Daily he saw the butler steal milk, sugar, and tea, for his own use; the *hamal* steal oil when he filled the lamps, for sale; the *malli* steal flowers, for sale; the coachman steal carriage-candles; the cook steal a moiety of everything that passed through his hands—every one in that black underworld stealing, lying, back-biting, cheating, intriguing (and all meanwhile strictly and stoutly religious, even the sweeper-descended Goanese cook, the biggest thief of all, purging his Christian soul on Sunday mornings by Confession, and fortifying himself against the temptations of the Evil One at early Mass).

Between these *nowker log*, the servant-people, and his own *jat* or class, the *Sahib-log*, the master-people, were the troopers, splendid Sikhs, Rajputs, Pathans and Punjabis, men of honour, courage, physique, tradition. Grand fighters, loyal as steel while properly understood and properly treated—in other words, while properly officered. (Men, albeit, with deplorably little understanding of, or regard for, Pagett, M.P., and his kind, who yearn to do so much for them.)

These men Damocles admired and loved, though even *they* were apt to be very naughty in the bazaar, to gamble and to toy with opium, bhang, and (alleged) brandy, to dally with houris and hearts'-delights, to use unkind measures towards the good *bunnia* and *sowkar* who had lent them monies, and to do things outside the Lines that were not known in the Officers' Mess.

The boy preferred the Rissaldar-Major even to some Sahibs of his acquaintance—that wonderful old man-at-arms, horseman, *shikarri*, athlete, gentleman. (Yet how strange and sad to see him out of his splendid uniform, in sandals, *dhotie*, untrammelled shirt-tails, dingy old cotton coat and loose *puggri*, undistinguishable from a school-master, clerk, or post-man; so *un*-sahib-like.)

And what a fine riding-master he made for an ambitious, fearless boy—though Ochterlonie Sahib said he was too cruel to be a good *horse*-master.

How *could* people be civilians and live away from regiments? Live without ever touching swords, lances, carbines, saddles?

What a queer feeling it gave one to see the regiment go past the saluting base on review-days, at the gallop, with lances down. One wanted to shout, to laugh—to *cry*. (It made one's mouth twitch and chin work.)

Oh, to *lead* the regiment as Father did—horse and man one welded piece of living mechanism.

Father said you couldn't ride till you had taken a hundred tosses, been pipped a hundred times. A hundred falls! Surely Father had *never* been thrown—it must be impossible for such a rider to come off. See him at polo.

By his sixth birthday Damocles de Warrenne, stout and sturdy, was an accomplished rider and never so happy (save when fencing) as when flogging his active and spirited little pony along the "rides" or over the dusty *maidans* and open country of Bimariabad. To receive a quarter-mile start on the race-course and ride a mile race against Khodadad Khan on his troop-horse, or with one of the syces on one of the Colonel's polo-ponies, or with some obliging male or female early morning rider, was the joy of his life. Should he suspect the competitor of "pulling" as he came alongside, that the tiny pony might win, the boy would lash at both horses impartially.

People who pitied him (and they were many) wondered as to how soon he would break his neck, and remonstrated with his father for allowing him to ride alone, or in charge of an attendant unable to control him.

In the matter of his curious love of fencing Major John Decies was deeply concerned, obtained more and more details of his "dweam," taught him systematically and scientifically to fence, bought him foils and got them shortened. He also interested him in a series of muscle-developing exercises which the boy called his "dismounted squad-dwill wiv'out arms," and performed frequently daily, and with gusto.

Lieutenant Lord Ochterlonie (Officers' Light-Weight Champion at Aldershot) rigged him up a small swinging sand-bag and taught him to punch with either hand, and drilled him in foot-work for boxing.

Later he brought the very capable ten-year-old son of a boxing Troop-Sergeant and set him to make it worth Dam's while to guard smartly, to learn to keep his temper, and to receive a blow with a grin.

28

(Possibly a better education than learning declensions, conjugations, and tables from a Eurasian "governess".)

He learnt to read unconsciously and automatically by repeating, after Nurse Beaton, the jingles and other letter-press beneath the pictures in the books obtained for him under Major Decies' censorship.

On his sixth birthday, Major John Decies had Damocles over to his bungalow for the day, gave him a box of lead soldiers and a schooner-rigged ship, helped him to embark them and sail them in the bath to foreign parts, trapped a squirrel and let it go again, allowed him to make havoc of his possessions, fired at bottles with his revolver for the boy's delectation, shot a crow or two with a rook-rifle, played an improvised game of fives with a tennis-ball, told him tales, and generally gave up the day to his amusement. What he did *not* do was to repeat the experiment of a year ago, or make any kind of reference to snakes....

A few days later, on the morning of the New-Year's-Day Review, Colonel Matthew de Warrenne once again strode up and down his verandah, arrayed in full review-order, until it should be time to ride to the regimental parade-ground.

He had coarsened perceptibly in the six years since he had lost his wife, and the lines that had grown deepest on his hard, handsome face were those between his eyebrows and beside his mouth—the mouth of an unhappy, dissipated, cynical man....

He removed his right-hand gauntlet and consulted his watch.... Quarter of an hour yet.

He continued the tramp that always reminded Damocles of the restless, angry to-and-fro pacing of the big bear in the gardens. Both father and the bear seemed to fret against fate, to suffer under a sense of injury; both seemed dangerous, fierce, admirable. Hearing the clink and clang and creak of his father's movement, Damocles scrambled from his cot and crept down the stairs, pink-toed, blue-eyed, curly-headed, night-gowned, to peep through the crack of the drawing-room door at his beautiful father. He loved to see him in review uniform—so much more delightful than plain khaki—pale blue, white, and gold, in full panoply of accoutrement, jackbooted and spurred, and with the great turban that made his English face look more English still.

Yes—he would ensconce himself behind the drawing-room door and watch. Perhaps "Fire" would be bobbery when the Colonel mounted him, would get "what-for" from whip and spur, and be put over the compound wall instead of being allowed to canter down the drive and out at the gate....

Colonel de Warrenne stepped into his office to get a cheroot. Re-appearing in the verandah with it in his mouth he halted and thrust his hand inside his tunic for his small match-case. Ere he could use the match his heart was momentarily chilled by the most blood-curdling scream he had ever heard. It appeared to come from the drawing-room. (Colonel de Warrenne never lit the cheroot that he had put to his lips—nor ever another again.) Springing to the door, one of a dozen that opened into the verandah, he saw his son struggling on the ground, racked by convulsive spasms, with glazed, sightless eyes and foaming mouth, from which issued appalling, blood-curdling shrieks. Just above him, on the fat satin cushion in the middle of a low settee, a huge half-coiled cobra swayed from side to side in the Dance of Death.

"It's under my foot—it's moving—moving—moving out," shrieked the child.

Colonel de Warrenne attended to the snake first. He half-drew his sword and then slammed it back into the scabbard. No—his sword was not for snakes, whatever his son might be. On the wall was a trophy of Afghan weapons, one of which was a sword that had played a prominent part on the occasion of the Colonel's winning of the Victoria Cross.

Striding to the wall he tore the sword down, drew it and, with raised arm, sprang towards the cobra. A good "Cut Three" across the coils would carve it into a dozen pieces. No. Lenore made that cushion—and Lenore's cushion made more appeal to Colonel de Warrenne than did Lenore's son. No. A neat horizontal "Cut Two," just below the head, with the deadly "drawing" motion on it, would meet the case nicely. Swinging it to the left, the Colonel subconsciously placed the sword, "resting flat on the left shoulder, edge to the left, hand in front of the shoulder and square with the elbow, elbow as high as the hand," as per drill-book, and delivered a lightning stroke—thinking as he did so that the Afghan *tulwar* is an uncommonly well-balanced, handy cutting-weapon, though infernally small in the hilt.

The snake's head fell with a thud upon the polished boards between the tiger-skins, and the body dropped writhing and twitching on to the settee.

Damocles appeared to be dead. Picking him up, the callous-hearted father strode out to where Khodadad Khan held "Fire's" bridle, handed him to the orderly, mounted, received him again from the man, and, holding him in his strong right arm, cantered to the bungalow of Major John Decies—since it lay on the road to the parade-ground.

Would the jerking hurt the little beggar in his present comatose state? Well, brats that couldn't stand a little jerking were better dead, especially when they screamed and threw fits at the sight of a common snake.

Turning into Major Decies' compound and riding up to his porch, the Colonel saw the object of his search, arrayed in pyjamas, seated in his long cane chair beside a tray of tea, toast, and fruit, in the verandah.

"Morning, de Warrenne," he cried cheerily.

"How's little—" and caught sight of the inanimate child.

"Little coward's fainted after throwing a fit—over a common snake," observed the Colonel coolly.

"Give him here," answered the Major, taking the boy tenderly in his arms,—"and kindly—er—clear out."

He did not wish to strike his friend and senior. How the black rage welled up in his heart against the callous brute who had dared to marry Lenore Seymour Stukeley.

Colonel de Warrenne wheeled his horse without a word, and rode out of Major Decies' life and that of his son.

Galloping to the parade-ground he spoke a few curt words to his Adjutant, inspected the *rissala*, and then rode at its head to the brigade parade-ground where it took up its position on the left flank of the Guns and the Queen's Greys, "sat at ease," and awaited the arrival of the Chief Commissioner at the saluting-base. A British Infantry regiment marched to the left flank of the 118th (Bombay) Lancers, left-turned and stood at ease. Another followed and was followed in turn by Native Infantry Regiments—grand Sikhs in scarlet tunics, baggy black breeches and blue putties; hefty Pathans and Baluchis in green tunics, crimson breeches and high white gaiters, sturdy little Gurkhas in rifle-green, stalwart Punjabi Mahommedans.

The great double line grew and grew, and stood patiently waiting, Horse, Foot, and Guns, facing the sun and a dense crowd of spectators ranked behind the rope-encircled, guard-surrounded saluting-base over which flew the Flag of England.

The Brigadier and his Staff rode on to the ground, were saluted by the mile of troops, and took up their position.

Followed the Chief Commissioner in his state carriage, accompanied by a very Distinguished Guest, and surrounded by his escort. The mile of men again came to attention and the review began. Guns boomed, massed bands played the National Anthem, the crackling rattle of the *feu-de-joie* ran up the front rank and down the rear.

After the inspection and the salutes came the march-past by the regiments.

Now the Distinguished Visitor's wife had told the Chief Commissioner that she "did not want to see the cavalry go past at the gallop as it raised such a dreadful dust". But her maid bungled, her toilette failed, and she decided not to accompany her husband to the Review at all. Her husband, the Distinguished Visitor, *did* desire to see the cavalry go past at the gallop, and so the Chief Commissioner's Distinguished Visitor's wife's maid's bungling had a tremendous influence upon the fate of Damocles de Warrenne, as will be seen.

Passed the massed Guns at the walk, followed by the Cavalry at the walk in column of squadrons and the Infantry in column of companies, each unit saluting the Chief Commissioner by turning "eyes right" as it passed the spot where he sat on horseback surrounded by the civil and military staffs.

Wheeling to the left at the end of the ground the Guns and Cavalry again passed, this time at the trot, while the Infantry completed its circular march to its original position.

Finally the Cavalry passed for the third time, and now at the gallop, an orderly whirlwind, a controlled avalanche of men and horses, with levelled lances, and the hearts of all men were stirred at one of the most stirring sights and sounds in the world—a cavalry charge.

At the head of the leading squadron galloped Colonel de Warrenne, cool, methodical, keeping a distant flag-staff in line with a still more distant church spire, that he might lead the regiment in a perfectly straight line. (Few who have not tried it realize the difficulty of leading a galloping line of men absolutely straight and at true right-angles to the line of their ranks.)

On thundered the squadrons unbending of rank, uncrowded, unopened, squadron-leaders maintaining distance, the whole mass as ordered, shapely, and precisely correct as when at the walk.

Past the saluting-base thundered the squadrons and in full career Colonel de Warrenne's charger put his near fore into ground honey-combed by insect, reptile, or burrowing beast, crashed on its head, rolled like a shot rabbit, and Colonel Matthew Devon de Warrenne lay dead—killed by his own sword.

Like his ancestors of that fated family, he had died by the sword, but unlike them, he had died by the *hilt* of it.

Major John Decies, I.M.S., Civil Surgeon of Bimariabad, executor of the will of the late Colonel de Warrenne and guardian of his son, cabled the sad news of the Colonel's untimely death to Sir Gerald Seymour Stukeley at Monksmead, he being, so far as Major Decies knew, the boy's only male relative in England—uncle of the late Mrs. de Warrenne.

The reply, which arrived in a day or two, appeared from its redundancy and incoherence to be the composition of Miss Yvette Seymour Stukeley, and bade Major Decies either send or bring the infant Damocles to Monksmead *immediately*.

The Major decided to apply forthwith for such privilege-leave and furlough as were due to him, and to proceed to England with the boy. It would be as well that his great-uncle should hear from him, personally, of the matter of the child's mental condition resultant upon the tragedy of his own birth and his mother's death. The

Major was decidedly anxious as to the future in this respect—all might be well in time, and all might be very far indeed from well.

Nurse Beaton absolutely and flatly refused to be parted from her charge, and the curious party of three set sail for England in due course.

"Hm!—He's every inch a Stukeley," remarked the General when Damocles de Warrenne was ushered into his presence in the great library at Monksmead. "Hope he's Stukeley by nature too. Sturdy young fella! 'Spose he's vetted sound in wind and limb?"

The Major replied that the boy was physically rather remarkably strong, mentally very sound, and in character all that could be desired. He then did his best to convey to the General an understanding of the psychic condition that must be a cause of watchfulness and anxiety on the part of those who guarded his adolescence.

At dinner, over the General's wonderful Clos Vougeot, the Major again returned to the subject and felt that his words of advice fell upon somewhat indifferent and uncomprehending ears.

It was the General's boast that he had never feed a doctor in his life, and his impression that a sound resort for any kind of invalid is a lethal chamber....

The seven years since the Major had last seen her, seemed to have dealt lightly with the sad-faced, pretty Miss Yvette, gentle, good, and very kind. Over the boy she rhapsodized to her own content and his embarrassment. Effusive endearments and embraces were new to Dam, and he appeared extraordinarily ignorant of the art of kissing.

"Oh, how like his dear Father!" she would exclaim afresh every few minutes, to the Major's slight annoyance and the General's plain disgust.

"Every inch a Stukeley!" he would growl in reply.

But Yvette Seymour Stukeley had prayed for Colonel de Warrenne nightly for seven years and had idealized him beyond recognition. Possibly Fate's greatest kindness to her was to ordain that she should not see him as he had become in fact, and compare him with her wondrous mental image.... The boy was to her, must be, should be, the very image of her life's hero and beloved....

The depolarized and bewildered Damocles found himself in a strange and truly foreign land, a queer, cold, dismal country inhabited by vast quantities of "second-class sahibs," as he termed the British lower middle-class and poor, a country of a strange greenness and orderedness, where there were white servants, strangely conjoined rows of houses in the villages, dangerous-looking fires inside the houses, a kind of tomb-stones on all house-tops, strange horse-drawn vehicles, butlerless and *ghari*[9]-less sahibs, and an utter absence of "natives," sepoys, *byle-gharies*,[10] camels, monkeys, kites, squirrels, bulbuls, *minahs*,[11] mongooses, palm-trees, and temples. Cattle appeared to have no humps, crows to have black heads, and trees to have no fruit. The very monsoon seemed inextricably mixed with the cold season. Fancy the rains coming in the cold weather! Perhaps there was no hot weather and nobody went to the hills in this strange country of strange people, strange food, strange customs. Nobody seemed to have any tents when they left the station for the districts, nor to take any bedding when they went on tour or up-country. A queer, foreign land.

But Monksmead was a most magnificent "bungalow" standing in a truly beautiful "compound"—wherein the very *bhistis*[12] and *mallis* were European and appeared to be second-class sahibs.

Marvellous was the interior of the bungalow with its countless rooms and mountainous stair-cases (on the wall of one of which hung *the Sword* which he had never seen but instantly recognized) and its army of white servants headed by the white butler (so like the Chaplain of Bimariabad in grave respectability and solemn pompousness) and its extraordinary white "ayahs" or maids, and silver-haired Mrs. Pont, called the "house-keeper". Was she a *pukka* Mem-Sahib or a *nowker*[13] or what? And how did she "keep" the house?

A wonderful place—but far and away the most thrilling and delightful of its wonders was the little white girl, Lucille—Damocles' first experience of the charming genus.

The boy never forgot his first meeting with Lucille.

On his arrival at Monksmead he had been "vetted," as he expressed it, by the Burra-Sahib, the General; and then taken to an attractive place called "the school-room" and there had found Lucille....

"Hullo! Boy," had been her greeting. "What's your name?" He had attentively scrutinized a small white-clad, blue-sashed maiden, with curling chestnut hair, well-opened hazel eyes, decided chin, Greek mouth and aristocratic cheek-bones. A maiden with a look of blood and breed about her. (He did not sum her up in these terms at the time.)

"Can you ride, Boy?"

"A bit."

"Can you fight?"

"A bit."

"Can you swim?"

34

"Not well."

"*I* can—ever so farther. D'you know French and German?"

"Not a word."

"Play the piano?"

"Never heard of it. D'you play it with cards or dice?"

"Lucky dog! It's music. I have to practise an hour a day."

"What for?"

"Nothing ... it's lessons. Beastly. How old are you?"

"Seven—er—nearly."

"So'm I—nearly. I've got to be six first though. I shall have a birthday next week. A big one. Have you brought any ellyfunts from India?"

"I've never seen a nellyfunt—only in pictures."

A shudder shook the boy's sturdy frame.

"Why do you go like that? Feel sick?"

"No. I don't know. I seemed to remember something—in a book. I dream about it. There's a nasty blue room with a mud floor. And *Something*. Beastly. Makes you yell out and you can't. You can't run away either. But the Sword dream is lovely."

Lucille appeared puzzled and put this incoherence aside.

"What a baby never to see ellyfunts! I've seen lots. Hundreds. Zoo. Circuses. Persessions. Camels, too."

"Oh, I used to ride a camel every day. There was one in the compound with his *oont-wallah*,[14] Abdul Ghaffr; and Khodadad Khan used to beat the *oont-wallah* on cold mornings to warm himself."

"What's an *oont-wallah*?"

"Don't you *know*? Why, he's just the *oont-wallah*, of course. Who'd graze the camel or load it up if there wasn't one?"

At tea in the nursery the young lady suddenly remarked:—

"I like you, Boy. You're worth nine Haddocks."

This cryptic valuation puzzled Damocles the more in that he had never seen or heard of a haddock. Had he been acquainted with the fowl he might have been yet more astonished.

Later he discovered that the comparison involved the fat boy who sat solemnly stuffing on the other side of the table, his true baptismal name being Haddon.

Yes, Lucille was a revelation, a marvel.

Far quicker of mind than he, cleverer at games and inventing "make believe," very strong, active, and sporting, she was the most charming, interesting, and attractive experience in his short but eventful life.

How he loved to make her laugh and clap her hands! How he enjoyed her quaint remarks, speculations, fairy-tales and jokes. How he yearned to win her approval and admiration. How he strove to please her!

In Lucille and his wonderful new surroundings he soon forgot Major Decies, who returned to live (and, at a ripe old age, to die) at Bimariabad, where had lived and died the woman whom he had so truly and purely loved. The place where he had known her was the only place for him.

On each of his birthdays Damocles received a long fatherly letter and a handsome present from the Major, and by the time he went away to school at Wellingborough, he wondered who on earth the Major might be.

To his great delight Damocles found that he was not doomed to discontinue his riding, fencing, boxing, and "dismounted drill without arms".

General Seymour Stukeley sent for a certain Sergeant Havlan (once a trooper in his own regiment), rough-rider, swordsman, and boxer, now a professional trainer, and bade him see that the boy learned all he could teach him of arms and horsemanship, boxing, swimming, and general physical prowess and skill. Lucille and Haddon Berners were to join in to the extent to which their age and sex permitted.

The General intended his great-nephew to be worthy of his Stukeley blood, and to enter Sandhurst a finished man-at-arms and horseman, and to join his regiment, Cavalry, of course, with nothing much to learn of sword, lance, rifle, revolver, and horse.

36

Sergeant Havlan soon found that he had little need to begin at the beginning with Damocles de Warrenne in the matter of riding, fencing or boxing, and was unreasonably annoyed thereat.

In time, it became the high ambition and deep desire of Dam to overcome Sergeant Havlan's son in battle with the gloves. As young Havlan was a year his senior, a trained infant prodigy, and destined for the Prize Ring, there was plenty for him to learn and to do.

With foil or sabre the boy was beneath Dam's contempt.

Daily the children were in Sergeant Havlan's charge for riding and physical drill, Dam getting an extra hour in the evening for the more manly and specialized pursuits suitable to his riper years.

He and Lucille loved it all, and the Haddock bitterly loathed it.

Until Miss Smellie came Dam was a happy boy—but for queer sudden spasms of terror of Something unknown; and, after her arrival, he would have been well content could he have been assured of an early opportunity of attending her obsequies and certain of a long-postponed resurrection; well content, and often wildly happy (with Lucille) ... but for the curious undefinable fear of Something ... Something about which he had the most awful dreams ... Something in a blue room with a mud floor. Something that seemed at times to move beneath his foot, making his blood freeze, his knees smite together, the sunlight turn to darkness....

CHAPTER IV.

THE SWORD AND THE SOUL.

One of the very earliest of all Dam's memories in after life—for in a few years he forgot India absolutely—was of *the Sword* (that hung on the oak-panelled wall of the staircase by the portrait of a cavalier), and of a gentle, sad-eyed lady, Auntie Yvette, who used to say:—

"Yes, sonny darling, it is more than two-hundred-and-fifty years old. It belonged to Sir Seymour Stukeley, who carried the King's Standard at Edgehill and died with that sword in his hand ... *You* shall wear a sword some day."

(He did—with a difference.)

The sword grew into the boy's life and he would rather have owned it than the mechanical steamboat with real brass cannon for which he prayed to God so often, so earnestly, and with such faith. On his seventh birthday he preferred a curious request, which had curious consequences.

"Can I take the sword to bed with me to-night, Dearest, as it is my birthday?" he begged. "I won't hurt it."

And the sword was taken down from the oak-panelled wall, cleaned, and laid on the bed in his room.

"Promise you will not try to take it out of the sheath, sonny darling," said the gentle, sad-eyed lady as she kissed him "Good night".

"I promise, Dearest," replied the boy, and she knew that she need have no fear.

He fell asleep fondling and cuddling the sword that had pierced the hearts of many men and defended the honour of many ancestors, and dreamed, with far greater vividness and understanding, the dream he had so often dreamt before.

Frequently as he dreamed it during his chequered career, it was henceforth always most vivid and real. It never never varied in the slightest detail, and he generally dreamed it on the night before some eventful, dangerful day on which he risked his life or fought for it.

Of the early dreamings, of course, he understood little, but while he was still almost a boy he most fully understood the significance of every word, act, and detail of the marvellous, realistic dream.

It began with a view of a camp of curious little bell-tents about which strode remarkable, big-booted, long-haired, bedizened men—looking strangely effeminate and strangely fierce, with their feathered hats, curls, silk sashes, velvet coats, and with their long swords, cruel faces, and savage oaths.

Some wore steel breastplates, like that of the suit of armour in the hall, and steel helmets. The sight of the camp thrilled the boy in his dream, and yet he knew that he had seen it all before actually, and in real life—in some former life.

Beside one of a small cluster of tents that stood well apart from the rest sat a big man who instantly reminded the boy of his dread "Grandfather," whom he would have loved to have loved had he been given the chance.

The big man was even more strangely attired than those others who clumped and clattered about the lower part of the camp.

Fancy a great big strong man with long curls, a lace collar, and a velvet coat—like a kid going to a party!

The velvet coat had the strangest sleeves, too—made to button to the elbow and full of slits that seemed to have been mended underneath with blue silk. There was a regular pattern of these silk-mended slits about the body of the coat, too, and funny silk-covered buttons.

On his head the man had a great floppy felt hat with a huge feather—a hat very like one that Dearest wore, only bigger.

One of his long curls was tied with a bow of ribbon—like young Lucille wore—and the boy felt quite uncomfortable as he noted it. A grown man—the silly ass! And, yes! he had actually got lace round the bottoms of his quaint baggy knickerbockers— as well as lace cuffs!

The boy could see it, where one of the great boots had sagged down below the knee.

Extraordinary boots they were, too. Nothing like "Grumper's" riding-boots. They were yellowish in colour, and dull, not nicely polished, and although the square-toed, ugly foot part looked solid as a house, the legs were more like wrinkled leather stockings, and so long that the pulled-up one came nearly to the hip.

Spurs had made black marks on the yellow ankles, and saddle and stirrup-leather had rubbed the legs....

And a sash! Whoever heard of a grown-up wearing a sash? It was a great blue silk thing, wound round once or twice, and tied with a great bow, the ends of which hung down in front.

Of all the Pip-squeaks!

And yet the big man's face was not that of a Pip-squeak—far from it.
It was very like Grumper's in fact.

The boy liked the face. It was strong and fierce, thin and clean-cut—marred only, in
his estimation, by the funny little tuft of hair on the lower lip. He liked the wavy,
rough, up-turned moustache, but not that silly tuft. How nice he would look with his
hair cut, his lower lip shaved, and his ridiculous silks, velvet, and lace exchanged for
a tweed shooting-suit or cricketing-flannels! How Grumper, Father, Major Decies,
and even Khodadad Khan and the sepoys would have laughed at the get-up. Nay,
they would have blushed for the fellow—a Sahib, a gentleman—to tog himself up
so!

The boy also liked the man's voice when he turned towards the tent and called:—

"Lubin, you drunken dog, come hither," a call which brought forth a servant-like
person, who, by reason of his clean-shaven face and red nose, reminded the boy of
Pattern the coachman.

He wore a dark cloth suit, cotton stockings, shoes that had neither laces nor buttons,
but fastened with a kind of strap and buckle, and, queer creature, a big Eton collar!

"Sword and horse, rascal," said the gentleman, "and warn Digby for duty. Bring me
wine and a manchet of bread."

The man bowed and re-entered the tent, to emerge a moment later bearing *the Sword*.

How the cut-steel hilt sparkled and shone! How bright and red the leather
scabbard—now black, dull, cracked and crumbling. But it was unmistakeably *the*
Sword.

It hung from a kind of broad cross-belt and was attached to it by several parallel
buckled straps—not like Father's Sam Browne belt at all.

As the gentleman rose from his stool (he must have been over six feet in height)
Lubin passed the cross-belt over his head and raised left arm so that it rested on his
right shoulder, and the Sword hung from hip to heel.

To the boy it had always seemed such a huge, unwieldy thing. At this big man's side
it looked—just right.

Lubin then went off at a trot to where long lines of bay horses pawed the ground,
swished their tails, tossed their heads, and fidgeted generally....

From a neighbouring tent came the sounds of a creaking camp-bed, two feet striking the ground with violence, and a prodigious, prolonged yawn.

A voice then announced that all parades should be held in Hell, and that it was better to be dead than damned. Why should gentlemen drill on a fine evening while the world held wine and women?

After a brief space, occupied with another mighty yawn, it loudly and tunefully requested some person or persons unknown to superintend its owner's obsequies.

"Lay a garland on my hearse
Of the dismal yew;
Maidens, willow branches bear;
Say I died true.
My love was false, but I was firm
From my hour of birth.
Upon my buried body lie
Lightly, gentle earth...."

"May it do so soon," observed the tall gentleman distinctly.

"What ho, without there! That you, Seymour, lad?" continued the voice. "Tarry a moment. Where's that cursed ..." and sounds of hasty search among jingling accoutrements were followed by a snatch of song of which the boy instantly recognized the words. He had often heard Dearest sing them.

"Drink to me only with thine eyes
And I will pledge with mine:
Or leave a kiss within the cup
And I'll not look for wine.
The thirst that from the soul doth rise
Doth ask a drink divine;
But might I of Jove's nectar sup,
I would not change for thine."

Lubin appeared, bearing a funny, fat, black bottle, a black cup (both appeared to be of leather), and a kind of leaden plate on which was a small funnily-shaped loaf of bread.

"'Tis well you want none," observed the tall gentleman, "I had asked you to help me crush a flask else," and on the word the singer emerged from the tent.

"Jest not on solemn subjects, Seymour," he said soberly, "Wine may carry me over one more pike-parade.... Good lad.... Here's to thee.... Why should gentlemen drill?... I came to fight for the King, not to ... But, isn't this thy day for de Warrenne? Oh, ten million fiends! Plague and pest! And I cannot see thee stick him, Seymour ..." and the speaker dashed the black drinking-vessel violently on the ground, having carefully emptied it.

The boy did not much like him.

His lace collar was enormous and his black velvet coat was embroidered all over with yellow silk designs, flowers, and patterns. It was like the silly mantel-borders and things that Mrs. Pont, the housekeeper, did in her leisure time. ("Cruel-work" she called it, and the boy quite agreed.)

This man's face was pink and fair, his hair golden.

"Warn him not of the hilt-thrust, Seymour, lad," he said suddenly. "Give it him first—for a sneering, bullying, taverning, chambering knave."

The tall gentleman glanced at his down-flung cup, raised his eyebrows, and drank from the bottle.

"Such *would* annoy *you*, Hal, of course," he murmured.

A man dressed in what appeared to be a striped football jersey under a leather waistcoat and steel breast-plate, high boots and a steel helmet led up a great horse.

The boy loved the horse. It was very like "Fire".

The gentleman (called Seymour) patted it fondly, stroked his nose, and gave it a piece of his bread.

"Well, Crony Long-Face?" he said fondly.

He then put his left foot in the great box-stirrup and swung himself into the saddle— a very different kind of saddle from those with which the boy was familiar.

It reminded him of Circuses and the Lord Mayor's Show. It was big enough for two and there was a lot of velvet and stuff about it and a fine gold *C.R.*—whatever that might mean—on a big pretty cloth under it (perhaps the gentleman's initials were C.R. just as his own were D. de W. and on some of his things).

The great fat handle of a great fat pistol stuck up on each side of the front of the saddle.

"Follow," said the gentleman to the iron-bound person, and moved off at a walk towards a road not far distant.

42

"Stap him! Spit him, Seymour," called the pink-faced man, "and warn him not of the hilt-thrust."

As he passed the corner of the camp, two men with great axe-headed spear things performed curious evolutions with their cumbersome weapons, finally laying the business ends of them on the ground as the gentleman rode by.

He touched his hat to them with his switch.

Continuing for a mile or so, at a walk, he entered a dense coppice and dismounted.

"Await me," he said to his follower, gave him the curb-rein, and walked on to an open glade a hundred yards away.

(It was a perfect spot for Red Indians, Smugglers, Robin Hood, Robinson Crusoe or any such game, the boy noted.)

Almost at the same time, three other men entered the clearing, two together, and one from a different quarter.

"For the hundredth time, Seymour, lad, *mention not the hilt-thrust*, as you love me and the King," said this last one quietly as he approached the gentleman; and then the two couples behaved in a ridiculous manner with their befeathered hats, waving them in great circles as they bowed to each other, and finally laying them on their hearts before replacing them.

"Mine honour is my guide, Will," answered the gentleman called Seymour, somewhat pompously the boy considered, though he did not know the word.

Sir Seymour then began to remove the slashed coat and other garments until he stood in his silk stockings, baggy knickerbockers, and jolly cambric shirt—nice and loose and free at the neck as the boy thought.

He rolled up his right sleeve, drew the sword, and made one or two passes—like Sergeant Havlan always did before he began fencing.

The other two men, meantime, had been behaving somewhat similarly—talking together earnestly and one of them undressing.

The one who did this was a very powerful-looking man and the arm he bared reminded the boy of that of a "Strong Man" he had seen recently at Monksmead Fair, in a tent, and strangely enough his face reminded him of that of his own Father.

He had a nasty face though, the boy considered, and looked like a bounder because he had pimples, a swelly nose, a loud voice, and a swanky manner. The boy disapproved of him wholly. It was like his cheek to resemble Father, as well as to have the same name.

His companion came over to the gentleman called Will, carrying the strong man's bared sword and, bowing ridiculously (with his hat, both hands, and his feet) said:—

"Shall we measure, Captain Ormonde Delorme?"

Captain Delorme then took the sword from Sir Seymour, bowed as the other had done, and handed him the sword with a mighty flourish, hilt first.

It proved to be half an inch shorter than the other, and Captain Delorme remarked that his Principal would waive that.

He and the strong man's companion then chose a spot where the grass was very short and smooth, where there were no stones, twigs or inequalities, and where the light of the setting sun fell sideways upon the combatants—who tip-toed gingerly, and rather ridiculously, in their stockinged feet, to their respective positions. Facing each other, they saluted with their swords and then stood with the right arm pointing downwards and across the body so that the hilt of the sword was against the right thigh and the blade directed to the rear.

"One word, Sir Matthew de Warrenne," said Sir Seymour as they paused in this attitude. "If my point rests for a second on your hilt *you are a dead man*."

Sir Matthew laughed in an ugly manner and replied:—

"And what is your knavish design now, Sir Seymour Stukeley?"

"My design *was* to warn you of an infallible trick of fence, Sir Matthew. It *now* is to kill you—for the insult, and on behalf of ... your own unhappy daughter."

The other yawned and remarked to his friend:—

"I have a parade in half an hour."

"On guard," cried the person addressed, drawing his sword and striking an attitude.

"Play," cried Captain Delorme, doing similarly.

Both principals crouched somewhat, held their swords horizontal, with point to the adversary's breast and hilt drawn back, arm sharply bent—for both, it appeared, had perfected the Art of Arts in Italy.

44

These niceties escaped the boy in his earlier dreamings of the dream—but the time came when he could name every pass, parry, invitation, and riposte.

The strong man suddenly threw his sword-hand high and towards his left shoulder, keeping his sword horizontal, and exposing the whole of his right side.

Sir Seymour lunged hard for his ribs, beneath the right arm-pit and, as the other's sword swooped down to catch his, twist it over, and riposte, he feinted, cleared the descending sword, and thrust at the throat. A swift ducking crouch let the sword pass over the strong man's head, and only a powerful French circular parry saved the life of Sir Seymour Stukeley.

As the boy realized later, he fought Italian in principle, and used the best of French parries, ripostes, and tricks, upon occasion—and his own perfected combination of the two schools made him, according to Captain Delorme, the best fencer in the King's army. So at least the Captain said to the other second, as they amicably chatted while their friends sought to slay each other before their hard, indifferent-seeming eyes.

To the boy their talk conveyed little—as yet.

The duellists stepped back as the "phrase" ended, and then Sir Seymour gave an "invitation," holding his sword-arm wide to the right of his body. Sir Matthew lunged, his sword was caught, carried out to the left, and held there as Sir Seymour's blade slid inward along it. Just in time, Sir Matthew's inward pressure carried Sir Seymour's sword clear to the right again. Sir Matthew disengaged over, and, as the sudden release brought Sir Seymour's sword springing in, he thrust under that gentleman's right arm and scratched his side.

As he recovered his sword he held it for a moment with the point raised toward Sir Seymour's face. Instantly Sir Seymour's point tinkled on his hilt, and Captain Delorme murmured "Finis" beneath his breath.

Sir Stukeley Seymour's blade shot in, Sir Matthew's moved to parry, and the point of the advancing sword flickered under his hand, turned upward, and pierced his heart.

"Yes," said Captain Delorme, as the stricken man fell, "if he parries outward the point goes under, if he anticipates a feint it comes straight in, and if he parries a lunge-and-feint-under, he gets feint-over before he can come up. I have never seen Stukeley miss when once he rests on the hilt. *Exit* de Warrenne—and Hell the worse for it——" and the boy awoke.

He kissed the sword and fell asleep again.

One day, when receiving his morning fencing and boxing lessons of Sergeant Havlan, he astonished that warrior (and made a bitter enemy of him) by warning him against allowing his blade to rest on the Sergeant's hilt, and by hitting him clean and fair whenever it was allowed to happen. Also, by talking of "the Italian school of fence" and of "invitations"—the which were wholly outside the fencing-philosophy of the French-trained swordsman. At the age of fifteen the boy was too good for the man who had been the best that Aldershot had known, who had run a *salle d'armes* for years, and who was much sought by ambitious members of the Sword Club.

The Sword, from the day of that newly vivid dream, became to the boy what his Symbol is to the religious fanatic, and he was content to sit and stare at it, musing, for hours.

The sad-eyed, sentimental lady encouraged him and spoke of Knights, Chivalry, Honour, *Noblesse Oblige*, and Ideals such as the nineteenth century knew not and the world will never know again.

"Be a real and true Knight, sonny darling," she would say, "and live to *help*. Help women—God knows they need it. And try to be able to say at the end of your life, 'I have never made a woman weep'. Yes—be a Knight and have 'Live pure, Speak true, Right wrong' on your shield. Be a Round Table Knight and ride through the world bravely. Your dear Father was a great swordsman. You may have the sword down and kiss it, the first thing every morning—and you must salute it every night as you go up to bed. You shall wear a sword some day."

(Could the poor lady but have foreseen!)

She also gave him over-copiously and over-early of her simple, fervent, vague Theology, and much Old and New Testament History, with the highest and noblest intentions—and succeeded in implanting a deep distrust and dislike of "God" in his acutely intelligent mind.

To a prattling baby, *Mother* should be God enough—God and all the angels and paradise in one ... (but he had never known a mother and Nurse Beaton had ever been more faithfully conscientious in deed than tenderly loving in manner).

She filled his soul with questionings and his mouth with questions which she could not answer, and which he answered for himself. The questions sometimes appalled her.

If God so loved the world, why did He let the Devil loose in it?

If God could do *anything*, why didn't He lay the Devil out with one hand?

If He always rewarded the Good and punished the Bad, why was Dearest so unhappy, and drunken Poacher Iggulsby so very gay and prosperously naughty?

He knew too that his dead Father had not been "good," for he heard servant-talk, and terrible old "Grandfather" always forgot that "Little Pitchers have Long Ears".

If God always answered devout and faith-inspired prayer, why did He not

1. Save Caiaphas the cat when earnestly prayed for—having been run over by Pattern in the dog-cart, coming out of the stables?

2. Send the mechanical steam-boat so long and earnestly prayed for, with Faith and Belief?

3. Help the boy to lead a higher and a better life, to eat up his crusts and fat as directed, to avoid chivvying the hens, inking his fingers, haunting the stables, stealing green apples in the orchard, tearing his clothes, and generally doing evil with fire, water, mud, stones and other tempting and injurious things?

And was it entirely decent of God to be eternally spying on a fellow, as appeared to be His confirmed habit?

As for that awful heart-rending Crucifixion, was that the sort of thing for a Father to look on at.... As bad as that brutal old Abraham with Isaac his son ... were *all* "Good" Fathers like that ...?

And nightmare dreams of Hell—a Hell in which there was a *Snake*—wrought no improvement.

And the Bible! How strangely and dully they talked, and what people! That nasty Jacob and Esau business, those horrid Israelites, the Unfaithful Steward; the Judge who let himself be pestered into action; those poor unfortunate swine that were made to rush violently down the steep place into the sea; Ananias and Sapphira. No—not a nice book at all.

The truth is that Theology, at the age of seven, is not commendable—setting aside the question of whether (at any age) Theology is a web of words, ritual, dogma, tradition, invention, shibboleth; a web originally spun by interested men to obscure God from their dupes.

So the boy worshipped Dearest and distrusted and disliked the God she gave him, a big sinister bearded Man who hung spread-eagled above the world, covering the entire roof of the Universe, and watched, watched, watched, with unwinking, all-seeing eye, and remembered with unforgetting, unrelenting mind. Cruel. Ungentlemanly. *Jealous!* Cold.

Also the boy fervently hoped it might never be his lot to go to Heaven—a shockingly dreary place where it was always Sunday and one must, presumably, be very quiet except when singing hymns. A place tenanted by white-robed Angels, unsympathetic towards dirty-faced little sinners who tore their clothes. Angels, cold, superior, unhuggable, haughty, given to ecstatic throes, singers of *Hallelujah* and other silly words—always *praising*.

How he loathed and dreaded the idea of Dearest being an Angel! Fancy sweet Dearest or his own darling Lucille with silly wings (like a beastly goose or turkey in dear old Cook's larder), with a long trumpet, perhaps, in a kind of night-gown, flying about the place, it wasn't decent at all—Dearest and Lucille, whom he adored and hugged—unsympathetic, cold, superior, unhuggable, haughty; and the boy who was very, *very* tender-hearted, would throw his arms round Dearest's neck and hug and hug and hug, for he abhorred the thought of her becoming a beastly angel.

Surely, if God knew His business, Dearest would be always happy and bright and live ever so long, and be ever so old, forty years and more.

And Dearest, fearing that her idolized boy might grow up a man like—well, like "Grumper" had been—hard, quarrelsome, adventurous, flippant, wicked, pleasure-loving, drunken, Godless ... redoubled her efforts to Influence-the-child's-mind-for-good by means of the Testaments and Theology, the Covenant, the Deluge, Miracles, the Immaculate Conception, the Last Supper, the Resurrection, Pentecost, Creeds, Collects, Prayers.

And the boy's mind weighed these things deliberately, pondered them, revolted—and rejected them one and all.

Dearest had been taken in....

He said the prayers she taught him mechanically, and when he felt the need of real prayer—(as he did when he had dreamed of the Snake)—he always began, "If you *are* there, God, and *are* a good, kind God" ... and concluded, "Yours sincerely, Damocles de Warrenne".

He got but little comfort, however, for his restless and logical mind asked:—

"If God *knows* best and will surely *do* what is best, why bother Him? And if He does not and will not, why bother yourself?"

But Dearest succeeded, at any rate, in filling his young soul with a love of beauty, romance, high adventure, honour, and all physical, mental, and moral cleanliness.

She taught him to use his imagination, and she made books a necessity. She made him a gentleman in soul—as distinct from a gentleman in clothes, pocket, or position.

She gave him a beautiful veneration for woman that no other woman was capable of destroying—though one or two did their best. Then the sad-eyed lady was superseded and her professional successor, Miss Smellie, the governess, finding the boy loved the Sword, asked Grumper to lock it away for the boy's Good.

Also she got Grumper to dismiss Nurse Beaton for impudence and not "knowing her place".

But Damocles entered into an offensive and defensive alliance with Lucille, on whom he lavished the whole affection of his deeply, if undemonstratively, affectionate nature, and the two "hunted in couples," sinned and suffered together, pooled their resources and their wits, found consolation in each other when harried by Miss Smellie, spent every available moment in each other's society and, like the Early Christians, had all things in common.

On birthdays, "high days and holidays" he would ask "Grumper" to let him have the Sword for an hour or two, and would stand with it in his hand, rapt, enthralled, ecstatic. How strange it made one feel! How brave, and anxious to do fine deeds. He would picture himself bearing an unconscious Lucille in his left arm through hostile crowds, while with the Sword he thrust and hewed, parried and guarded.... Who could fear *anything* with the Sword in his hand, the Sword of the Dream! How glorious to die wielding it, wielding it in a good cause ... preferably on behalf of Lucille, his own beloved little pal, staunch, clever, and beautiful. And he told Lucille tales of the Sword and of how he loved it!

CHAPTER V.

LUCILLE.

"If you drinks a drop more, Miss Lucy, you'll just go like my pore young sister goed," observed Cook in a warning voice, as Lucille paused to get her second wind for the second draught.

(Lucille had just been tortured at the stake by Sioux and Blackfeet—thirsty work on a July afternoon.)

"And how did she go, Cookie-Bird—*Pop?*" inquired Lucille politely, with round eyes, considering over the top of the big lemonade-flagon as it rose again to her determined little mouth.

"No, Miss Lucy," replied Cook severely. "Pop she did not. She swole ... swole and swole."

"You mean 'swelled,' Cookoo," corrected Lucille, inclined to be a little didactic and corrective at the age of ten.

"Well, she were *my* sister after all, Miss Lucy," retorted Cook, "and perhaps I may, or may not, know what she done. *I* say she swole—and what is more she swole clean into a dropsy. All along of drinking water.... *Drops* of water—*Dropsy.*"

"Never drink water," murmured Dam, absentmindedly annexing, and pocketing, an apple.

"Ah, water, but you see this is lemonade," countered Lucille. "Home-made, too, and not—er—gusty. It doesn't make you go——" and here it is regrettable to have to relate that Lucille made a shockingly realistic sound, painfully indicative of the condition of one who has imbibed unwisely and too well of a gas-impregnated liquor.

"No more does water in my experiants," returned Cook, "and I was not allooding to wulgarity, Miss Lucy, which you should know better than to do such. My pore young sister's systerm turned watery and they tapped her at the last. All through drinking too much water, which lemonade ain't so very different either, be it never so 'ome-made.... Tapped 'er they did—like a carksk, an' 'er a Band of 'Oper, Blue Ribander, an' Sunday Schooler from birth, an' not departin' from it when she grew up. Such be the Ways of Providence," and Cook sighed with protestive respectfulness....

"Tapped 'er systerm, they did," she added pensively, and with a little justifiable pride.

"Were they hard taps?" inquired Lucille, reappearing from behind the flagon. "I hate them myself, even on the funny-bone or knuckles—but on the *cistern!* Ugh!"

"*Hard* taps; they was *silver* taps," ejaculated Cook, "and drawed gallings and gallings—and nothing to laugh at, Master Dammicles, neether.... So don't you drink no more, Miss Lucy."

"I can't," admitted Lucille—and indeed, to Dam, who regarded his "cousin" with considerable concern, it did seem that, even as Cook's poor young sister of unhappy memory, Lucille had "swole"—though only locally.

"Does *beer* make you swell or swole or swellow when you swallow, Cooker?" he inquired; "because, if so, *you* had better be—" but he was not allowed to conclude his deduction, for cook, bridling, bristling, and incensed, bore down upon the children and swept them from her kitchen.

To the boy, even as he fled *via* a dish of tartlets and cakes, it seemed remarkable that a certain uncertainty of temper (and figure) should invariably distinguish those who devote their lives to the obviously charming and attractive pursuit of the culinary art.

Surely one who, by reason of unfortunate limitations of sex, age, ability, or property, could not become a Colonel of Cavalry could still find infinite compensation in the career of cook or railway-servant.

Imagine, in the one case, having absolute freedom of action with regard to raisins, tarts, cream, candy-peel, jam, plum-puddings and cakes, making life one vast hamper, and in the other case, boundless opportunity in the matter of leaping on and off moving trains, carrying lighted bull's-eye lanterns, and waving flags.

One of the early lessons that life taught him, without troubling to explain them, and she taught him many and cruel, was that Cooks are Cross.

"What shall we do now, Dam?" asked Lucille, and added, "Let's raid the rotten nursery and rag the Haddock. Little ass! Nothing else to do. How I *hate* Sunday afternoon.... No work and no play. Rotten."

The Haddock, it may be stated, owed his fishy title to the fact that he once possessed a Wealthy Relative of the name of Haddon. With far-sighted reversionary intent his mother, a Mrs. Berners *nee* Seymour Stukeley, had christened him Haddon.

But the Wealthy Relative, on being informed of his good fortune, had bluntly replied that he intended to leave his little all to the founding of Night-Schools for illiterate Members of Parliament, Travelling-Scholarships for uneducated Cabinet Ministers, and Deportment Classes for New Radical Peers. He was a Funny Man as well as a Wealthy Relative.

And, thereafter, Haddon Berners' parents had, as Cook put it, "up and died" and "Grandfather" had sent for, and adopted, the orphan Haddock.

Though known to Dam and Lucille as "The Haddock" he was in reality an utter Rabbit and esteemed as such. A Rabbit he was born, a Rabbit he lived, and a Rabbit he died. Respectable ever. Seen in the Right Place, in the Right Clothes, doing the Right Thing with the Right People at the Right Time.

Lucille was the daughter of Sylvester Bethune Gavestone, the late and lamented Bishop of Minsterbury (once a cavalry subaltern), a school, Sandhurst, and life-long friend of "Grandfather," and husband of "Grandfather's" cousin, Geraldine Seymour Stukeley.

Poor "Grandfather," known to the children as "Grumper," the ferocious old tyrant who loved all mankind and hated all men, with him adoption was a habit, and the inviting of other children to stay as long as they liked with the adopted children, a craze.

And yet he rarely saw the children, never played with them, and hated to be disturbed.

He had out-lived his soldier-contemporaries, his children, his power to ride to hounds, his pretty taste in wine, his fencing, dancing, flirting, and all that had made life bearable—everything, as he said, but his gout and his liver (and, it may be added, except his ferocious, brutal temper).

"Yes.... Let us circumvent, decoy, and utterly destroy the common Haddock," agreed Dam.

The entry into the nursery was an effective night-attack by Blackfeet (not to mention hands) but was spoilt by the presence of Miss Smellie who was sitting there knitting relentlessly.

"Never burst into rooms, children," she said coldly. "One expects little of a boy, but a *girl* should try to appear a Young Lady. Come and sit by me, Lucille. What did you come in for—or rather for what did you burst in?"

"We came to play with the Haddock," volunteered Dam.

"Very kind and thoughtful of you, I am sure," commented Miss Smellie sourly. "Most obliging and benevolent," and, with a sudden change to righteous anger and bitterness, "Why don't you speak the truth?"

"I am speaking the truth, Miss—er—Smellie," replied the boy. "We did come to play with the dear little Haddock—like one plays with a football or a frog. I didn't say we came for Haddock's *good*."

"We needed the Haddock, you see, Miss Smellie," confirmed Lucille.

"How many times am I to remind you that Haddon Berners' name *is* Haddon, Lucille," inquired Miss Smellie. "Why must you always prefer vulgarity? One expects vulgarity from a boy—but a girl should try to appear a Young Lady."

With an eye on Dam, Lucille protruded a very red tongue at surprising length, turned one eye far inward toward her nose, wrinkled that member incredibly, corrugated her forehead grievously, and elongated her mouth disastrously. The resultant expression of countenance admirably expressed the general juvenile view of Miss Smellie and all her works.

Spurred to honourable emulation, the boy strove to excel. Using both hands for the elongation of his eyes, the extension of his mouth, and the depression of his ears, he turned upon the Haddock so horrible a mask that the stricken child burst into a howl, if not into actual tears.

"What's the matter, Haddon?" demanded Miss Smellie, looking up with quick suspicion.

"Dam made a *fathe* at me," whimpered the smitten one.

"Say 'made a grimace' not 'made a face,'" corrected Miss Smellie. "Only God can make *faces*."

Dam exploded.

"At what are you laughing, Damocles?" she asked sternly.

"Nothing, Miss Smellie. What you said sounded rather funny and a little irrevilent or is it irrembrant?"

"Damocles! Should *I* be likely to say anything Irreverent? Should *I* ever dream of Irreverence? What *can* you mean? And never let me see you make faces again."

"I didn't let you see me, Miss Smellie, and only God can make faces—"

"Leave the room at once, Sir, I shall report your impudence to your great-uncle," hissed Miss Smellie, rising in wrath—and the bad abandoned boy had attained his object. Detention in the nursery for a Sunday afternoon was no part of his programme.

Most unobtrusively Lucille faded away also.

"*Isn't* she a hopeless beast," murmured she as the door closed.

"Utter rotter," admitted the boy. "Let's slope out into the garden and dig some worms for bait."

"Yes," agreed Lucille, and added, "Parse *Smellie*," whereupon, with one voice and heart and purpose the twain broke into a pæan, not of praise—a kind of tribal lay, and chanted:—

"*Smellie*—Very common noun, absurd person, singular back number, tutor gender, objectionable case governed by the word *I*," and so *da capo*.

And yet the poor lady strove to do her duty in that station of life in which it had pleased Providence (or a drunken father) to place her—and to make the children "genteel". Had she striven to win their love instead, her ministrations might have had some effect (other than infinite irritation and bitter dislike).

She was the Compleat Governess, on paper, and all that a person entrusted with the training of young children should not be, in reality. She had innumerable and admirable testimonials from various employers of what she termed "aristocratic standing"; endless certificates that testified unto her successful struggles in Music, Drawing, Needlework, German, French, Calisthenics, Caligraphy, and other mysteries, including the more decorous Sciences (against Physiology, Anatomy, Zoology, Biology, and Hygiene she set her face as subjects apt to be, at times, improper), and an appearance and manner themselves irrefragible proofs of the highest moral virtue.

She also had the warm and unanimous witness of the children at Monksmead that she was a Beast.

To those who frankly realize with open eyes that the student of life must occasionally encounter indelicacies upon the pleasant path of research, it may be revealed, in confidence, that they alluded to Miss Smellie as "Sniffy" when not, under extreme provocation, as "Stinker".

She taught them many things and, prominently, Deceit, Hate, and an utter dislike of her God and her Religion—a most disastrous pair.

Poor old "Grumper"; advertising, he got her, paid her highly, and gave her almost absolute control of the minds, souls, and bodies of his young wards and "grandchildren".

"The best of everything" for them—and they, at the average age of eight, a band of depressed, resentful babes, had "hanged, drawed, and quartered" her in effigy, within a month of coming beneath her stony ministrations.

In appearance Miss Smellie was tall, thin, and flat. Most exceedingly and incredibly flat. Impossibly flat. Her figure, teeth, voice, hair, manner, hats, clothes, and whole life and conduct were flat as Euclid's plane-surface or yesterday's champagne.

To counter-balance the possession, perhaps, of so many virtues, gifts, testimonials, and certificates she had no chin, no eyebrows, and no eyelashes. Her eyes were weak and watery; her spectacles strong and thick; her nose indeterminate, wavering, erratic; her ears large, her teeth irregular and protrusive, her mouth unfortunate and not guaranteed to close.

An ugly female face is said to be the index and expression of an ugly mind. It certainly was so in the case of Miss Smellie. Not that she had an evil or vicious mind in any way—far from it, for she was a narrowly pious and dully conscientious woman. Her mind was ugly as a useful building may be very ugly—or as a room devoid of beautiful furniture or over-crowded with cheap furniture may be ugly.

And her mind was devoid of beautiful thought-furniture, and over-crowded with cheap and ugly furniture of text-book facts. She was an utterly loveless woman, living unloving, and unloved—a terrible condition.

One *could not* like her.

Deadly dull, narrow, pedantic, petty, uninspiring, Miss Smellie's ideals, standards, and aims were incredibly low.

She lived, and taught others to live, for appearances.

The children were so to behave that they might appear "genteel". If they were to do this or that, no one would think they were young ladies or young gentlemen.

"If we were out at tea and you did that, I *should* be ashamed," she would cry when some healthy little human licked its jarnmy fingers, and "*Do* you wish to be considered vulgar or a little gentleman, Damocles?"

Damocles was profoundly indifferent on the point and said so plainly.

They were not to be clean of hand for hygienic reasons—but for fear of what people might "think"; they were not to be honourable, gentle, brave and truthful because these things are fine—but because of what the World might dole out in reward; they were not to eat slowly and masticate well for their health's sake—but by reason of "good manners"; they were not to study that they might develop their powers of reasoning, store their minds, and enlarge their horizons—but that they might pass some infernal examination or other, *ad majorem Smelliae gloriam*; they were not to practise the musical art that they might have a soul-developing aesthetic training, a means of solace, delight, and self-expression—but that they might "play their piece" to the casual visitor to the school-room with priggish pride, expectant of praise; they were not to be Christian for any other reason than that it was the recommended way to Eternal Bliss and a Good Time Hereafter—the whole duty of canny and respectable man being to "save his soul" therefore.

Her charges were skilfully, if unintentionally, trained in hypocrisy and mean motive, to look for low reward and strive for paltry ends—to do what looked well, say what sounded well, to be false, veneered, ungenuine.

And Miss Smellie was giving them the commonly accepted "education" of their class and kind.

The prize product of the Smellie system was the Haddock whose whole life was a pose, a lie, a refusal to see the actual. Perhaps she influenced him more strongly than the others because he was caught younger and was of weaker fibre. Anyhow he grew up the perfect and heartless snob, and by the time he left Oxford, he would sooner have been seen in a Black Maria with Lord Snooker than in a heavenly chariot with a prophet of unmodish garment and vulgar ancestry.

To the finished Haddock, a tie was more than a character, and the cut of a coat more than the cutting of a loving heart.

To him a "gentleman" was a person who had the current accent and waistcoat, a competence, the entree here and there—a goer unto the correct places with the correct people. Manners infinitely more than conduct; externals everything; let the whitening be white and the sepulchre mattered not.

The Haddock had no bloodful vice, but he was unstable as water and could not excel, a moral coward and weakling, a liar, a borrower of what he never intended to return, undeniably and incurably mean, the complete parasite.

From the first he feared and blindly obeyed Miss Smellie, propitiated while loathing her; accepted her statements, standards, and beliefs; curried favour and became her spy and informer.

"What's about the record cricket-ball throw, Dam?" inquired Lucille, as they strolled down the path to the orchard and kitchen-garden, hot-houses, stream and stables, to seek the coy, reluctant worm.

"Dunno," replied the boy, "but a hundred yards wants a lot of doing."

"Wonder if *I* could do it," mused Lucille, picking up a tempting egg-shaped pebble, nearly as big as her fist, and throwing it with remarkably neat action (for a girl) at the first pear-tree over the bridge that spanned the trout-stream.

At, but not into.

With that extraordinary magnetic attraction which glass has for the missile of the juvenile thrower, the orchid-house, on the opposite side of the path from the pear-tree, drew the errant stone to its hospitable shelter.

Through the biggest pane of glass it crashed, neatly decapitated a rare, choice exotic, the pride of Mr. Alastair Kenneth MacIlwraith, head gardener, released from its hold a hanging basket, struck a large pot (perched high in a state of unstable equilibrium), and passed out on the other side with something accomplished, something done, to earn a long repose.

So much for the stone.

The descending pot lit upon the edge of one side of the big glass aquarium, smashed it, and continued its career, precipitating an avalanche of lesser pots and their priceless contents.

The hanging basket, now an unhung and travelling basket, heavy, iron-ribbed, anciently mossy, oozy of slime, fell with neat exactitude upon the bald, bare cranium of Mr. Alastair Kenneth MacIlwraith, head gardener, and dour, irascible child and woman hater.

"Bull's-eye!" commented Dam—always terse when not composing fairy-tales.

"Crikey!" shrieked Lucille. "That's done it," and fled straightway to her room and violent earnest prayer, not for forgiveness but for salvation, from consequences. (What's the good of Saying your Prayers if you can't look for Help in Time of Trouble such as this?)

The face of Mr. Alastair Kenneth MacIlwraith was not pleasant to see as he pranced forth from the orchid-house, brandishing an implement of his trade.

"Ye'll be needing a wash the day, Mon Sandy, and the Sawbath but fower days syne," opined Dam, critically observing the moss-and-mud streaked head, face and neck of the raving, incoherent victim of Lucille's effort.

When at all lucid and comprehensible Mr. MacIlwraith was understood to say he'd give his place (and he twenty-twa years in it) to have the personal trouncing of Dam, that Limb, that Deevil, that predestined and fore-doomed Child of Sin, that—

Dam pocketed his hands and said but:—

"*Havers*, Mon Sandy!"

"I'll tak' the hide fra y'r bones yet, ye feckless, impident—"

Dam shook a disapproving head and said but:—

"*Clavers*, Mon Sandy!"

"I'll *see* ye skelped onny-how—or lose ma job, ye—"

More in sorrow than in anger Dam sighed and said but:—

"*Hoots*, Mon Sandy!"

"I'll go straight to y'r Grandfer the noo, and if ye'r not flayed alive! Aye! I'll gang the noo to Himself——"

"*Wi' fower an twanty men, an' five an' thairrty pipers*," suggested Dam in tuneful song.

Mr. Alastair Kenneth MacIlwraith did what he rarely did—swore violently.

"*Do you think at your age it is right?*" quoted the wicked boy ... the exceedingly bad and reprehensible boy.

The maddened gardener turned and strode to the house with all his imperfections on his head and face and neck.

Taking no denial from Butterson, he forced his way into the presence of his master and clamoured for instant retributive justice—or the acceptance of his resignation forthwith, and him twenty-twa years in the ane place.

"Grandfather," roused from slumber, gouty, liverish, ferociously angry, sent for Dam, Sergeant Havlan, and Sergeant Havlan's cane.

"What's the meaning of this, Sir," he roared as Dam, cool, smiling, friendly ever, entered the Sanctum. "What the Devil d'ye mean by it, eh? Wreckin' my orchid-houses, assaultin' my servants, waking me up, annoying ME! Seven days C.B.[15] and bread and water, on each count. What d'ye mean by it, ye young hound? Eh? Answer me before I have ye flogged to death to teach ye better manners! Guilty or Not Guilty? and I'll take your word for it."

"The missile, describing a parabola, struck its subjective with fearful impact, Sir," replied the bad boy imperturbably, misquoting from his latest fiction (and calling it a "parry-bowler," to "Grandfather's" considerable and very natural mystification).

"*What?*" roared that gentleman, sitting bolt upright in astonishment and wrath.

"No. It's *ob*jective," corrected Dam. "Yes. With fearful impact. Fearful also were the words of the Mon Sandy."

"Grandfather" flushed and smiled a little wryly.

"You'd favour *me* with pleasantries too, would you? I'll reciprocate to the best of my poor ability," he remarked silkily, and his mouth set in the unpleasant Stukeley grimness, while a little muscular pulse beat beneath his cheek-bone.

"A dozen of the very best, if you please, Sergeant," he added, turning to Sergeant Havlan.

"Coat off, Sir," remarked that worthy, nothing loath, to the boy who could touch him almost as he would with the foil.

Dam removed his Eton jacket, folded his arms, turned his back to the smiter and assumed a scientific arrangement of the shoulders with tense muscles and coyly withdrawn bones. He had been there before....

The dozen were indeed of the Sergeant's best and he was a master. The boy turned not a hair, though he turned a little pale.... His mouth grew extraordinarily like that of his grandfather and a little muscular pulse beat beneath his cheek-bone.

"And what do you think of *my* pleasantries, my young friend?" inquired Grandfather. "Feeling at all witty *now*?"

"Havlan is failing a bit, Sir," was the cool reply. "I have noticed it at fencing too— Getting old—or beer perhaps. I scarcely felt him and so did not see or feel the point of your joke."

"Grandfather's" flush deepened and his smile broadened crookedly. "Try and do yourself justice, Havlan," he said. "'Nother dozen. 'Tother way."

Sergeant Havlan changed sides and endeavoured to surpass himself. It was a remarkably sound dozen.

He mopped his brow.

The bad boy did not move, gave no sign, but retained his rigid, slightly hunched attitude, as though he had not counted the second dozen and expected another stroke.

"Let that be a lesson to you to curb your damned tongue," said "Grandfather," his anger evaporating, his pride in the stiff-necked, defiant young rogue increasing.

The boy changed not the rigid, slightly hunched attitude.

"Be pleased to wreck no more of my orchid-houses and to exercise your great wit on your equals and juniors," he added.

Dam budged not an inch and relaxed not a muscle.

"You may go," said "Grandfather".... "Well—what are you waiting for?"

"I was waiting for Sergeant Havlan to *begin*," was the reply. "I thought I was to have a second dozen."

With blazing eyes, bristling moustache, swollen veins and bared teeth, "Grandfather" rose from his chair. Resting on one stick he struck and struck and struck at the boy with the other, passion feeding on its own passionate acts, and growing to madness— until, as the head gardener and Sergeant rushed forward to intervene, Dam fell to the ground, stunned by an unintentional blow on the head.

"Grandfather" stood trembling.... "*Quite* a Stukeley," observed he. "Oblige me by flinging his carcase down the stairs."

"'Angry Stookly's mad Stookly' is about right, mate, wot?" observed the Sergeant to the gardener, quoting an ancient local saying, as they carried Dam to his room after dispatching a groom for Dr. Jones of Monksmead.

"Dammy Darling," whispered a broken and tear-stained voice outside Dam's locked and keyless door the next morning, "are you dead yet?"

"Nit," was the prompt reply, "but I'm starving to death, fast."

"I am so glad," was the sobbed answer, "for I've got some flat food to push under the door."

"Shove it under," said Dam. "Good little beast!"

"I didn't know anything about the fearful fracass until tea-time," continued Lucille, "and then I went straight to Grumper and confessed, and he sent me to bed on an empty stummick and I laid upon it, the bed I mean, and howled all night, or part of it anyhow. I howled for your sake, not for the empty stummick. I thought my howls would break or at least soften his hard heart, but I don't think he heard them. I'm sure he didn't, in fact, or I should not have been allowed to howl so loud and long.... Did he blame you with anger as well as injustice?"

"With a stick," was the reply. "What about that grub?"

"I told him you were an innocent unborn babe and that Justice had had a miscarriage, but he only grinned and said you had got C.B. and dry bread for insilence in the Orderly Room. What is 'insilence'?"

"Pulling Havlan's leg, I s'pose," opined Dam. "What about that *grub*? There comes a time when you are too hungry to eat and then you die. I—"

"Here it is," squealed Lucille, "don't go and die after all my trouble. I've got some thin ice-wafer biscuits, sulphur tablets, thin cheese, a slit-up apple and three sardines. They'll all come under the door—though the sardines may get a bit out of shape. I'll come after lessons and suck some brandy-balls here and breathe through the key-hole to comfort you. I could blow them through the key-hole when they are small too."

"Thanks," acknowledged Dam gratefully, "and if you could tie some up and a sausage and a tart or two and some bread-and-jam and some chicken and cake and toffee and things in a handkerchief, and climb on to the porch with Grumper's longest fishing-rod, you might be able to relieve the besieged garrison a lot. If the silly Haddock were any good he could fire sweets up with a catapult."

"I'd try that too," announced Lucille, "but I'd break the windows. I feel I shall never have the heart to throw a stone or anything again. My heart is broken," and the penitent sinner groaned in deep travail of soul.

"Have you eaten everything, Darling? How do you feel?" she suddenly asked.

"Yes. Hungrier than ever," was the reply. "I like sulphur tablets with sardines. Wonder when they'll bring that beastly dry bread?"

"If there's a sulphur tablet left I could eat one myself," said Lucille. "They are good for the inside and I have wept mine sore."

"Too late," answered Dam. "Pinch some more."

"They were the last," was the sad rejoinder. "They were for Rover's coat, I think. Perhaps they will make your coat hairy, Dam. I mean your skin."

"Whiskers to-morrow," said Dam.

After a pregnant silence the young lady announced:—

"Wish I could hug and kiss you, Darling. Don't you?... I'll write a kiss on a piece of paper and push it under the door to you. Better than spitting it through the key-hole."

"Put it on a piece of *ham,*—more sense," answered Dam.

The quarter-inch rasher that, later, made its difficult entry, pulled fore and pushed aft, was probably the only one in the whole history of Ham that was the medium of a kiss—located and indicated by means of a copying-ink pencil and a little saliva.

Before being sent away to school at Wellingborough Dam had a very curious illness, one which greatly puzzled Dr. Jones of Monksmead village, annoyed Miss Smellie, offended Grumper, and worried Lucille.

Sitting in solitary grandeur at his lunch one Sabbath, sipping his old Chambertin, Grumper was vexed and scandalized by a series of blood-curdling shrieks from the floor above his breakfast-room. Butterson, dispatched in haste to see "who the Devil was being killed in that noisy fashion," returned to state deferentially as how Master Damocles was in a sort of heppiletic fit, and foaming at the mouth. They had found him in the General's study where he had been reading a book, apparently; a big Natural History book.

A groom was galloping for Dr. Jones and Mrs. Pont was doin' her possible.

No. Nothing appeared to have hurt or frightened the young gentleman—but he was distinctly 'eard to shout: "*It is under my foot. It is moving—moving—moving out....*" before he became unconscious.

No, Sir. Absolutely nothing under the young gentleman's foot.

Dr. Jones could shed no light and General Sir Gerald Seymour Stukeley hoped to God that the boy was not going to grow up a wretched epileptic. Miss Smellie appeared to think the seizure a judgment upon an impudent and deceitful boy who stole into his elders' rooms in their absence and looked at their books.

Lucille was troubled in soul for, to her, Damocles confessed the ghastly, terrible, damning truth that he was a Coward. He said that he had hidden the fearful fact for all these years within his guilty bosom and that now it had emerged and convicted him. He lived in subconscious terror of the Snake, and in its presence—nay even in that of its counterfeit presentment—he was a gibbering, lunatic coward. Such, at least, was her dimly realized conception resultant upon the boy's bald, stammering confession.

But how could her dear Dammy be a *coward*—the vilest thing on earth! He who was willing to fight anyone, ride anything, go anywhere, act anyhow. Dammy the boxer, fencer, rider, swimmer. Absurd! Think of the day "the Cads" had tried to steal their boat from them when they were sailing it on the pond at Revelmead. There had been five of them, two big and three medium. Dam had closed the eye of one of them, cut the lip of another, and knocked one of the smaller three weeping into the dust.

62

They had soon cleared off and flung stones until Dam had started running for them and then they had fled altogether.

Think of the time when she set fire to the curtains. Why, he feared no bull, no dog, no tramp in England.

A coward! Piffle.

And yet he had screamed and kicked and cried—yes *cried*—as he had shouted that it was under his foot and moving out. Rum! *Very* rum!

On the day that Dam left Monksmead for school Lucille wept till she could weep no more. Life for the next few years was one of intermittent streaks of delirious joy and gloomy grief, vacation time when he was at Monksmead and term time when he was at school. All the rest of the world weighed as a grain of dust against her hero, Dam.

CHAPTER VI.

THE SNAKE'S "MYRMIDON".

For a couple of years and more, in the lower School at Wellingborough, Damocles de Warrenne, like certain States, was happy in that he had no history. In games rather above the average, and in lessons rather below it, he was very popular among his fellow "squeakers" for his good temper, modesty, generous disposition, and prowess at football and cricket.

Then, later, dawned the day when from this comfortable high estate a common adder, preserved in spirits of wine, was the cause of his downfall and Bully Harberth the means of his reinstatement....

One afternoon Mr. Steynker, the Science Master, for some reason and without preliminary mention of his intent, produced a bottled specimen of a snake. He entered the room with the thing under his arm and partly concealed by the sleeve of his gown. Watching him as he approached the master's desk and spoke with Mr. Colfe, the form-master, Dam noted that he had what appeared to be a long oblong glass box of which the side turned towards him was white and opaque.

When Mr. Steynker stepped on to the dais, as Mr. Colfe took up his books and departed, he placed the thing on the desk with the other side to the class....

And there before Dam's starting, staring eyes, fastened to the white back of the tall glass box, and immersed in colourless liquid was the Terror.

He rose, gibbering, to his feet, pale as the dead, and pointed, mopping and mowing like an idiot.

How should a glass box restrain the Fiend that had made his life a Hell upon earth? What did Steynker and Colfe and these others—all gaping at him open-mouthed—know of the Devil with whom he had wrestled deep beneath the Pit itself for ten thousand centuries of horror—centuries whose every moment was an aeon?

What could these innocent men and boys know of the living Damnation that made him pray to die—provided only that he could be *really* dead and finished, beyond all consciousness and fear. The fools!... to think that it was a harmless, concrete thing. It would emerge in a moment like the Fisherman's Geni from the Brass Bottle and grow as big as the world. He felt he was going mad again.

"Help!" he suddenly shrieked. "*It is under my foot. It is moving ... moving ... moving out.*" He sprang to his astounded friend, Delorme, and screamed to him for help—and then realizing that there was *no* help, that neither man nor God could save him, he fled from the room screaming like a wounded horse.

Rushing madly down the corridor, falling head-long down the stone stairs, bolting blindly across the entrance-hall, he fled until (unaware of his portly presence up to the moment when he rebounded from him as a cricket-ball from a net) he violently encountered the Head.

Scrambling beneath his gown the demented boy flung his arms around the massy pillar of the Doctor's leg, and prayed aloud to him for help, between heart-rending screams.

Now it is undeniable that no elderly gentleman, of whatsoever position or condition, loves to be butted violently upon a generous lunch as he makes his placid way to his arm-chair, cigar, book, and ultimate pleasant doze. If he be pompous by profession, precise by practice, dignified as a duty, a monument of most stately correctness and, to small boys and common men, a great and distant, if tiny, God—he may be expected to resent it.

The Doctor did. Almost before he knew what he was doing, he struck the sobbing, gasping child twice, and then endeavoured to remove him by the ungentle application of the untrammelled foot, from the leg to which, limpet-like, he clung.

To Dam the blows were welcome, soothing, reassuring. Let a hundred Heads flog him with two hundred birch-rods, so they could keep him from the Snake. What are mere blows?

Realizing quickly that something very unusual was in the air, the worthy Doctor repented him of his haste and, with what dignity he might, inquired between a bleat and a bellow:—

"What is the matter, my boy? Hush! Hush!"

"The Snake! The Snake!" shrieked Dam. "Save me! Save me! *It is under my foot! It is moving ... moving ... moving out*," and clung the tighter.

The good Doctor also moved with alacrity—but saw no snake. He was exceedingly perturbed, between a hypothetical snake and an all too actual lunatic boy.

Fortunately, "Stout" (so called because he was Porter), passing the big doors without, was attracted by the screams.

Entering, he hastened to the side of the agitated Head, and, with some difficulty, untied from that gentleman's leg, a small boy—but not until the small boy had fainted....

When Dam regained consciousness he had a fit, recovered, and found himself in the Head's study, and the object of the interested regard of the Head, Messrs. Colfe and Steynker, the school medico, and the porter.

It was agreed (while the boy fought for his sanity, bit his hand for the reassuring pleasure of physical pain, and prayed for help to the God in whom he had no reason to believe) that the case was "very unusual, very curious, v-e-r-y interesting indeed". Being healthier and stronger than at the time of previous attacks, Dam more or less recovered before night and was not sent home. But he had fallen from his place, and in the little republics of the dormitory and class-room, he was a thing to shun, an outcast, a disgrace to the noble race of Boy.

Not a mere liar, a common thief, a paltry murderer or vulgar parricide—but a COWARD, a blubberer, a baby. Even Delorme, more in sorrow than in anger, shunned his erstwhile bosom-pal, and went about as one betrayed.

The name of "Funky Warren" was considered appropriate, and even the Haddock, his own flesh and blood, and most junior of "squeakers," dared to apply it!....

The infamy of the Coward spread abroad, was talked of in other Houses, and fellows made special excursions to see the cry-baby, who funked a dead snake, a blooming bottled, potted, dead snake, and who had blubbed aloud in his terror.

And Bully Harberth of the Fifth, learning of these matters, revolved in his breast the thought that he who fears dead serpents must, even more, fear living bullies, put Dam upon his list as a safe and pliant client, and thereby (strange instrument of grace!) gave him the chance to rehabilitate himself, clear the cloud of infamy from about his head, and live a bearable life for the rest of his school career....

One wet Wednesday afternoon, as Dam, a wretched, forlorn Ishmael, sat alone in a noisy crowd, reading a "penny horrible" (admirable, stimulating books crammed with brave deeds and noble sentiments if not with faultless English) the Haddock entered the form-room, followed by Bully Harberth.

"That's him, Harberth, by the window, reading a penny blood," said the Haddock, and went and stood afar off to see the fun.

Harberth, a big clumsy boy, a little inclined to fat, with small eyes, heavy low forehead, thick lips, and amorphous nose, lurched over to where Dam endeavoured to read himself into a better and brighter world inhabited by Deadwood Dick, Texas Joe, and Red Indians of no manners and nasty customs.

"I want you, Funky Warren. I'm going to torture you," he announced with a truculent scowl and a suggestive licking of blubber lips.

Dam surveyed him coolly.

Of thick build, the bully was of thicker wit and certainly of no proven courage. Four years older than Dam and quite four inches taller, he had never dreamed of molesting him before. Innumerable as were the stories of his brutalities to the smallest "squeakers" and of his cruel practical jokes on new boys, there were no stories of his fighting, such as there were about Ormond Delorme, of Dam's form, whose habit it was to implore bigger boys of their courtesy to fight him, and to trail his coat where there were "chaws" about.

"I'm going to torture you, Funky. Every day you must come to me and *beg* me to do it. If you don't come and pray for it I'll come to *you* and you'll get it double and treble. If you sneak you'll get it quadru—er—quadrupedal—and also be known as Sneaky as well as Funky. See?" he continued.

"How will you torture me, Harberth, please?" asked Dam meekly, as he measured the other with his eye, noted his puffiness, short reach, and inward tendency of knee.

"Oh! lots of ways," was the reply. "Dry shaves, tweaks, scalpers, twisters, choko, tappers, digs, benders, shinners, windos, all sorts."

"I don't even know what they are," moaned Dam.

"Poor Kid!" sympathized the bully, "you soon will, though. Dry shaves are beautiful. You die dotty in about five minutes if I don't see fit to stop. Twisters break your wrists and you yell the roof off—or would do if I didn't gag you first with a cake of soap and a towel. Tappers are very amusing, too, for me that is—not for you. They are done on the side of your knee with a cricket stump. Wonderful how kids howl when you understand knee-treatment. Choko is good too. Makes you black in the face and your eyes goggle out awful funny. Done with a silk handkerchief and a stick. Windos and benders go together and really want two fellows to do it properly. I hit you in the wind and you double up, and the other fellow un-doubles you from behind—with a cane—so that I can double you up again. Laugh! I nearly died over young Berners. Shinners, scalpers, and tweaks are good too—jolly good!... but of course all this comes after lamming and tunding.... Come along with me...."

"Nit," was Dam's firm but gentle reply, and a little pulse began to beat beneath his cheek bone.

"Oh! Ho!" smiled Master Harberth, "then I'll *begin* here, and when you're broke and blubbing you'll come with me—and get just double for a start."

Dam's spirits rose and he felt almost happy—certainly far better than he had done since the hapless encounter with the bottled adder and his fall from grace. It was a positive, *joy* to have an enemy he could tackle, a real flesh-and-blood foe and tormentor that came upon him in broad daylight and in mere human form.

After countless thousands of centuries of awful nightmare struggling—in which he was bound hand-and-foot and doomed to failure and torture from the outset, the sport, plaything, and victim of a fearful, intangible Horror—this would be sheer amusement and recreation. What could mere man do to *him*, much less mere boy! Why, the most awful torture-chamber of the Holy Inquisition of old was a pleasant recreation-room compared with *any* place where the Snake could enter.

Oh, if the Snake could only be met and fought in the open with free hands and untrammelled limbs, as Bully Harberth could!

Oh, if it could only inflict mere physical pain instead of such agonies of terror as made the idea of any bodily injury—mere cutting, burning, beating, blinding—a trifling nothing-at-all. Anyhow, he could *imagine* that Bully Harberth was the Snake or Its emissary and, since he was indirectly brought upon him by the Snake, regard him as a myrmidon—and deal with him accordingly....

"How do you like this?" inquired that young gentleman as he suddenly seized the seated and unsuspecting Dam by the head, crushed him down with his superior weight and dug cruelly into the sides of his neck, below the ears, with his powerful thumb and fingers. "It is called 'grippers'. You'll begin to enjoy it in a minute." ... In a few seconds the pain became acute and after a couple of minutes, excruciating.

Dam kept absolutely still and perfectly silent.

To Harberth this was disappointing and after a time he grew tired. Releasing his impassive victim he arose preparatory to introducing the next item of his programme of tortures.

"How do you like *this*?" inquired Dam rising also—and he smote his tormentor with all his strength beneath the point of his chin. Rage, pain, rebellion, and undying hatred (of the Snake) lent such force to the skilful blow—behind which was the weight and upward spring of his body—that Bully Harberth went down like a nine-pin, his big head striking the sharp edge of a desk with great violence.

He lay still and white with closed eyes. "Golly," shrilled the Haddock, "Funky Warren has murdered Bully Harberth. Hooray! Hooray!" and he capered with joy.

A small crowd quickly collected, and, it being learned from credible eye-witnesses that the smaller boy had neither stabbed the bully in the back nor clubbed him from behind, but had well and truly smitten him on the jaw with his fist, he went at one bound from despised outcast coward to belauded, admired hero.

"You'll be hung, of course, Warren," said Delorme.

"And a jolly good job," replied Dam, fervently and sincerely.

As he spoke, Harberth twitched, moved his arms and legs, and opened his eyes.

68

Sitting up, he blinked owl-like and inquired as to what was up.

"You are down is what's up," replied Delorme.

"Oh—he's not dead," squeaked the Haddock, and there was a piteous break in his voice.

"What's up?" asked Harberth again.

"Why, Funky—that is to say, Warren—knocked you out, and you've got to give him best and ask for *pax*, or else fight him," said Delorme, adding hopefully, "but of course you'll fight him."

Harberth arose and walked to the nearest seat.

"He hit me a 'coward's poke' when I wasn't looking," quoth he. "It's well known he is a coward."

"You are a liar, Bully Harberth," observed Delorme. "He hit you fair, and anyhow he's not afraid of *you*. If you don't fight him you become Funky Harberth *vice*. Funky Warren—no longer Funky. So you'd better fight. See?" The Harberth bubble was evidently pricked, for the sentiment was applauded to the echo.

"I don't fight cowards," mumbled Harberth, holding his jaw—and, at this meanness, Dam was moved to go up to Harberth and slap him right hard upon his plump, inviting cheek, a good resounding blow that made his hand tingle with pain and his heart with pleasure.

He still identified him somehow with the Snake, and had a glorious, if passing, sensation of successful revolt and some revenge.

He felt as the lashed galley-slave must have felt when, during a lower-deck mutiny, he broke from his oar and sprang at the throat of the cruel overseer, the embodiment and source of the agony, starvation, toil, brutality, and hopeless woe that had thrust him below the level of the beasts (fortunate beasts) that perish.

"Now you've *got* to fight him, of course," said Delorme, and fled to spread the glad tidings far and wide.

"I—I—don't feel well now," mumbled Harberth. "I'll fight him when I'm better," and shambled away, outraged, puzzled, disgusted. What was the world coming to? The little brute! He had a punch like the kick of a horse. The little cad—to *dare*! Well, he'd show him something if he had the face to stand up to his betters and olders and biggers in the ring....

News of the affair spread like wild-fire, and the incredible conduct of the extraordinary Funky Warren—said to be no longer Funky—became the topic of the hour.

At tea, Dam was solemnly asked if it were true that he had cast Harberth from a lofty window and brought him to death's door, or that of the hospital; whether he had strangled him with the result that he had a permanent squint; if he had so kicked him as to break both his thigh bones; if he had offered to fight him with one hand.

Even certain more or less grave and reverend seniors of the upper school took a well-disguised interest in the matter and pretended that the affair should be allowed to go on, as it would do Harberth a lot of good if de Warrenne could lick him, and do the latter a lot of good to reinstate himself by showing that he was not really a coward in essentials. Of course they took no interest in the fight as a fight. Certainly not (but it was observed that Flaherty of the Sixth stopped the fight most angrily and peremptorily when it was over, and that no sign of anger or peremptoriness escaped him until it was over—and he happened to pass behind the gymnasium, curiously enough, just as it started)....

Good advice was showered upon Dam from all sides. He was counselled to live on meat, to be a vegetarian, to rise at 4 a.m. and swim, to avoid all brain-fag, to run twenty miles a day, to rest until the fight, to get up in the night and swing heavy dumb-bells, to eat no pudding, to drink no tea, to give up sugar, avoid ices, and deny himself all "tuck" and everything else that makes life worth living.

He did none of these things—but simply went on as usual, save in one respect.

For the first time since the adder episode, he was really happy. Why, he did not know, save that he was about to "get some of his own back," to strike a blow against the cruel coward Incubus (for he persisted in identifying Harberth with the Snake and in regarding him as a materialization of the life-long Enemy), and possibly to enjoy a brief triumph over what had so long triumphed over him.

If he were at this time a little mad the wonder is that he was still on the right side of the Lunatic Asylum gates.

Mad or not, he was happy—and the one thing wanting was the presence of Lucille at the fight. How he would have loved to show her that he was not really a coward—given a fair chance and a tangible foe.

If only Lucille could be there—dancing from one foot to the other, and squealing. (Strictly *between*, and not during, the rounds, of course.)

"Buck up, Dammy! Ginger for pluck! Never say croak!"

A very large and very informal committee took charge of the business of the fight, and what was alluded to as "a friendly boxing contest between Bully Harberth of the Fifth and de Warrenne—late Funky—" was arranged for the following Saturday afternoon. On being asked by a delegate of the said large and informal committee as to whether he would be trained by then or whether he would prefer a more distant date, Dam replied that he would be glad to fight Harberth that very moment—and thus gained the reputation of a fierce and determined fellow (though erstwhile "funky"—the queer creature).

Those who had been loudest in dubbing him Funky Warrenne were quickest in finding explanations of his curious conduct and explained it well away.

It was at this time that Dam's heart went wholly and finally out to Ormonde Delorme who roundly stated that his father, a bemedalled heroic Colonel of Gurkhas, was "in a blind perishing funk" during a thunderstorm and always sought shelter in the wine cellar when one was in progress in his vicinity.

Darn presented Delorme with his knife and a tiger's tooth forthwith. Saturday came and Dam almost regretted its advent, for, though a child in years, he was sufficiently old, weary, and cynical in spirit to know that all life's fruit contains dust and ashes, that the joys of anticipation exceed those of realization, and that with possession dies desire.

With the fight would end the glorious feeling of successful revolt, and if he overcame one emissary of the Snake there would be a million more to take his place.

And if Providence should be, as usual, on the side of the "big battalions," and the older, taller, stronger, heavier boy should win? Why—then he would bully the loser to his heart's content and the limit of his ingenuity.

Good! Let him! He would fight him every day with the greatest pleasure. A chance to fight the Snake on fair terms was all he asked....

Time and place had been well chosen and there was little likelihood of interference.

Some experienced youth, probably Cokeson himself, had made arrangements as to seconds, time-keeper, judges, and referee; and, though there was no ring of ropes and stakes, a twenty-four-foot square had been marked out and inclosed by forms and benches. Seating was provided for the "officials" and seniors, and two stools for the principals. A couple of bowls of water, sponges, and towels lent a business-like air to the scene.

To his delight, Dam discovered that Delorme was to be his second—a person of sound advice, useful ministrations, and very present help in time of trouble....

Delorme led him to his stool in an angle of the square of benches, bade him spread wide his arms and legs and breathe deeply "for all he was worth, with his eyes closed and his thoughts fixed on jolly things".

Feeling himself the cynosure of neighbouring eyes and able to hear the comments of the crowd, the last part of his second's instructions was a little difficult of strict observation. However, he continued to think of licking Harberth—the "jolliest" thing he could conceive, until his mind wandered home to Lucille, and he enhanced the imaginary jollity by conceiving her present.... "Sturdy little brute," observed a big Fifth Form boy seated with a couple of friends on the bench beside him, "but I'd lay two to one in sovs. (if I had 'em) that he doesn't last a single round with Harberth".

"Disgrace to Harberth if he doesn't eat the kid alive," responded the other.

"Got a good jaw and mouth, though," said the third. "Going to die hard, you'll see. Good little kid."

"Fancy funking a bottled frog or something and fighting a chap who can give him about four years, four inches, and four stone," observed the first speaker.

"Yes. Queer little beast. He knocked Harberth clean out, they say. Perhaps his father has had him properly taught and he can really box. Ever seen him play footer? Nippiest little devil *I* ever saw. Staunch too. Rum go," commented his friend.

Dam thought of Sergeant Havlan and his son, the punching-ball, and the fighting days at Monksmead. Perhaps he could "really" box, after all. Anyhow he knew enough to hit straight and put his weight into it, to guard chin and mark, to use his feet, duck, dodge, and side step. Suppose Harberth knew as much? Well—since he was far stronger, taller, and heavier, the only hope of success lay in the fact that he was connected with the Snake—from whom mere blows in the open would be welcome.

Anyhow he would die or win.

The positive joy of fighting *It* in the glorious day and open air, instead of in the Bottomless Pit—bound, stifled, mad with Fear—none could realize....

Bully Harberth entered the ring accompanied by Shanner, who looked like a Sixth Form boy and was in the Shell.

Harberth wore a thick sweater and looked very strong and heavy.

"If the little kid lasts three rounds with *that*" observed Cokeson to Coxe Major, "he ought to be chaired."

72

Dam was disposed to agree with him in his heart, but he had no fear. The feeling that *his* brief innings had come—after the Snake had had Its will of him for a dozen years—swallowed up all other feelings.

Coxe Major stepped into the ring. "I announce a friendly boxing contest between Harberth of the Fifth, nine stone seven, and Funky Warren (said to be no longer Funky) of Barton's House, weight not worth mentioning," he declaimed.

"Are the gloves all right," called Cokeson (whose father owned racehorses, was a pillar of the National Sporting Club, and deeply interested in the welfare of a certain sporting newspaper).

"No fault can be found with Warren's gloves," said Shanner, coming over to Dam.

"There's nothing wrong with the gloves here," added Delorme, after visiting Harberth's corner.

This was the less remarkable in that there were no gloves whatsoever.

Presumably the fiction of a "friendly boxing contest" was to be stoutly maintained. The crowd of delighted boys laughed.

"Then come here, both of you," said Cokeson.

The combatants complied.

"Don't hold and hit. Don't butt nor trip. Don't clinch. Don't use knee, elbow, nor shoulder. When I call 'Break away,' break without hitting. If you do any of these things you will be jolly well disqualified. Fight fair and God have mercy on your souls." To Dam it seemed that the advice was superfluous—and of God's mercy on his soul he had had experience.

Returning to their corners, the two stripped to the waist and sat ready, arrayed in shorts and gymnasium shoes.

Seen thus, they looked most unevenly matched, Harberth looking still bigger for undressing and Dam even smaller. But, as the knowing Coxe Major observed, what there was of Dam was in the right place—and was muscle. Certainly he was finely made.

"Seconds out of the ring. *Time!*" called the time-keeper and Dam sprang to his feet and ran at Harberth who swung a mighty round-arm blow at his face as Dam ducked and smote him hard and true just below the breast-bone and fairly on the "mark ".

The bully's grunt of anguish was drowned in howls of "Shake hands!" "They haven't shaken hands!"

"Stop! Stop the fight," shouted Cokeson, and as they backed from each other he inquired with anger and reproach in his voice:—

"Is this a friendly boxing-contest or a vulgar fight?" adding, "Get to your corners and when *Time* is called, shake hands and then begin."

Turning to the audience he continued in a lordly and injured manner: "And there is only *one* Referee, gentlemen, please. Keep silence or I shall stop the fight—I mean—the friendly boxing contest."

As Dam sat down Delorme whispered:—

"Splendid! *In*fighting is your tip. Duck and go for the body every time. He knows nothing of boxing I should say. Tire him—and remember that if he gets you with a swing like that you're out."

"Seconds out of the ring. *Time!*" called the time-keeper and Dam walked towards Harberth with outstretched hand, met him in the middle of the ring and shook hands with great repugnance. As Harberth's hand left Dam's it rose swiftly to Dam's face and knocked him down.

"Shame! Foul poke! Coward," were some of the indignant cries that arose from the spectators.

"Silence," roared the referee. "*Will* you shut up and be quiet. Perfectly legitimate—if not very sporting."

Dam sprang to his feet, absolutely unhurt, and, if possible, more determined than ever. It was only because he had been standing with feet together that he had been knocked down at all. Had he been given time to get into sparring position the blow would not have moved him. Nor was Harberth himself in an attitude to put much weight behind the blow and it was more a cuff than a punch.

Circling round his enemy, Dam sparred for an opening and watched his style and methods.

Evidently the bully expected to make short work of him, and he carried his right fist as though it were a weapon and not a part of his body.

As he advanced with his right extended, quivering, menacing, and poised for a knock-out blow, his left did not appear in the matter at all.

Suddenly he aimed his fist at Dam like a stone and with great force. Dam side-stepped and it brushed his ear; with his right he smote with all his force upon Harberth's ribs and with his left he drove at his eye as he came up. Both blows were well and truly laid and with good sounding thuds that seemed to delight the audience.

Bully Harberth changed his tactics and advanced upon his elusive opponent with his left in the position of guard and his right drawn back to the arm-pit. Evidently he was going to hold him off with the one and smash him with the other. Not waiting for him to develop his attack, but striking the bully's left arm down with his own left, Dam hit over it with his right and reached his nose and—so curious are the workings of the human mind—thought of Moses striking the rock and bringing forth water.

The sight of blood seemed to distress Harberth and, leaping in as the latter drew his hand across his mouth, Dam drove with all his strength at his mark and with such success that Harberth doubled up and fetched his breath with deep groans. Dam stood clear and waited.

Delorme called out, "You've a right to finish him," and was sternly reproved by the referee.

As Harberth straightened up, Dam stepped towards him, but the bully turned and ran to his stool. As he reached it amid roars of execration the time-keeper arose and cried "*Time!*"

"You had him, you little ass," said Delorme, as he squeezed a sponge of water on Dam's head. "Why on earth didn't you go in and finish him?"

"It didn't seem decent when he was doubled up," replied Dam.

"Did it seem decent his hitting you while you shook hands?" returned the other, beginning to fan his principal with a towel.

"Anyhow he's yours if you go on like this. Keep your head and don't worry about his. Stick to his body till you have a clear chance at the point of his jaw."

"Seconds out of the ring. *Time!*" cried the time-keeper.

This round was less fortunate for the smaller boy. Harberth's second had apparently given him some good advice, for he kept his mark covered and used his left both to guard and to hit.

Also he had learned something from Dam, and, on one occasion as the latter went at his face with a straight left, he dropped the top of his head towards him and made a fierce hooking punch at Dam's body. Luckily it was a little high, but it winded him for a moment, and had his opponent rushed him then, Dam could have done nothing at all.

Just as "Time" was called, Harberth swung a great round-arm blow at Dam which would have knocked him head over heels had not he let his knees go just in time and ducked under it, hitting his foe once again on the mark with all his strength.

"How d'you feel?" asked Delorme as Dam went to his stool.

"Happy," said he.

"Don't talk piffle," was the reply. "How do you feel? Wind all right? Groggy at all?"

"Not a bit," said Dam. "I am enjoying it."

And so he was. Hitherto the Snake had had him bound and helpless. As it pursued him in nightmares, his knees had turned to water, great chains had bound his arms, devilish gags had throttled him, he could not breathe, and he had not had a chance to escape nor to fight. He could not even scream for help. He could only cling to a shelf. *Now* he had a chance. His limbs were free, his eyes were open, he could breathe, think, act, defend himself and *attack*.

"Seconds out of the ring. *Time!*" called the time-keeper and Delorme ceased fanning with the towel, splashed a spongeful of water in Dam's face and backed away with his stool.

Harberth seemed determined to make an end.

He rushed at his opponent whirling his arms, breathing stertorously, and scowling savagely.

Guarding hurt Dam's arms, he had no time to hit, and in ducking he was slow and got a blow (aimed at his chin) in the middle of his forehead. Down he went like a nine-pin, but was up as quickly, and ready for Harberth who had rushed at him in the act of rising, while the referee shouted "Stand clear".

As he came on, Dam fell on one knee and drove at his mark again.

Harberth grunted and placed his hands on the smitten spot.

Judging time and distance well, Dam hit with all his force at the bully's chin and he went down like a log.

Rising majestically, the time-keeper lifted up his voice and counted: "*One—two—three—four—five—six*"—and Harberth opened his eyes, sat up, "*seven—eight—nine*"—and lay down again; and just as Dam was about to leap for joy and the audience to roar their approval—instead of the fatal *"OUT"* the time-keeper called *"Time"*.

Had Dam struck the blow a second sooner, the fight would have been over and he would have won. As it was, Harberth had the whole interval in which to recover. Dam's own luck! (But Miss Smellie had always said there is no such thing as Luck!) Well—so much the better. *Fighting* the Snake was the real joy, and victory would end it. So would defeat and he must not get cock-a-hoop and careless.

Delorme filled his mouth with water and ejected it in a fine spray over Dam's head and chest. He was very proud of this feat, but, though most refreshing, Dam could have preferred that the water had come from a sprayer.

"Seconds out of the ring, *Time!*" called the referee.

Harberth appeared quite recovered, but he was of a curious colour and seemed tired.

Acting on his second's advice, Dam gave his whole attention to getting at his opponent's body again, and overdid it. As Harberth struck at him with his left, he ducked, and as he was aiming at Harberth's mark, he was suddenly knocked from day into night, from light into darkness, from life into death....

Years passed and Dam strove to explain that the mainspring had broken and that he had heard it click—when suddenly a great black drop-curtain rolled up, while some one snapped back some slides that had covered his ears, and had completely deafened him.

Then he saw Harberth and heard the voice of the time-keeper saying: *"five—six—seven"*.

He scrambled to his knees, *"eight"* swayed and staggered to his feet, collapsed, rose, *"nine"* and was knocked down by Harberth.

The time-keeper again stood up and counted, *"One—two—three"*. But this blow actually helped him.

He lay collecting his strength and wits, breathing deeply and taking nine seconds' rest.

On the word *"nine"* he sprang to his feet and as Harberth rushed in, side-stepped, and, as that youth instinctively covered his much-smitten "mark," Dam drove at his chin and sent him staggering. As he went after him he saw that Harberth was breathing hard, trembling, and swaying on his feet. Springing in, he rained short-arm blows until Harberth fell and then he stepped well back.

Harberth sat shaking his head, looking piteous, and, in the middle of the time-keeper's counting, he arose remarking, "I've had enough"—and walked to his chair.

Bully Harberth was beaten—and Dam felt that the Snake was farther from him than ever it had been since he could remember.

"De Warrenne wins," said Cokeson, and then Flaherty of the Sixth stepped into the ring and stopped the fight with much show of wrath and indignation.

Dam was wildly cheered and chaired and thence-forth was as popular and as admired as he had been shunned and despised.

Nor did he have another Snake seizure by day (though countless terrible nightmares in what must be called his sleep) till some time after he had left school.

When he did, it had a most momentous influence upon his career.

She is mine! She is mine!
By her soul divine
By her heart's pure guile
By her lips' sweet smile
She is mine! She is mine.

Encapture? Aye
In dreams as fair
As angel whispers, low and rare,
In thoughts as pure
As childhood's innocent allure
In hopes as bright
In deeds as white
As altar lilies, bathed in light.

She is mine! She is mine!
By seal as true
To spirit view
As holy scripture writ in dew,
By bond as fair
To vision rare
As holy scripture writ in air,
By writ as wise to spirit eyes
As holy scripture in God's skies v
She is mine! She is mine!

Elude me? Nay,
Ere earth reclaimed
In joy unveils a Heaven regained,

Ere sea unbound,
Unfretting, rolls in mist—nor sound,
Ere sun and star repentent crash
In scattered ash, across the bar
She is *mine* I She is *mine*!

A. L. WREN.

CHAPTER VII.

LOVE—AND THE SNAKE.

Damocles de Warrenne, gentleman-cadet, on the eve of returning from Monksmead to the Military Academy of Sandhurst, appeared to have something on his mind as he sat on the broad coping of the terrace balustrade and idly kicked his heels. Every time he had returned to Monksmead from Wellingborough and Sandhurst, he had found Lucille yet more charming, delightful, and lovable. As her skirts and hair lengthened she became more and more the real companion, the pal, the adviser, without becoming any less the sportsman.

He had always loved her quaint terms of endearment, slang, and epithets, but as she grew into a beautiful and refined and dignified girl, it was still more piquant to be addressed in the highly unladylike (or un-Smelliean) terms that she affected.

Dam never quite knew when she began to make his heart beat quicker, and when her presence began to act upon him as sunshine and her absence as dull cloud; but there came a time when (whether she were riding to hounds in her neat habit, rowing with him in sweater and white skirt, swinging along the lanes in thick boots and tailor-made costume, sitting at the piano after dinner in simple white dinner-gown, or waltzing at some ball—always the belle thereof for him) he *did* know that Lucille was more to him than a jolly pal, a sound adviser, an audience, a confidant, and ally. Perhaps the day she put her hair up marked an epoch in the tale of his affections. He found that he began to hate to see other fellows dancing, skating, or playing golf or tennis with her. He did not like to see men speaking to her at meets or taking her in to dinner. He wanted the blood of a certain neighbouring spring-Captain, a hunter of "flappers" and molester of parlour-maids, home on furlough, who made eyes at her at the Hunt Ball and followed her about all Cricket Week and said something to her which, as Dam heard, provoked her coolly to request him "not to be such a priceless ass". What it was she would not tell Dam, and he, magnifying it, called, like the silly raw boy he was, upon the spring-Captain, and gently requested him to "let my cousin alone, Sir, if you don't mind, or—er—I'll jolly well make you". Dam knew things about the gentleman, and considered him wholly unfit to come within a mile of Lucille. The spring-Captain was obviously much amused and inwardly much annoyed—but he ceased his scarce-begun pursuit of the hoydenish-queenly girl, for Damocles de Warrenne had a reputation for the cool prosecution of his undertakings and the complete fulfilment of his promises. Likewise he had a reputation for Herculean strength and uncanny skill. Yet the gay Captain had been strongly attracted by the beauty and grace of the unspoilt, unsophisticated, budding woman, with her sweet freshness and dignity (so quaintly enhanced by lapses into the slangy, unfettered schoolgirl ...). Not that he was a marrying man at all, of course.... Yes—Dam had it weightily on his mind that he might come down from Sandhurst at any time and find Lucille engaged to some other fellow. Girls did get engaged.... It was the natural and obvious thing for them to do. She'd get engaged to some brainy clever chap worth a dozen of his own mediocre self.... Of course she liked him dearly as a pal and all that, an ancient crony and chum—but how should he hope to compete with the brilliant fellers she'd meet as she went about more, and knew them. She was going to have a season in London next year. Think of the kind of chaps she'd run across in Town in the season. Intellectual birds, artists, poets, authors, travellers, distinguished coves, rising statesmen, under-secretaries, soldiers, swells, all sorts. Not much show for him against that lot!

Gad! What a rotten look-out! What a rotten world to be sure! Fancy losing Lucille!... Should he put his fortunes to the touch, risk all, and propose to her. Fellows did these things in such circumstances.... No—hardly fair to try to catch her like that before she had had at least one season, and knew what was what and who was who.... Hardly the clean potato—to take advantage of their long intimacy and try to trap her while she was a country mouse.

It was not as though he were clever and could hope for a great career and the power to offer her the position for which she was fitted. Why, he was nearly bottom of his year at Sandhurst—not a bit brilliant and brainy. Suppose she married him in her inexperience, and then met the right sort of intellectual, clever feller too late. No, it wouldn't be the straight thing and decent at all, to propose to her now. How would Grumper view such a step? What had he to offer her? What was he? Just a penniless orphan. Apart from Grumper's generosity he owned a single five-pound note in money. Never won a scholarship or exam-prize in his life. Mere Public Schools boxing and fencing champion, and best man-at-arms at Sandhurst, with a score or so of pots for running, jumping, sculling, swimming, shooting, boxing, fencing, steeple-chasing and so forth. His total patrimony encashed would barely pay for his Army outfit. But for Grumper's kindness he couldn't go into the Army at all. And Grumper, the splendid old chap, couldn't last very much longer. Why—for many a long year he would not earn more than enough to pay his mess-bills and feed his horses. Not in England certainly.... Was he to ask Lucille to leave her luxurious home in a splendid mansion and live in a subaltern's four-roomed hut in the plains in India? (Even if he could scrape into the Indian army so as to live on his pay—more or less.) Grumper, her guardian, and executor of the late Bishop's will, might have very different views for her. Why, she might even be his heiress—he was very fond of her, the daughter of his lifelong friend and kinsman. Fancy a pauper making up to a very rich girl—if it came to her being that, which he devoutly hoped it would not. It would remove her so hopelessly beyond his reach. By the time he could make a position, and an income visible to the naked eye, he would be grey-haired. Money was not made in the army. Rather was it becoming no place for a poor gentleman but the paradise of rich bounders, brainy little squits of swotters, and commission-without-training nondescripts—thanks to the growing insecurity of things among the army class and gentry generally. If she were really penniless he might—as a Captain—ask her to share his poverty—but was it likely shed be a spinster ten years hence—even if he were a Captain so soon? Promotion is not violently rapid in the Cavalry.... And yet he simply hated the bare thought of life without Lucille. Better to be a gardener at Monksmead, and see her every day, than be the Colonel of a Cavalry Corps and know her to be married to somebody else.... Yes—he would come home one of these times from Sandburst or his Regiment and find her engaged to some other fellow. And what then? Well—nothing—only life would be of no further interest. It was bound to happen. Everybody turned to look at her. Even women gave generous praise of her beauty, grace, and sweetness. Men raved about her, and every male creature who came near her was obviously dpris in five minutes. The curate, plump "Holy Bill," was well known to be fading away, slowly and beautifully, but quite surely, on her account. Grumper's old pal, General Harringport, had confided to Dam himself in the smoking-room, one very late night, that since he was fifty years too old for hope of success in that direction he'd go solitary to his lonely grave (here a very wee hiccup), damn his eyes, so he would, unwed, unloved, uneverything. Very trag(h)ic, but such was life, the General had declared, the one alleviation being the fact that he might die any night now, and ought to have done so a decade ago.

Why, even the little useless snob and tuft-hunter, the Haddock, that tailor's dummy and parody of a man, cast sheep's eyes and made what he called "love" to her when down from Oxford (and was duly snubbed for it and for his wretched fopperies, snobberies, and folly). He'd have to put the Haddock across his knee one of these days.

Then there was his old school pal and Sandhurst senior, Ormonde Delorme, who frequently stayed at, and had just left, Monksmead —fairly dotty about her. She certainly liked Delorme—and no wonder, so handsome, clever, accomplished, and so fine a gentleman. Rich, too. Better Ormonde than another—but, God! what pain even to think of it.... Why had he cleared off so suddenly, by the way, and obviously in trouble, though he would not admit it?...

Lucille emerged from a French window and came swinging across the terrace. The young man, his face aglow, radiant, rose to meet her. It was a fine face—with that look on it. Ordinarily it was somewhat marred by a slightly cynical grimness of the mouth and a hint of trouble in the eyes—a face a little too old for its age.

"Have a game at tennis before tea, young Piggy-wig?" asked Lucille as she linked her arm in his.

"No, young Piggy-wee," replied Dam. "Gettin' old an' fat. Joints stiffenin'. Come an' sit down and hear the words of wisdom of your old Uncle Dammiculs, the Wise Man of Monksmead."

"Come off it, Dammy. Lazy little beast. Fat little brute," commented the lady.

As Damocles de Warrenne was six feet two inches high, and twelve stone of iron-hard muscle, the insults fell but lightly upon him.

"I will, though," she continued. "I shan't have the opportunity of hearing many more of your words of wisdom for a time, as you go back on Monday. And you'll be the panting prey of a gang of giggling girls at the garden party and dance to-morrow.... Why on earth must we muck up your last week-day with rotten 'functions'. You don't want to dance and you don't want to garden-part in the least."

"Nit," interrupted Dam.

" ... Grumper means it most kindly but ... we want you to ourselves the last day or two ... anyhow...."

"D'you want me to yourself, Piggy-wee?" asked Dam, trying to speak lightly and off-handedly.

"Of course I do, you Ass. Shan't see you for centuries and months. Nothing to do but weep salt tears till Christmas. Go into a decline or a red nose very likely. Mind you write to me twice a week at the very least," replied Lucille, and added:—

"Bet you that silly cat Amelia Harringport is in your pocket all to-morrow afternoon and evening. *All* the Harringport crowd are coming from Folkestone, you know. If you run the clock-golf she'll *adore* clock-golf, and if you play tennis she'll *adore* tennis.... Can't think what she sees in you...."

"Don't be cattish, Lusilly," urged the young man. "'Melier's all right. It's you she comes to see, of course."

To which, it is regrettable to have to relate, Lucille replied "Rodents".

Talk languished between the young people. Both seemed unwontedly ill at ease and nervous.

"D'you get long between leaving Sandhurst and joining the Corps you're going to distinguish, Dammy?" asked the girl after an uneasy and pregnant silence, during which they had furtively watched each other, and smiled a little uncomfortably and consciously when they had caught each other doing so.

"Dunno. Sure not to. It's a rotten world," replied Dam gloomily. "I expect I shall come back and find you—"

"Of course you'll come back and find me! What do you mean, Dam?" said the girl. She flushed curiously as she interrupted him. Before he could reply she continued:—

"You won't be likely to have to go abroad directly you join your Regiment, will you?"

"I shall try for the Indian Army or else for a British Regiment in India," was the somewhat sullen answer.

"Dam! What ever for?"

"More money and less expenses."

"Dam! You mercenary little toad! You grasping, greedy hog!... Why! I thought...."

Lucille gazed straight and searchingly at her life-long friend for a full minute and then rose to her feet.

"Come to tea," she said quietly, and led the way to the big lawn where, beneath an ancient cedar of Lebanon, the pompous Butterton and his solemn satellite were setting forth the tea "things".

Aunt Yvette presided at the tea-table and talked bravely to two woolly-witted dames from the Vicarage who had called to consult her anent the covering of a foot-stool "that had belonged to their dear Grandmamma".

("'Time somebody shot it," murmured Dam to Lucille as he handed her cup.)

Anon Grumper bore down upon the shady spot; queer old Grumper, very stiff, red-faced, dapper, and extremely savage.

Having greeted the guests hospitably and kindly he confined his subsequent conversation to two grunts and a growl.

Lucille and Damocles could not be said to have left the cane-chaired group about the rustic tables and cake-stands at any given moment. Independently they evaporated, after the manner of the Cheshire Cat it would appear, really getting farther and farther from the circle by such infinitely small degrees and imperceptible distances as would have appealed to the moral author of "Little by Little". At length the intervening shrubbery seemed to indicate that they were scarcely in the intimate bosom of the tea-party, if they had never really left it.

"Come for a long walk, Liggy," remarked Dam as they met, using an ancient pet-name.

"Right-O, my son," was the reply. "But we must start off mildly. I have a lovely feeling of too much cake. Too good to waste. Wait here while I put on my clod-hoppers."

The next hour was *the* Hour of the lives of Damocles de Warrenne and Lucille Gavestone—the great, glorious, and wonderful hour that comes but once in a lifetime and is the progenitor of countless happy hours—or hours of poignant pain. The Hour that can come only to those who are worthy of it, and which, whatever may follow, is an unspeakably precious blessing, confuting the cynic, shaming the pessimist, confounding the atheist, rewarding the pure in heart, revealing God to Man.

Heaven help the poor souls to whom that Hour never comes, with its memories that nothing can wholly destroy, its brightness that nothing can ever wholly darken. Heaven especially help the poor purblind soul that can sneer at it, the greatest and noblest of mankind's gifts, the countervail of all his cruel woes and curses.

As they walked down the long sweep of the elm-avenue, the pair encountered the vicar coming to gather up his wife and sister for the evening drive, and the sight of the two fine young people gladdened the good man's heart. He beheld a tall, broad-shouldered, narrow-hipped young man, with a frank handsome face, steady blue eyes, fair hair and determined jaw, a picture of the clean-bred, clean-living, out-door Englishman, athletic, healthy-minded, straight-dealing; and a slender, beautiful girl, with a strong sweet face, hazel-eyed, brown-haired, upright and active of carriage, redolent of sanity, directness, and all moral and physical health.

"A well-matched pair," he smiled to himself as they passed him with a cheery greeting.

For a mile or two both thought much and spoke little, the man thinking of the brilliant, hated Unknown who would steal away his Lucille; the woman thinking of the coming separation from the friend, without whom life was very empty, dull, and poor. Crossing a field, they reached a fence and a beautiful view of half the county. Stopping by mutual consent, they gazed at the peaceful, familiar scene, so ennobled and etherealized by the moon's soft radiance.

"I shall think of this walk, somehow, whenever I see the full moon," said Dam, breaking a long silence.

"And I," replied Lucille.

"I hate going away this time, somehow, more than usual," he blurted out after another spell of silence. "I can't help wondering whether you'll be—the same—when I come back at Christmas."

"Why—how should I be different, Dammy?" asked the girl, turning her gaze upon his troubled face, which seemed to twitch and work as though in pain.

"How?... Why, you might be—"

"Might be what, dear?"

"You might be—engaged."

The girl saw that in the man's eyes to which his tongue could not, or would not, give utterance. As he spoke the word, with a catch in his breath, she suddenly flung her arms round his neck, pressed her lips to his white face, and, with a little sob, whispered:—

"Not unless to you, Dam, darling—there is no other man in the world but you," and their lips met in their first lover's kiss.... Oh, the wonderful, glorious world!... The grand, beautiful old world! Place of delight, joy, wonder, beauty, gratitude. How the kind little stars sang to them and the benign old moon looked down and said: "Never despair, never despond, never fear, God has given you Love. What matters else?" How the man swore to himself that he would be worthy of her, strive for her, live for her; if need be—die for her. How the woman vowed to herself that she would be worthy of her splendid, noble lover, help him, cheer him, watch over him. Oh, if he might only need her some day and depend on her for something in spite of his strength and manhood. How she yearned to do something for him, to give, to give, to give. Their hour lasted for countless ages, and passed in a flash. The world intruded, spoiling itself as always.

"Home to dinner, darling," said the girl at last. "Hardly time to dress if we hurry. Grumper will simply rampage and roar. He gets worse every day." She disengaged herself from the boy's arms and her terribly beautiful, painfully exquisite, trance.

"Give me one more kiss, tell me once more that you love me and only me, for ever, and let us go.... God bless this place. I thank God. I love God—now ..." she said.

Dam could not speak at all.

They walked away, hand in hand, incredulous, tremulous, bewildered by the beauty and wonder and glory of Life.

Alas!

As they passed the Lodge and entered the dark avenue, Dam found his tongue.

"Must tell Grumper," he said. Nothing mattered since Lucille loved him like that. She'd be happier in the subaltern's hut in the plains of India than in a palace. If Grumper didn't like it, he must lump it. Her happiness was more important than Grumper's pleasure.

"Yes," acquiesced Lucille, "but tell him on Monday morning when you go. Let's have this all to ourselves, darling, just for a few hours. I believe he'll be jolly glad. Dear old bear, isn't he—really."

In the middle of the avenue Lucille stopped.

"Dammy, my son," quoth she, "tell me the absolute, bare, bald truth. Much depends upon it and it'll spoil everything if you aren't perfectly, painfully honest."

"Right-O," responded Dam. "Go it."

"Am I the very very loveliest woman that ever lived?"

"No," replied Dam, "but I wouldn't have a line of your face changed."

"Am I the cleverest woman in the world?"

"No. But you're quite clever enough for me. I wouldn't have you any cleverer. God forbid."

"Am I absolutely perfect and without flaw—in character."

"No. But I love your faults."

"Do you wish to enshrine me in a golden jewel-studded temple and worship me night and day?"

"No. I want to put you in a house and live with you."

"Hurrah," cried the surprising young woman. "That's *love*, Dam. It's not rotten idealizing and sentimentalizing that dies away as soon as facts are seen as such. You're a man, Dam, and I'm going to be a woman. I loathe that bleating, glorified nonsense that the Reverend Bill and Captain Luniac and poor old Ormonde and people talk when they're 'in love'. *Love!* It's just sentimental idealizing and the worship of what does not exist and therefore cannot last. You love *me*, don't you, Dammy, not an impossible figment of a heated imagination? This will last, dear.... If you'd idealized me into something unearthly and impossible you'd have tired of me in six months or less. You'd have hated me when you saw the reality, and found yourself tied to it for life."

"Make a speech, Daughter," replied Damocles. "Get on a stump and make a blooming speech."

Both were a little unstrung.

"I must wire this news to Delorme," said he suddenly. "He'll be delighted." Lucillemade no reply.

As they neared the end of the drive and came within sight of the house, the girl whispered:—

"My own pal, Dammy, for always. And you thought I could be engaged to anyone but *you*. There *is* no one but you in the world, dear. It would be quite empty if you left it. Don't worry about ways and means and things, Dam, I shall enjoy waiting for *you*—twenty years."

He thought of that, later.

On the morrow of that incredible day, Damocles de Warrenne sprang from his bed at sunrise and sought the dew-washed garden below the big south terrace.

The world contained no happier man. Sunrise in a glorious English summer and a grand old English garden, on the day after the Day of Days. He trod on air as he lived over again every second of that wonderful over-night scene, and scarcely realized the impossible truth.

Lucille loved him, as a lover! Lucille the *alter ego*, the understanding, splendid friend; companion in play and work, in idle gaiety and serious consideration; the *bon camarade*, the real chum and pal.

Life was a Song, the world a Paradise, the future a long-drawn Glory.

He would like to go and hold the Sword in his hand for a minute, and—something seemed to stir beneath his foot, and a shudder ran through his powerful frame.

The brightness of the morning was dimmed, and then Lucille came towards him blushing, radiant, changed, and all was well with the world, and God in high heaven.

* * * * *

After breakfast they again walked in the garden, the truly enchanted garden, and talked soberly with but few endearments though with over-full hearts, and with constant pauses to eye the face of the other with wondering rapture. They came of a class and a race not given to excessive demonstrativeness, but each knew that the other loved—for life.

In the afternoon, guests began to arrive soon after lunch, duties usurped the place of pleasures, and the lovers met as mere friends in the crowd. There was meaning in the passing glances, however, and an occasional hand-touch in the giving of tennis-ball, or tea-cup.

"Half the County" was present, and while the younger fry played tennis, croquet, clock-golf, and bowls, indulged in "mixed cricket," or attempted victory at archery or miniature-rifle shooting, the sedate elders strolled o'er velvet lawns beneath immemorial elms, sat in groups, or took tea by carpet-spread marquees.

Miss Amelia Harringport, seeing Dam with a croquet-mallet in his hand, observed that she *adored* croquet. Dam stated in reply that Haddon Berners was a fearful dog at it, considered there should be a croquet Blue in fact, and would doubtless be charmed to make up a set with her and the curate, the Reverend William Williamson Williams (Holy Bill), and Another. Dam himself was cut off from the bliss of being the Other—did not know the game at all.

Miss Amelia quickly tired of her croquet with the Haddock, Holy Bill and the Vicar's Wife's Sister, who looked straitly after Holy Bill on this and all other occasions. Seeing Dam shepherding a flock of elders to the beautifully-mown putting-tracks radiating from the central circle of "holes" for the putting competition, she informed him that she *adored* putting, so much so that she wanted lessons from him, the local amateur golf-champion.

"I just want a little *personal tuition* from the Champion and I shall be quite a classy putter," she gurgled.

"I will personally tuit," replied Dam, "and when you are tuited we will proceed to win the prize."

Carefully posing the maiden aspirant for putting excellence at the end of the yard-wide velvety strip leading to the green and "hole," Dam gave his best advice, bade her smite with restraint, and then proceeded to the "hole" to retrieve the ball for his own turn. Other couples did "preliminary canters" somewhat similarly on the remaining spokes of the great wheel of the putting "clock".

The canny and practised Amelia, who had designs upon the handsome silver prize as well as upon the handsome Damocles, smote straight and true with admirable judgment, and the ball sped steadily down the track direct for the "hole," a somewhat large and deep one.

"By Jove! Magnificent!" cried Dam, with quick and generous appreciation of the really splendid putt. "You'll hole out in one this time, anyhow." As the slowing ball approached the "hole" he inserted his hand therein, laughing gaily, to anticipate the ball which with its last grain of momentum would surely reach it and topple in.

Then the thing happened!

As he put his hand to the grass-encircled goal of the maiden's hopes and ball, its gloomy depths appeared to move, swirl round, rise up, as a small green snake uncoiled in haste and darted beneath Dam's approaching upturned hand, and swiftly undulated across the lawn.

With a shriek that momentarily paralysed the gay throng, turned all eyes in his direction, and brought the more cool and helpful running to the spot, Dam fell writhing, struggling, and screaming to the ground.

"The SNAKE! The SNAKE!" he howled, while tears gushed from his eyes and he strove to dig his way into the ground for safety.

"There it goes!" squealed the fair Amelia pointing tragically. Ladies duly squeaked, bunched their skirts tightly, jumped on chairs or sought protection by the side of stalwart admirers.

Men cried "Where?" and gathered for battle. One sporting character emitted an appalling "View Halloo" and there were a few "Yoicks" and "Gone Aways" to support his little solecism. Lucille, rushing to Dam, encountered the fleeing reptile and with a neat stroke of her putter ended its career.

"It's all right, old chap," sneered Haddon Berners, as the mad, convulsed, and foaming Dam screamed: "*It's under my foot. It's moving, moving, moving out,*" and doubled up into a knot.

"Oh no, it isn't," he continued. "Lucille has killed it. Nothing to be terrified about.... Oh, chuck it, man! Get up and blow your nose...." He was sent sprawling on his back as Lucille dropped by Dam's side and strove to raise his face from the grass.

"Come off it, Dam! You're very funny, we know," adjured the sporting character, rather ashamed and discomfortable at seeing a brother man behaving so. There are limits to acting the goat—especially with wimmin about. Why couldn't Dam drop it?...

Lucille was shocked and horrified to the innermost fibres of her being. Her dignified, splendid Dam rolling on the ground, shrieking, sobbing, writhing.... Ill or well, joke or seizure, it was horrible, unseemly.... Why couldn't the gaping fools be obliterated?...

"Dam, dear," she whispered in his ear, as she knelt over the shuddering, gasping, sobbing man. "What is it, Dam? Are you ill? Dam, it's Lucille.... The snake is quite dead, dear. I killed it. Are you joking? Dam! *Dam!*" ...

The stricken wretch screamed like a terrified child.

"Oh, won't somebody fetch Dr. Jones if he's not here yet," she wailed, turning to the mystified crowd of guests. "Get some water quickly, somebody, salts, brandy, anything! Oh, *do* go away," and she deftly unfastened the collar of the spasm-wracked sufferer. "Haddon," she cried, looking up and seeing the grinning Haddock, "go straight for Dr. Jones. Cycle if you're afraid of spoiling your clothes by riding. Quick!"

"Oh, he'll be all right in a minute," drawled the Haddock, who did not relish a stiff ride along dusty roads in his choicest confection. "He's playing the fool, I believe— or a bit scared at the ferocious serpent."

Lucille gave the youth a look that he never forgot, and turned to the sporting person.

"You know the stables, Mr. Fellerton," she said. "Would you tell Pattern or somebody to send a man for Dr. Jones? Tell him to beat the record."

The sporting one sprinted toward the shrubbery which lay between the grounds and the kitchen-gardens, beyond which were the stables.

Most people, with the better sort of mind, withdrew and made efforts to recommence the interrupted games or to group themselves once more about the lawns and marquees.

Others remained to make fatuous suggestions, to wonder, or merely to look on with feelings approaching awe and fascination. There was something uncanny here—a soldier and athlete weeping and screaming and going into fits at the sight of a harmless grass-snake, probably a mere blind worm! Was he a hysterical, neurotic coward, after all—a wretched decadent?

Poor Lucille suffered doubly—every pang, spasm, and contortion that shook and wrung the body of her beloved, racked her own frame, and her mind was tortured by fear, doubts, and agony. "Oh, please go away, dear people," she moaned. "It is a touch of sun. He is a little subject to slight fits—very rarely and at long intervals, you know. He may never have another." A few of the remaining onlookers backed away a little shamefacedly. Others offered condolences while inwardly scoffing at the "sun" explanation. Did not de Warrenne bowl, bat, or field, bare-headed, throughout the summer's day without thinking of the sun? Who had heard of the "fits" before? Why had they not transpired during the last dozen years or so? "Help me carry him indoors, somebody," said the miserable, horrified Lucille. That would get rid of the silly staring "helpers" anyhow—even if it brought matters to the notice of Grumper, who frankly despised and detested any kind of sick person or invalid.

What would he say and do? What had happened to the glowing, glorious world that five minutes ago was fairy-land and paradise? Was her Dam a wretched coward, afraid of things, screaming like a girl at the sight of a common snake, actually terrified into a fit? Better be a pick-pocket than a.... Into the thinning, whispering circle came General Sir Gerald Seymour Stukeley, apoplectically angry. Some silly fool, he understood, had fainted or something—probably a puling tight-laced fool of a woman who starved herself to keep slim. People who wanted to faint should stay and do it at home—not come creating disturbances and interruptions at Monksmead garden-parties....

And then he saw a couple of young men and Lucille striving to raise the recumbent body of a man. The General snorted as snorts the wart-hog in love and war, or the graceful hippopotamus in the river.

"What the Devil's all this?" he growled. "Some poor fella fainted with the exertions of putting?" A most bitter old gentleman.

Lucille turned to him and his fierce gaze fell upon the pale, contorted, and tear-stained face of Dam.

The General flushed an even deeper purple, and the stick he held perpendicularly slowly rose to horizontal, though he did not raise his hand.

He made a loud but wholly inarticulate sound.

Haddon Berners, enjoying himself hugely, volunteered the information.

"He saw a little grass-snake and yelled out. Then he wept and fainted. Coming round now. Got the funks, poor chap."

Lucille's hands closed (the thumbs correctly on the knuckles of the second fingers), and, for a moment, it was in her heart to smite the Haddock on the lying mouth with the straight-from-the-shoulder drive learned in days of yore from Dam, and practised on the punching-ball with great assiduity. Apparently the Haddock realized the fact for he skipped backward with agility.

"He is ill, Grumper dear," she said instead. "He has had a kind of fit. Perhaps he had sunstroke in India, and it has just affected him now in the sun...."

Grumper achieved the snort of his life.

It may have penetrated Dam's comatose brain, indeed, for at that moment, with a moan and a shudder, he struggled to a sitting posture.

"The Snake," he groaned, and collapsed again.

"What the Devil!" roared the General. "Get up, you miserable, whining cur! Get indoors, you bottle-fed squalling workhouse brat! Get out of it, you decayed gentlewoman!" ... The General bade fair to have a fit of his own.

Lucille flung herself at him.

"Can't you see he's very ill, Grumper? Have you no heart at all? Don't be so cruel ... and ... stupid."

The General gasped.... Insults!... From a chit of a girl!... "Ill!" he roared. "What the Devil does he want to be ill for now, here, to-day? I never ..."

Dam struggled to his feet with heroic efforts at self-mastery, and stood swaying, twitching, trembling in every limb, and obviously in an agony of terror.

"The Snake!" he said again.

"Ha!" barked General Stukeley. "Been fighting forty boa-constrictors, what? Just had a fearful struggle with five thousand fearful pythons, what? There'll be another Victoria Cross in your family soon, if you're not careful."

"You are an unjust and cruel old man," stormed Lucille, stamping her foot at the hitherto dread Grumper. "He is ill, I tell you! You'll be ill yourself someday. He had a fit. He'll be all right in a minute. Let him go in and lie down. It wasn't the snake at all. There wasn't any snake—where he was. He is just ill. He has been working too hard. Let him go in and lie down."

"Let him go to the Devil," growled the infuriated General, and turned to such few of the guests as had not displayed sufficient good sense and good taste to go elsewhere and resume their interrupted games, tea, or scandal, to remark:—

"I really apologize most sincerely and earnestly for this ridiculous scene. The boy should be in petticoats, apparently. I hope he won't encounter a mouse or a beetle to-night. Let's all—er—come and have a drink."

Lucille led her shaking and incoherent lover indoors and established him on a sofa, had a fire lit for him as he appeared to be deathly cold, and sat holding his clammy hand until the arrival of Dr. Jones.

As well as his chattering teeth and white frozen lips would allow, he begged for forgiveness, for understanding. "He wasn't really wholly a coward in essentials." ...

The girl kissed the contorted face and white lips passionately. Dr. Jones prescribed bed and "complete mental and bodily rest". He said he would "send something," and in a cloud of wise words disguised the fact that he did not in the least know what to do. It was not in his experience that a healthy young Hercules, sound as a bell, without spot or blemish, should behave like an anæmic, neurotic girl....

Dam passed the night in the unnameable, ghastly hell of agony that he knew so well and that he wondered to survive.

In the morning he received a note from Sir Gerald Seymour Stukeley. It was brief and clear:—"Sandhurst is scarcely the place for a squealing coward, still less the Army. Nor is there room for one at Monksmead. I shall not have the pleasure of seeing you before you catch the 11.15 train; I might say things better left unsaid. I thank God you do not bear our name though you have some of our blood. This will be the one grain of comfort when I think that the whole County is gibing and jeering. No—your name is no more Seymour Stukeley than is your nature. If you will favour my Solicitors with your address, they will furnish you with an account of your patrimony and such balance thereof as may remain—if any. But I believe you came to England worth about fifty pounds—which you have probably spent as pocket-money. I beg of you to communicate with me or my household in no way whatsoever.

Hastily dressing, Dam fled from the house on foot, empty handed and with no money but a five-pound note legitimately his own private property. On his dressing-table he left the cheque given to him by his "grandfather" for ensuing Sandhurst expenses. Hiding in the station waiting-room, he awaited the next train to London—with thoughts of recruiting-sergeants and the Guards. From force of habit he travelled first-class, materially lessening his five pounds. In the carriage, which he had to himself, he sat stunned. He was rather angry than dismayed and appalled. He was like the soldier, cut down by a sabre-slash or struck by a bullet, who, for a second, stares dully at the red gash or blue hole—waiting for the blood to flow and the pain to commence.

He was numbed, emotionally dead, waiting the terrible awakening to the realization that he had *lost Lucille*. What mattered the loss of home, career, friends, honour—mere anti-climax to glance at it.

Yesterday!... To-day!

What was Lucille thinking? What would she do and say? Would she grow to hate the coward who had dared to make love to her, dared to win her love!

Would she continue to love him in spite of all?

I shall enjoy waiting twenty years for you, she had said yesterday, and *The world would be quite empty if you left it*. What would it be while he remained in it a publicly disgraced coward? A coward ridiculed by the effeminate, degenerate Haddock, who had no soul above club-ribbons, and no body above a Piccadilly crawl!

Could she love him in spite of all? She was great-hearted enough for anything. Perhaps for anything but that. To her, cowardice must be the last lowest depths of degradation. Anyhow he had done the straight thing by Grumper, in leaving the house without any attempt to let her know, to say farewell, to ask her to believe in him for a while. If there had been any question as to the propriety of his trying to become engaged to her when he was the penniless gentleman-cadet, was there any question about it when he was the disgraced out-cast, the publicly exposed coward?

Arrived at the London terminus he sought a recruiting-sergeant and, of course, could not find one.

However, Canterbury and Cavalry were indissolubly connected in his mind, and it had occurred to him that, in the Guards, he would run more risk of coming face to face with people whom he knew than in any other corps. He would go for the regiment he had known and loved in India (as he had been informed) and about which he had heard much all his life. It was due for foreign service in a year or two, and, so far as he knew, none of its officers had ever heard of him. Ormonde Delorme was mad about it, but could not afford its expensive mess. Dam had himself thought how jolly it would be if Grumper "came down" sufficiently handsomely for him to be able to join it on leaving Sandhurst. He'd join it *now*!

He hailed a hansom and proceeded to Charing Cross, whence he booked for the noble and ancient city of Canterbury.

Realizing that only one or two sovereigns would remain to him otherwise, he travelled in a third-class carriage for the first time in his hitherto luxurious life. Its bare discomfort and unpleasant occupants (one was a very malodorous person indeed, and one a smoker of what smelt like old hats and chair-stuffing in a rank clay pipe) brought home to him more clearly than anything had done, the fact that he was a homeless, destitute person about to sell his carcase for a shilling, and seek the last refuge of the out-of-work, the wanted-by-the-police, the disgraced, and the runaway.

That carriage and its occupants showed him, in a blinding flash, that his whole position, condition, outlook, future, and life were utterly and completely changed.

He was Going Under. Had anybody else ever done it so quickly?...

He went Under, and his entrance to the Underworld was through the great main-gates of the depot of the Queen's Own (2nd) Regiment of Heavy Cavalry, familiarly known as the Queen's Greys.

CHAPTER VIII.

TROOPERS OF THE QUEEN.

GLIMPSES OF CERTAIN "POOR DEVILS" AND THE HELL THEY INHABITED.

The Queen's Own (2nd) Regiment of Heavy Cavalry (The Queen's Greys) were under orders for India and the influence of great joy. That some of its members were also under the influence of potent waters is perhaps a platitudinous corollary.

... "And phwat the Divvle's begone of me ould pal Patsy Flannigan, at all, at all?" inquired Trooper Phelim O'Shaughnessy, entering the barrack-room of E Troop of the Queen's Greys, lying at Shorncliffe Camp. "Divvle a shmell of the baste can I see, and me back from furlough-leaf for minnuts. Has the schamer done the two-shtep widout anny flure, as Oi've always foretould? Is ut atin' his vegetables by the roots he now is in the bone-orchard, and me owing the poor bhoy foive shillin'? Where is he?"

"In 'orsepittle," laconically replied Trooper Henry Hawker, late of Whitechapel, without looking up from the jack-boot he was polishing.

"Phwat wid?" anxiously inquired the bereaved Phelim.

"Wot wiv'? Wiv' callin' 'Threes abaht' after one o' the Young Jocks,"[16] was the literal reply.

"Begob that same must be a good hand wid his fisties—or was it a shillaleigh?" mused the Irishman.

"'Eld the Helliot belt in Hinjer last year, they say," continued the Cockney. "*Good?* Not'arf. I wouldn't go an' hinsult the bloke for the price of a pot. No. 'Erbert 'Awker would not. (Chuck us yore button-stick, young 'Enery Bone.) *Good?* 'E's a 'Oly Terror—and I don't know as there's a man in the Queen's Greys as could put 'im to sleep—not unless it's Matthewson," and here Trooper Herbert Hawker jerked his head in the direction of Trooper Damocles de Warrenne (*alias* D. Matthewson) who, seated on his truckle-bed, was engaged in breathing hard, and rubbing harder, upon a brass helmet from which he had unscrewed a black horse-hair plume.

Dam, arrayed in hob-nailed boots, turned-up overalls "authorized for grooming," and a "grey-back" shirt, looked indefinably a gentleman.

Trooper Herbert Hawker, in unlaced gymnasium shoes, "leathers," and a brown sweater (warranted not to show the dirt), looked quite definably what he was, a Commercial Road ruffian; and his foreheadless face, greasy cow-lick "quiff" (or fringe), and truculent expression, inspired more disgust than confidence in the beholder.

His reference to Dam as the only likely champion of the Heavy Cavalry against the Hussar was a tribute to the tremendous thrashing he had received from "Trooper D. Matthewson" when the same had become necessary after a long course of unresented petty annoyance. Hawker was that very rare creature, a boaster, who made good, a bully of great courage and determination, and a loud talker, who was a very active doer; and the battle had been a terrible one.

The weary old joke of having a heavy valise pulled down on to one's upturned face from the shelf above, by means of a string, as one sleeps, Dam had taken in good part. Being sent to the Rough-Riding Sergeant-Major for the "Key of the Half Passage" by this senior recruit, he did not mind in the least (though he could have kicked himself for his gullibility when he learned that the "Half Passage" is not a place, but a Riding-School manoeuvre, and escaped from the bitter tongue of the incensed autocrat—called untimely from his tea! How the man had *bristled*. Hair, eyebrows, moustache, buttons even—the Rough-Riding Sergeant-Major had been rough indeed, and had done his riding rough-shod over the wretched lad).

Being instructed to "go and get measured for his hoof-picker" Dam had not resented, though he had considered it something of an insult to his intelligence that Hawker should expect to "have" him so easily as that. He had taken in good part the arrangement of his bed in such a way that it collapsed and brought a pannikin of water down with it, and on to it, in the middle of a cold night. He had received with good humour, and then with silent contempt, the names of "Gussie the Bank Clurk," references to "broken-dahn torfs" and "tailor's bleedn' dummies," queries as to the amount of "time" he had got for the offence that made him a "Queen's Hard Bargain," and various the other pleasantries whereby Herbert showed his distaste for people whose accent differed from his own, and whose tastes were unaccountable.

Dam had borne these things because he was certain he could thrash the silly animal when the time came, and because he had a wholesome dread of the all-too-inevitable military "crimes" (one of which fighting is—as subversive of good order and military discipline).

It had come, however, and for Dam this exotic of the Ratcliffe Highway had thereafter developed a vast admiration and an embarrassing affection. It was a most difficult matter to avoid his companionship when "walking-out" and also to avoid hurting his feelings.

It was a humiliating and chastening experience to the man, who had supported himself by boxing in booths at fairs and show-grounds, to find this "bloomin' dook of a 'Percy,'" this "lah-de-dar 'Reggie'" who looked askance at good bread-and-dripping, this finnicky "Clarence" without a "bloody" to his conversation, this "blasted, up-the-pole[17] 'Cecil'"—a man with a quicker guard, a harder punch, a smarter ring-craft, a better wind, and a tougher appetite for "gruel" than himself.

97

The occasion was furnished by a sad little experience.

Poor drunken Trooper Bear (once the Honourable MacMahon FitzUrse), kindliest, weakest, gentlest of gentlemen, had lurched one bitter soaking night (or early morning) into the barrack-room, singing in a beautiful tenor:—

"Menez-moi" dit la belle,
"A la rive fidele
Ou l'on aime toujours."
...—"Cette rive ma chere
On ne la connait guere
Au pays des amours."....

Trooper Herbert Hawker had no appreciation for Théophile Gautier—or perhaps none for being awakened from his warm slumbers.

"'Ere! stow that blarsted catawaulin'," he roared, with a choice selection from the Whitechapel tongue, in which he requested the adjectived noun to be adverbially "quick about it, too".

With a beatific smile upon his weak handsome face, Trooper Bear staggered toward the speaker, blew him a kiss, and, in a vain endeavour to seat himself upon the cot, collapsed upon the ground.

"You're a...." (adverbially adjectived noun) shouted Hawker. "You ain't a man, you're a...." "[Greek: skias hovar havthropos]" ... "Man is the dream of a shadow," suggested Bear dreamily with a hiccup....

"D'yer know where you *are*, you ..." roared Hawker.

"Dear Heart, I am in hell," replied the recumbent one, "but by the Mercy of God I'm splendidly drunk. Yes, hell. *'Lasciate ogni speranza,'* sweet Amaryllis. I am Morag of the Misty Way. *Mos'* misty. Milky Way. Yesh. Milk Punchy Way." ...

"I'll give you all the *punch* you'll want, in abaht two ticks if you don't chuck it—you blarsted edjucated flea," warned Hawker, half rising.

Dam got up and pulled on his cloak preparatory to helping the o'er-taken one to bed, as a well-aimed ammunition boot took the latter nearly on the ear.

Struggling to his feet with the announcement that he was "the King's fair daughter, weighed in the balance and found—devilish heavy and very drunk," the unhappy youth lurched and fell upon the outraged Hawker—who struck him a cruel blow in the face.

98

At the sound of the blow and heavy fall, Dam turned, saw the blood—and went Stukeley-mad. Springing like a tiger upon Hawker he dragged him from his cot and knocked him across it. In less than a minute he had twice sent him to the boards, and it took half-a-dozen men on either side to separate the combatants and get them to postpone the finish till the morning. That night Dam dreamed his dream and, on the morrow, behind the Riding-School, and in fifteen rounds, became, by common consent, champion bruiser of the Queen's Greys—by no ambition of his own.

And so—as has been said—Trooper Henry Hawker ungrudgingly referred Trooper Phelim O'Shaughnessy to him in the matter of reducing the pride of the Young Jock who had dared to "desthroy" a dragoon.

Trooper Phelim O'Shaughnessy—in perfect-fitting glove-tight scarlet stable-jacket (that never went near a stable, being in fact the smart shell-jacket, shaped like an Eton coat, sacred to "walking-out" purposes), dark blue overalls with broad white stripe, strapped over half-wellington boots adorned with glittering swan-neck spurs, a pill-box cap with white band and button, perched jauntily on three hairs—also looked what he was, the ideal heavy-cavalry man, the swaggering, swashbuckling trooper, *beau sabreur*, good all round and all through....

The room in which these worthies and various others (varying also in dress, from shirt and shorts to full review-order for Guard) had their being, expressed the top note and last cry—or the lowest note and deepest groan—of bleak, stark utilitarianism. Nowhere was there hint or sign of grace and ornament. Bare deal-plank floor, bare white-washed walls, plank and iron truckle beds, rough plank and iron trestle tables, rough plank and iron benches, rough plank and iron boxes clamped to bedsteads, all bore the same uniform impression of useful ugliness, ugly utility. The apologist in search of a solitary encomium might have called it clean—save around the hideous closed stove where muddy boots, coal-dust, pipe-dottels, and the bitter-end of five-a-penny "gaspers"[18] rebuked his rashness.

A less inviting, less inspiring, less home-like room for human habitation could scarce be found outside a jail. Perhaps this was the less inappropriate in that a jail it was, to a small party of its occupants—born and bred to better things.

The eye was grateful even for the note of cheer supplied by the red cylindrical valise on the shelf above each cot, and by the occasional scarlet tunic and stable-jacket. But for these it had been, to the educated eye, an even more grim, grey, depressing, beauty-and-joy-forsaken place than it was....

Dam (*alias* Trooper D. Matthewson) placed the gleaming helmet upon his callous straw-stuffed pillow, carefully rubbed the place where his hand had last touched it, and then took from a peg his scarlet tunic with its white collar, shoulder-straps and facings. Having satisfied himself that to burnish further its glittering buttons would be to gild refined gold, he commenced a vigorous brushing—for it was now his high ambition to "get the stick"—in other words to be dismissed from guard-duty as reward for being the best-turned-out man on parade.... As he reached up to his shelf for his gauntlets and pipe-clay box, Trooper Phelim O'Shaughnessy swaggered over with much jingle of spur and playfully smote him, netherly, with his cutting whip.

"What-ho, me bhoy," he roared, "and how's me natty Matty—the natest foightin' man in E Troop, which is sayin' in all the Dhraghoons, which is sayin' in all the Arrmy! How's Matty?"

"Extant," replied Dam. "How's Shocky, the biggest liar in the same?"

As he extended his hand it was noticeable that it was much smaller than the hand of the smaller man to whom it was offered. "Ye'll have to plug and desthroy the schamin' divvle that strook poor Patsy Flannigan, Matty," said the Irishman. "Ye must bate the sowl out of the baste before we go to furrin' parts. Loife is uncertain an' ye moight never come back to do ut, which the Holy Saints forbid—an' the Hussars troiumphin' upon our prosprit coorpses. For the hanner an' glory av all Dhraghoons, of the Ould Seconds, and of me pore bed-ridden frind, Patsy Flannigan, ye must go an' plug the wicked scutt, Matty darlint."

"It was Flannigan's fault," replied Dam, daubing pipe-clay on the huge cuff of a gauntlet which he had drawn on to a weird-looking wooden hand, sacred to the purposes of glove-drying. "He got beastly drunk and insulted a better man than himself by insulting his Corps—or trying to. He called a silly lie after a total stranger and got what he deserved. He shouldn't seek sorrow if he doesn't want to find it, and he shouldn't drink liquor he can't carry."

"And the Young Jock beat Patsy when drunk, did he?" murmured O'Shaughnessy, in tones of awed wonder. "I riverince the man, for there's few can beat him sober. Knocked Patsy into hospital an' him foightin' dhrunk! Faith, he must be another Oirish gintleman himself, indade."

"He's a Scotchman and was middle-weight champion of India last year," rejoined Dam, and moistened his block of pipe-clay again in the most obvious, if least genteel, way.

"Annyhow he's a mere Hussar and must be rimonsthrated wid for darin' to assault and bathter a Dhraghoon—an' him dhrunk, poor bhoy. Say the wurrud, Matty. We'll lay for the spalpeen, the whole of E Troop, at the *Ring o' Bells*, an' whin he shwaggers in like he was a Dhraghoon an' a sodger, ye'll up an' say *'Threes about'* an' act accordin' subsequint, an' learn the baste not to desthroy an' insult his betthers of the Ould Second. Thread on the tail of his coat, Matty...."

"If I had anything to do with it at all I'd tread on Flannigan's coat, and you can tell him so, for disgracing the Corps.... Take off your jacket and help with my boots, Shocky. I'm for Guard."

100

"Oi'd clane the boots of no man that ud demane himself to ax it," was the haughty reply of the disappointed warrior. "Not for less than a quart at laste," he amended.

"A quart it is," answered Dam, and O'Shaughnessy speedily divested himself of his stable-jacket, incidentally revealing the fact that he had pawned his shirt.

"You have got your teeth ready, then?" observed Dam, noting the underlying bareness—and thereby alluded to O'Shaughnessy's habit of pawning his false teeth after medical inspection and redeeming them in time for the next, at the cost of his underclothing—itself redeemed in turn by means of the teeth. Having been compelled to provide himself with a "plate" he invariably removed the detested contrivance and placed it beside him when sitting down to meals (on those rare occasions when he and not his "uncle" was the arbiter of its destinies)....

A young and important Lance-Corporal, a shocking tyrant and bully, strode into the room, his sword clanking. O'Shaughnessy arose and respectfully drew him aside, offering him a "gasper". They were joined by a lean hawk-faced individual answering to the name of Fish, who said he had been in the American navy until buried alive at sea for smiling within sight of the quarter-deck.

"Yep," he was heard to say to some statement of O'Shaughnessy's. "We'll hatch a five-bunch frame-up to put the eternal kibosh on the tuberous spotty—souled skunklet. Some. We'll make him wise to whether a tippy, chew-the-mop, bandy-legged, moke-monkey can come square-pushing, and with his legs out, down *this* side-walk, before we ante out. Some."

"Ah, Yus," agreed the Lance-Corporal. "Damned if I wouldn't chawnce me arm[19] and go fer 'im meself before we leave—on'y I'm expectin' furver permotion afore long. But fer that I'd take it up meself"—and he glanced at Dam.

"Ketch the little swine at it," remarked Trooper Herbert Hawker, as loudly as he dared, to his "towny," Trooper Henry Bone. "'Chawnst 'is arm!' It's 'is bloomin' life 'e'd chawnce if that Young Jock got settin' abaht 'im. Not 'arf!" and the exotic of the Ratcliffe Highway added most luridly expressed improprieties anent the origins of the Lance-Corporal, his erstwhile enemy and, now, superior officer, in addition.

"That's enough," said Dam shortly.

"Yep. Quit those low-browed sounds, guttermut, or I'll get mad all over," agreed Fish, whose marvellous vocabulary included no foul words. There was no need for them.

"Hi halso was abaht ter request you not to talk beastial, Mr. 'Erbert 'Awker," chimed in Trooper "Henery" Bone, anxious to be on the side of the saints. "'Oo'd

taike you to be the Missin' Hair of a noble 'ouse when you do such—'Missin' Hair!'
Missin' Link more like," he added with spurious indignation.

The allusion was to the oft-expressed belief of Trooper Herbert Hawker, a belief that became a certainty and subject for bloodshed and battle after the third quart or so, that there was a mystery about his birth.

There was, according to his reputed papa....

The plotters plotted, and Dam completed the burnishing of his arms, spurs, buckles, and other glittering metal impedimenta (the quantity of which earned the Corps its barrack-room soubriquet of "the Polish Its"), finished the flicking of spots of pipe-clay from his uniform, and dressed for Guard.

Being ready some time before he had to parade, he sat musing on his truckle-bed.

What a life! What associates (outside the tiny band of gentlemen-rankers). What cruel awful *publicity* of existence—that was the worst of all. Oh, for a private room and a private coat, and a meal in solitude! Some place of one's own, where one could express one's own individuality in the choice and arrangement of property, and impress it upon one's environment.

One could not even think in private here.

And he was called a *private* soldier! A grim joke indeed, when the crying need of one's soul was a little privacy.

A *private* soldier!

Well—and what of the theory of Compensations, that all men get the same sum-total of good and bad, that position is really immaterial to happiness? What of the theory that more honour means also more responsibility and worry, that more pay also means more expenses and a more difficult position, that more seniority also means less youth and joy—that Fate only robs Peter to pay Paul, and, when bestowing a blessing with one hand, invariably bestows a curse with the other?

Too thin.

Excellent philosophy for the butterfly upon the road, preaching contentment to the toad, who, beneath the harrow, knows exactly where each tooth-point goes. Let the butterfly come and try it.

What a life!

Not so bad at first, perhaps, for a stout-hearted, hefty sportsman, during recruit days when everything is novel, there is something to learn, time is fully occupied, and one is too busy to think, too busy evading strange pit-falls, and the just or (more often) unjust wrath of the Room Corporal, the Squadron Orderly Sergeant, the Rough-Riding Corporal, the Squadron Sergeant-Major, the Rough-Riding Sergeant-Major, the Regimental Sergeant-Major, the Riding-Master.

But when, to the passed "dismissed soldier," everything is familiar and easy, weary, flat, stale and unprofitable?

The (to one gently nurtured) ghastly food, companions, environment, monotony—-the ghastly ambitions!

Fancy an educated gentleman's ambitions and horizon narrowed to a good-conduct "ring," a stripe in the far future (and to be a Lance-Corporal with far more duty and no more pay, in the hope of becoming a Corporal—that comfortable rank with the same duty and much more pay, and little of the costly gold-lace to mount, and heavy expenses to assume that, while putting the gilt on, takes it off, the position of Sergeant); and, for the present, to "keep off the peg," not to be "for it," to "get the stick," for smartest turn-out, to avoid the Red-Caps,[20] to achieve an early place in the scrimmage at the corn-bin and to get the correct amount of two-hundred pounds in the corn-sack when drawing forage and corn; to placate Troop Sergeants, the Troop Sergeant-Major and Squadron Sergeant-Major; to have a suit of mufti at some safe place outside and to escape from the branding searing scarlet occasionally; possibly even the terrible ambition to become an Officer's servant so as to have a suit of mufti as a right, and a chance of becoming Mess-Sergeant and then Quarter-Master, and perhaps of getting an Honorary Commission without doing a single parade or guard after leaving the troop!...

What a life for a man of breeding and refinement!... Fancy having to remember the sacred and immeasurable superiority of a foul-mouthed Lance-Corporal who might well have been your own stable-boy, a being who can show you a deeper depth of hell in Hell, wreak his dislike of you in unfair "fatigues," and keep you at the detested job of coal-drawing on Wednesdays; who can achieve a "canter past the beak"[21] for you on a trumped-up charge and land you in the "digger,"[22] who can bring it home to you in a thousand ways that you are indeed the toad beneath the harrow. Fancy having to remember, night and day, that a Sergeant, who can perhaps just spell and cypher, is a monarch to be approached in respectful spirit; that the Regimental Sergeant-Major, perhaps coarse, rough, and ignorant, is an emperor to be approached with fear and trembling; that a Subaltern, perhaps at school with you, is a god not to be approached at all. Fancy looking forward to being "branded with a blasted worsted spur," and, as a Rough-Riding Corporal, receiving a forfeit tip from each young officer who knocks off his cap with his lance in Riding-School....

Well! One takes the rough with the smooth—but perceives with great clearness that the (very) rough predominates, and that one does not recommend a gentleman to enlist, save when a Distinguished Relative with Influence has an early Commission ready in his pocket for him.

Lacking the Relative, the gently-nurtured man, whether he win to a Commission eventually or not, can only do one thing more rash than enlist in the British Army, and that is enlist in the French Foreign Legion.

Discipline for soul and body? The finest thing in all the world—in reason. But the discipline of the tram-horse, of the blinded bullock at the wheel, of the well-camel, of the galley-slave—meticulous, puerile, unending, unchanging, impossible ...? Necessary perhaps, once upon a time—but hard on the man of brains, sensibility, heart, and individuality.

Soul and body? Deadly for the soul—and fairly dangerous for the body in the Cavalry Regiment whose riding-master prefers the abominable stripped-saddle training to the bare-backed....

Dam yawned and looked at the tin clock on the shelf above the cot of the Room Corporal. Half an hour yet.... Did time drag more heavily anywhere in the world?...

His mind roamed back over his brief, age-long life in the Queen's Greys and passed it in review.

The interview with the Doctor, the Regimental Sergeant-Major, the Adjutant, the Colonel—the Oath on the Bible before that dread Superman.... How well he remembered his brief exordium—"Obey your Superiors blindly; serve your Queen, Country, and Regiment to the best of your ability; keep clean, don't drink, fear God, and—most important of all—take care of your horse. *Take care of your horse*, d'ye hear?"

Also the drawled remark of the Adjutant afterwards, "Ah—what—ah—University?"—his own prompt reply of "Whitechapel, sir," and the Adjutant's approving "Exactly.... You'll get on here by good conduct, good riding, and good drill—not by—ah—good accent or anything else."

How well he remembered the strange depolarized feeling consequent upon realizing that his whole worldly possessions consisted in three "grey-back" shirts, two pairs of cotton pants, two pairs of woollen socks, a towel; a hold-all containing razor, shaving-brush, spoon, knife and fork, and a button-stick; a cylindrical valise with hair-brush, clothes-brush, brass-brush, and boot-brushes; a whip, burnisher, and dandy-brush (all three, for some reason, to be paid for as part of a "free" kit); jack-boots and jack-spurs, wellington-boots and swan-neck box-spurs, ammunition boots; a tin of blacking and another of plate powder; blue, white-striped riding-breeches, blue, white-striped overalls, drill-suit of blue serge, scarlet tunic, scarlet stable-jacket, scarlet drill "frock," a pair of trousers of lamentable cut "authorized for grooming," brass helmet with black horse-hair plume, blue pill-box cap with white stripe and button, gauntlets and gloves, sword-belt and pouch-belt, a carbine and a sword. Also of a daily income of one loaf, butter, tea, and a pound of meat (often uneatable), and the sum of one shilling and twopence subject to a deduction of threepence a day "mess-fund," fourpence a month for delft, and divers others for library, washing, hair-cutting, barrack-damages, *etc.*

Yes, it had given one a strange feeling of nakedness, and yet of a freedom from the tyranny of things, to find oneself so meagrely and yet so sufficiently endowed.

Then, the strange, lost, homeless feeling that Home is nothing but a cot and a box in a big bare barrack-room, that the whole of God's wide Universe contains no private and enclosed spot that is one's own peculiar place wherein to be alone—at first a truly terrible feeling.

How one envied the Rough-Riding Sergeant-Major his Staff Quarters—without going so far as to envy the great Riding-Master his real separate and detached house!

No privacy—and a scarlet coat that encarnadined the world and made its wearer feel, as he so often thought, like a live coal glowing bright in Hell.

Surely the greatest of all an officer's privileges was his right of mufti, his daily escape from the burning cloth.

"Why does not the British officer wear his uniform always?" writes the perennial gratuitous ass to the Press, periodically in the Silly Season.... Dam could tell him.

Memories ...!

Being jerked violently from uneasy slumber and broken, vivid dreams at 5 a.m., by the thunderous banging of the Troop Sergeant's whip on the table, and his raucous roar of "Tumble out, you lazy swine, before you get sunstroke! Rise and shine! Rise and shine, you tripe-hounds!" ... Broken dreams on a smelly, straw-stuffed pillow and lumpy straw-stuffed pallet, dreams of *"Circle and cha-a-a-a-a-a-nge"* *"On the Fore-hand, Right About"* *"Right Pass, Shoulder Out"* *"Serpentine"* *"Order Lance"* *"Trail Lance"* *"Right Front Thrust"* (for the front rank of the Queen's Greys carry lances); dreams of riding wild mad horses to unfathomable precipices and at unsurmountable barriers....

Memories ...!

His first experience of "mucking out" stables at five-thirty on a chilly morning— doing horrible work, horribly clad, feeling horribly sick. Wheeling away intentionally and maliciously over-piled barrows to the muck-pits, upsetting them, and being cursed.

Being set to water a notoriously wild and vicious horse, and being pulled about like a little dog at the end of the chain, burning into frozen fingers.

Not much of the glamour and glow and glory left!

Better were the interesting and amusing experiences of the Riding-School where his trained and perfected hands and seat gave him a tremendous advantage, an early dismissal, and some amelioration of the roughness of one of the very roughest experiences in a very rough life.

Even he, though, knew what it was to have serge breeches sticking to abraided bleeding knees, to grip a stripped saddle with twin suppurating sores, and to burrow face-first in filthy tan *via* the back of a stripped-saddled buck-jumper. How he had pitied some of the other recruits, making their first acquaintance with the Trooper's "long-faced chum" under the auspices of a pitiless, bitter-tongued Rough-Riding Sergeant-Major! *Rough!* What a character the fellow was! Never an oath, never a foul word, but what a vocabulary and gift of invective, sarcasm and cruel stinging reproof! A well-educated man if not a gentleman. "Don't dismount again, Muggins—or is it Juggins?—without permission" when some poor fellow comes on his head as his horse (bare of saddle and bridle) refuses at a jump. "Get up (and SIT BACK) you—you—hen, you pierrot, you *Aard Vark,* you after-thought, you refined entertainer, you pimple, you performing water-rat, you mistake, you *byle,* you drip, you worm-powder.... What? You think your leg's broken? Well—*you've got another,* haven't you? Get up and break that. Keep your neck till you get a stripped saddle and no reins.... Don't embrace the horse like that, you pawn-shop, I can hear it blushing.... Send for the key and get inside it.... Keep those fine feet forward. Keep them *forward* (and SIT BACK), Juggins or Muggins, or else take them into the Infantry—what they were meant for by the look of them. Now then—over you go without falling if I have to keep you here all night.... Look at *that*" (as the poor fellow is thrown across the jump by the cunning brute that knows its rider has neither whip, spurs, saddle nor reins). "What? The *horse* refuse? One of *my* horses *refuse? If the man'll jump, the horse'll jump.* (All of you repeat that after me and don't forget it.) No. It's the *man* refuses, not the poor horse. Don't you know the ancient proverb 'Faint heart ne'er took fair jump'....? What's the good of coming here if your heart's the size of your eye-ball instead of being the size of your fist? *Refuse?* Put him over it, man. *Put* him over—SIT BACK and lift him, and *put* him over. I'll give you a thousand pounds if he refuses *me*...."

Then the day when poor bullied, baited, nervous Muggins had reached his limit and come to the end of his tether—or thought he had. Bumped, banged, bucketed, thrown, sore from head to foot, raw-kneed, laughed at, lashed by the Rough-Riding Sergeant-Major's cruel tongue, blind and sick with dust and pain and rage, he had at last turned his horse inward from his place in the ride to the centre of the School, and dismounted.

How quaintly the tyrant's jaw had dropped in sheer astonishment, and how his face had purpled with rage when he realized that his eyes had not deceived him and that the worm had literally turned—without orders.

Indian, African, and Egyptian service, disappointment, and a bad wife had left Rough-Riding Sergeant-Major Blount with a dangerous temper.

Poor silly Muggins. He had been Juggins indeed on that occasion, and, as the "ride" halted of its own accord in awed amazement, Dam had longed to tell him so and beg him to return to his place ere worse befell....

"I've 'ad enough, you bull-'eaded brute," shouted poor Muggins, leaving his horse and advancing menacingly upon his (incalculably) superior officer, "an' fer two damns I'd break yer b—— jaw, I would. You ..."

Even as the Rough-Riding Corporal and two other men were dragging the struggling, raving recruit to the door, *en route* for the Guard-room, entered the great remote, dread Riding-Master himself.

"What's this?" inquired Hon. Captain Style, Riding-Master of the Queen's Greys, strict, kind-hearted martinet.

Salute, and explanations from the Rough-Riding Sergeant-Major.

Torrent of accusation and incoherent complaint and threat from the baited Muggins.

"Mount that horse," says the Riding-Master.

"I'll go to Clink first," gasps Muggins. "I'll go to 'Ell first."

"No. *Afterwards,*" replies the Riding-Master and sends the Rough-Riding Corporal for the backboard—dread instrument of equestrian persuasion.

Muggins is forcibly mounted, put in the lunging ring and sent round and round till he throws himself off at full gallop and lies crying and sobbing like a child—utterly broken.

Riding-Master smiles, allows Muggins to grow calmer, accepts his apologies and promises, shows him he has had his Hell *after*, as promised, and that it is a better punishment than one that leaves him with a serious "crime" entry on his Defaulter's Sheet for life.... That vile and damning sheet that records the youthful peccadilloes and keeps it a life-long punishment after its own severe punishment.... To the Rough-Riding Sergeant-Major he quietly remarks: "No good non-com *makes* crimes ... and don't forget that the day of riding-school brutality is passing. You can carry a man further than you can kick him."

And the interrupted lesson continues.

"Sit *back* and you can't come off. Nobody falls off backwards." ...

Poor "Old Sit-Back"! (as he was called from his constant cry)—after giving that order and guarantee daily for countless days—was killed in the riding-school by coming off backwards from the stripped saddle of a rearing horse—(which promptly fell upon him and crushed his chest)—that had never reared before and would not have reared then, it was said, but for the mysterious introduction, under its saddle, of a remarkably "foreign" body.

Memories ...!

How certain old "Sit-Back" had been that Dam was a worthless "back-to-the-Army-again" when he found him a finished horseman, an extraordinarily expert swordsman, and a master of the lance.

"You aren't old enough for a 'time-expired,'" he mused, "nor for a cashiered officer. One of the professional 'enlist-desert-and-sell-me-kit,' I suppose. Anyhow you'll do time for one of the three if *I* don't approve of ye.... You've been in the Cavalry before. Lancer regiment, too. Don't tell *me* lies ... but see to it that I'm satisfied with your conduct. Gentlemen-rankers are better in their proper place—*Jail.*" ...

None the less it had given Dam a thrill of pride when, on being dismissed recruit-drills and drafted from the reserve troop to a squadron, the Adjutant had posted him to E Troop, wherein were congregated the seven other undoubted gentlemen-rankers of the Queen's Greys (one of whom would one day become a peer of the realm and, meantime, followed what he called "the only profession in the world" in discomfort for a space, the while his Commission ripened).

To this small band of "rankers" the accession of the finest boxer, swordsman, and horseman in the corps, was invaluable, and helped them notably in their endeavour to show that there are exceptions to all rules, and that a gentleman *can* make a first-class trooper. At least so "Peerson" had said, and Dam had been made almost happy for a day.

Memories ...!

His first walk abroad from barracks, clad in the "walking-out" finery of shell-jacket and overalls, with the jingle of spurs and effort at the true Cavalry swagger, or rather the first attempt at a walk abroad, for the expedition had ended disastrously ere well begun. Unable to shake off his admirer, Trooper Herbert Hawker, Dam had just passed the Main Guard and main gates in the company of Herbert, and the two recruits had encountered the Adjutant and saluted with the utmost smartness and respect....

108

"What the Purple Hell's that thing?" had drawled the Adjutant thereupon—pointing his whip at Trooper Henry Hawker, whose trap-like mouth incontinent fell open with astonishment. "It's got up in an imitation of the uniform of the Queen's Greys, I do believe!... It's not a rag doll either.... It's a God-forsaken undertaker's mute in a red and black shroud with a cake-tin at the back of its turnip head and a pair of chemises on its ugly hands.... Sergeant of the Guard!... Here!"

"Sir?" and a salute of incredible precision from the Sergeant of the Guard.

"What the name of the Devil's old Aunt is *this* thing? What are you on Guard for? To write hymns and scare crows—or to allow decayed charwomen to stroll out of barracks in a dem parody of your uniform? Look at her! Could turn round in the jacket without taking it off. Room for both legs in one of the overalls. Cap on his beastly neck. Gloves like a pair of ... *Get inside you!*... Take the thing in with a pair of tongs and bury it where it won't contaminate the dung-pits. Burn it! Shoot it! Drown it! D'ye hear?... And then I'll put you under arrest for letting it pass...."

It had been a wondrously deflated and chapfallen Herbert that had slunk back to the room of the reserve troop, and perhaps his reputation as a mighty bruiser had never stood him in so good stead as when it transpired that an Order had been promulgated that no recruit should leave barracks during the first three months of his service, and that the names of all such embryos should be posted in the Main Guard for the information of the Sergeant....

Memories ...!

His first march behind the Band to Church....

The first Review and March Past....

His first introduction to bread-and-lard....

His wicked carelessness in forgetting—or attempting to disregard—the law of the drinking-troughs. "So long as one horse has his head down no horse is to go." There had been over a score drinking and he had moved off while one dipsomaniac was having a last suck.

His criminal carelessness in not removing his sword and leaving it in the Guard-room, when going on sentry after guard-mounting—"getting the good Sergeant into trouble, too, and making it appear that *he* had been equally criminally careless ".

The desperate quarrel between Hawker and Bone as to whether the 10th Hussars were called the "Shiny Tenth" because of their general material and spiritual brilliance, or the "Chainy Tenth" because their Officers wore pouch-belts of gold chain-mail.... The similar one between Buttle and Smith as to the reason of a brother regiment being known as "The Virgin Mary's Body-guard," and their reluctant acceptance of Dam's dictum that they were both wrong, it having been earned by them in the service of a certain Maria Theresa, a lady unknown to Messrs. Buttle and Smith.... Dam had found himself developing into a positive bully in his determination to prevent senseless quarrelling, senseless misconduct, senseless humourless foulness, senseless humourless blasphemy, and all that unnecessary, avoidable ugliness that so richly augmented the unavoidable....

Memories ...!

Sitting throughout compulsory church, cursing and mutinous of heart, because after spending several hours of the Day of Rest in burnishing and pipe-claying, blacking and shining ("Sunday spit an' polish"), he was under orders for sharp punishment—-because at the last moment his tunic had been fouled by a passing pigeon! When would the Authorities realize that soldiers are still men, still Englishmen (even if they have, by becoming soldiers, lost their birthright of appeal to the Law of the Land, though not their amenability to its authority), and cease to make the Blessed Sabbath a curse, the worst day of the week, and to herd angry, resentful soldiers into church to blaspheme with politely pious faces? Oh, British, British, Pharisees and Humbugs—make Sunday a curse, and drive the soldier into church to do his cursing—make it the chief day of dress "crimes" and punishments, as well as the busiest day, and force the soldier into church to Return Thanks....

The only man in the world flung into church as though into jail for punishment! Shout it in the Soldier's ear, *"You are not a Man, you are a Slave,"* on Sundays also, on Sundays louder than usual.... And when he has spent his Sunday morning in extra hard labour, in suffering the indignity of being compulsorily marched to church, and very frequently of having been punished because it is a good day on which a Sergeant may decide that he is not sufficiently cleanly shaved or his boots of minor effulgence—then let him sit and watch his hot Sunday dinner grow stone cold before the Colonel stalks through the room, asks a perfunctory question, and he is free to fall to.

"O Day of Rest and Gladness,
  O Day of Joy most Bright...."

Yah!

A pity some of the energy that went to making the annual 20,000 military "criminals" out of honest, law-abiding, well-intending men could not go to harassing the Canteen instead of the soldier (whom the Canteen swindles right and left, and whence *he* gets salt-watery beer, and an "ounce" of tobacco that will go straight into his pipe in one "fill"—no need to wrap it up, thank you) and discovering how handsome fortunes, as well as substantial "illegal gratifications," are made out of his much-stoppaged one-and-tuppence-a-week.

Did the Authorities really yearn to *dis*courage enlistment and to *en*courage desertion and "crime"? When would they realize that making "crimes," and manufacturing "criminals" from honest men, is *not* discipline, is *not* making soldiers, is *not* improving the Army—is *not* common ordinary sanity and sense? When would they break their dull, unimaginative, hide-bound—no, tape-bound—souls from the ideas that prevailed before (and murdered) the Crimean Army.... The Army is not now the sweepings of the jails, and more in need of the wild-beast tamer than of the kind firm teacher, as once it was. How long will they continue to suppose that you make a fine fighting-man, and a self-reliant, intelligent soldier, by treating him as a depraved child, as a rightless slave, as a mindless automaton, and by encouraging the public (whom he protects) to regard him as a low criminal ruffian to be classed with the broad-arrowed convict, and to be excluded from places where any loafing rotten lout may go.... When would a lawyer-ridden Army Council realize that there is a trifle of significance in the fact that there are four times as many soldier suicides as there are civilian, and that the finest advertisement for the dwindling Army *is the soldier.* To think that sober men should, with one hand spend vast sums in lying advertisements for the Army, and with the other maintain a system that makes the soldier on furlough reply to the question "Shall I enlist, mate?" with the words "Not while you got a razor to cut yer throat".... Ah, well, common sense would reach even the Army some day, and the soldier be treated and disciplined as a man and a citizen—and perhaps, when it did, and the soldier gave a better description of his life, the other citizen, the smug knave who despises him while he shelters behind him, will become less averse from having his own round shoulders straightened, his back flattened and his muscles developed as he takes his part in the first fundamental elementary duty of a citizen—preparation for the defence of hearth and home.... Lucille! Well ... Thank God she could not see him and know his life. If *she* had any kindness left for him she would suffer to watch him eating well-nigh uneatable food, grooming a horse, sweeping a stable, polishing trestle-legs with blacklead, scrubbing floors, sleeping on damp straw, carrying coals, doing scullion-work for uneducated roughs, being brow-beaten, bullied, and cursed by them in tight-lipped silence—not that these things troubled him personally—the less idle leisure for thought the better, and no real man minds physical hardship—there is no indignity in labour *per se* any more than there is dignity....

"'Ere, Maffewson, you bone-idle, moonin' waster," bawled the raucous voice of Lance-Corporal Prag, and Dam's soaring spirit fell to earth.

The first officer to whom Trooper Matthewson gave his smart respectful salute as he stood on sentry-duty was the Major, the Second-in-Command of the Queen's Greys, newly rejoined from furlough,—a belted Earl, famous for his sporting habit of riding always and everywhere without a saddle—who, as a merry subaltern, had been Lieutenant Lord Ochterlonie and Adjutant of the Queen's Greys at Bimariabad in India. There, he had, almost daily, taken upon his knee, shoulder, saddle, or dog-cart, the chubby son of his polo and pig-sticking exemplar, Colonel Matthew Devon de Warrenne.

The sentry had a dim idea that he had seen the Major somewhere before.

CHAPTER IX.

A SNAKE AVENGES A HADDOCK AND LUCILLE BEHAVES IN AN UN-SMELLIEAN MANNER.

Finding himself free for the afternoon, and the proud possessor of several shillings, "Trooper Matthewson" decided to walk to Folkestone, attend an attractively advertised concert on the pier, and then indulge in an absolutely private meal in some small tea-room or confectioner's shop.

Arrayed in scarlet shell-jacket, white-striped overalls, and pill-box cap, he started forth, carrying himself as though exceeding proud to be what he was, and wondering whether a swim in the sea, which should end somewhere between Shorncliffe and Dieppe (and end his troubles too), would not be a better pastime.

Arrived at the Folkestone pier, Dam approached the ticket office at the entrance and tendered his shilling to the oily-curled, curly-nosed young Jew who sat at the receipt of custom.

"Clear out o' this," said Levi Solomonson.

"I want a ticket for the concert," said Dam, not understanding.

"Would you like a row o' stalls to sprawl your dirty carcase on?... Outside, I tell yer, Tommy Atkins, this ain't a music-'all nor yet a pub. Soldiers *not* ''alf-price to cheap seats' nor yet full-price—nor yet for ten pound a time. Out yer go, lobster."

The powerful hand of Damocles de Warrenne approached the window and, for a second, Mr. Levi Solomonson was in danger—but only for a second. Dam was being well-broken-in, and quickly realized that he was no longer a free British citizen entitled to the rights of such so long as he behaved as a citizen should, but a mere horrible defender of those of his countrymen, who were averse from the toils and possible dangers of self-defence. It was brought home to him, then and there, with some clearness, that the noble Britons who (perhaps) "never never will be slaves," have a fine and high contempt for those whose life-work is to save them from that distressing position; that the noble Briton, while stoutly (and truly Britishly) refusing to hear of universal service and the doing by each man of his first duty to the State, is informed with a bitter loathing of those who, for wretched hire and under wretched conditions, perform those duties for him. Dam did not mind, though he did not enjoy, doing housemaid's work in the barrack-room, scrubbing floors, blackleading iron table-legs and grates, sweeping, dusting, and certain other more unpleasant menial tasks; he did not mind, though he did not like, "mucking-out" stables and scavenging; he could take at their proper value the insults of ignorant boors set in authority over him; he could stand, if not enjoy, the hardships of the soldier's life—but he did *not* see why his doing his duty in that particular sphere—an arduous, difficult, and frequently dangerous sphere—should earn him the united insult of the united public! Why should an educated and cultured man, a gentleman in point of fact, be absolutely prohibited from hearing a "classical" concert because he wore the Queen's uniform and did that most important and necessary work which the noble Briton is too slack-baked, too hypocritically genteel, too degenerate, to perform, each man for himself?

In a somewhat bitter frame of mind the unfortunate young man strolled along the Leas and seated himself on a public bench, honestly wondering as he did so, whether he were sufficiently a member of the great and glorious public to have a right to do it while wearing the disgraceful and disgracing garb of a Trooper of the Queen.... Members of that great and glorious public passed him by in rapid succession. Narrow-chested youths of all classes, and all crying aloud in slack-lipped silence for the drill-sergeant to teach them how to stand and walk; for the gymnasium-instructor to make them, what they would never be, *men*; for some one to give them an aim and an ideal beyond cigarettes, socks, and giggling "gels" or "gals" or "garls" or "gyurls" or "gurrls" according to their social sphere. Vast-stomached middle-aged men of all classes, and all crying aloud in fat-lipped silence of indulgence, physical sloth, physical decay before physical prime should have been reached, of mental, moral, and physical decadence from the great Past incredible, and who would one and all, if asked, congratulate themselves on living in these glorious modern times of 'igh civilization and not in the dark, ignorant days of old.

(Decidedly a bitter young man, this.)

Place Mister Albert Pringle, Insurance Agent; Mister Peter Snagget, Grocer; Mister Alphonso Pumper, Rate Collector; Mister Bill 'Iggins, Publican; Mister Walter Weed, Clerk; Mister Jeremiah Ramsmouth, Local Preacher; Mr. 'Ookey Snagg, Loafer; Mister William Guppy, Potman—place them beside Hybrias, Goat-herd; Damon, Shepherd; Phydias, Writer; Nicarchus, Ploughman; Balbus, Bricklayer; Glaucus, Potter; Caius, Carter; Marcus, Weaver; Aeneas, Bronze-worker; Antonius, Corn-seller; Canidius, Charioteer—and then talk of the glorious modern times of high civilization and the dark ignorant days of old!...

And as he sat musing thus foolishly and pessimistically, who should loom upon his horizon but—of all people in the world—the Haddock, the fishy, flabby, stale, unprofitable Haddock! Most certainly Solomon in all his glory was not arrayed like this. A beautiful confection of pearly-grey, pearl-buttoned flannel draped his droopy form, a pearly-grey silk tie, pearl-pinned, encircled his lofty collar, pearly-grey silk socks spanned the divorcing gap 'twixt beautiful grey kid shoes and correctest trousers, a pearly-grey silk handkerchief peeped knowingly from the cuff of his pearly-grey silk shirt by his pearly-grey kid glove, and his little cane was of grey lacquer, and of pearl handle. One could almost have sworn that a pearl-grey smile adorned the scarce-shut mouth of the beautiful modern product of education and civilization, to carry on the so well-devised colour-scheme to the pearly-grey grey-ribboned soft hat.

The Haddock's mind wandered not in empty places, but wrestled sternly with the problem—*would* it not have been better, after all, perhaps, to have worn the pearly-grey spats (with the pearl buttons) instead of relying on the pearly-grey socks alone? When one sat down and modestly protruded an elegant foot as one crossed one's legs and gently drew up one's trouser (lest a baggy knee bring black shame), one could display both—the spat itself, *and*, above it, the sock. Of course! To the passer-by, awe-inspired, admiring, stimulated, would then have been administered the double shock and edification. While gratefully observing the so-harmonizing grey spat and grey shoe he would have noted the Ossa of grey silk sock piled upon that Pelion of ultra-fashionable foot-joy! Yes. He had acted hastily and had erred and strayed from the Perfect Way—and a cloud, at first no bigger than a continent or two, arose and darkened his mental sky.

But what of the cloud that settled upon him, black as that of the night's Plutonian shore, a cloud much bigger than the Universe, when a beastly, awful, ghastly, common private soldier arose from a seat—a common seat for which you do not pay a penny and show your selectitude—arose, I say, from a beastly common seat and SEIZED HIM BY THE ARM and remarked in horrible, affected, mocking tones:—

"And how's the charming little Haddock, the fourpenny, common breakfast Haddock?"

Yes, in full sight of the Leas of Folkestone, and the nobility, gentry, shopmen, nurse-girls, suburban yachtsmen, nuts, noisettes, bath-chairmen and all the world of rank and fashion, a common soldier took the pearly-grey arm of *the* Haddon Berners as he took the air and walked abroad to give the public a treat. And proved to be his shameful, shameless, disgraced, disgraceful, cowardly relative, Damocles de Warrenne!

The Haddock reeled, but did not fall.

On catching sight of the beautiful young man, Dam's first impulse was to spring up and flee, his second to complete the work of Mr. Levi Solomonson of the pier concert and see for himself, once again, how he was regarded by the eyes of all right-minded and respectable members of society, including those of a kinsman with whom he had grown up.

Yes, in his bitterness of soul, and foolish youthful revolt against Fate, he was attracted by the idea of claiming acquaintance with the superb Haddock in his triumphant progress, take him by the arm, and solemnly march him the whole length of the Leas! He would, by Jove! *He did.*

Confronting the resplendent languid loafer, he silkily observed, as he placed his cutting-whip beneath his left arm and extended his white cotton-gloved right hand:—

"And how's the charming little Haddock, the fourpenny, common breakfast Haddock?"

Had it been Ormonde Delorme, any friend of Monksmead days, any school or Sandhurst acquaintance, had it been any other relative, had it been Lucille, he would have fled for his life, he would have seen his hand paralysed ere he would have extended it, he would have been struck dumb rather than speak, he would have died before he would have inflicted upon them the indignity of being seen in the company of a common soldier. But the Haddock! 'twould do the Haddock a world of good; the Haddock who had mocked him as he fought for sanity and life on the lawn at Monksmead—the Haddock who "made love" to Lucille.

The Haddock affected not to see the hand.

"I—er—don't—ah—know you, surely, do I?" he managed to mumble as he backed away and turned to escape.

"Probably not, dear Haddock," replied the embittered desperate Dam, "but you're going to. We're going for a walk together."

"Are you—ah—dwunk, fellow? Do you suppose I walk with—ah—*soldiers?*"

"I don't, my Fish, but you're going to now—if I have to carry you. And if I have to do that I'll slap you well, when I put you down!"

"I'll call a policeman and give you in charge if you dare molest me. What do you—-ah—desire? Money?... If you come to my hotel this evening—" and the hapless young man was swung round, his limp thin arm tucked beneath a powerful and mighty one, and he was whirled along at five miles an hour in the direction of the pier, gasping, feebly struggling, and a sight to move the High Gods to pity.

"To the pier, my Haddock, and then back to the turnpike gate, and if you let a yell, or signal a policeman, I'll twist your little neck. Fancy our Haddock in a vulgar street row with a common soldier and in the Police Court! Step it out, you worm!"

Then the agonized Haddock dropped pretence.

"Oh, Dam, I'm awf'ly sorry. I apologize, old chap. *Let up*—I say—this is *awful....* Good God, here's Lady Plonk, the Mayor's wife!"

"You shall introduce me, Lovely One—but no, we mustn't annoy ladies. You must *not* go trying to introduce your low companions—nay, relations—to Lady Plonkses. Step out—and look happy."

"Dam—for God's sake, let me go! I didn't know you, old chap. I swear I didn't. The disgrace will kill me. I'll give you—"

"Look here, wee Fish, you offer me money again and I'll—I'll undress you and run away with your clothes. I will, upon my soul."

"I shall call to this policeman," gasped the Haddock.

"And appear with your low-class *relation* in Court? Not you, Haddock. I'd swear you were my twin brother, and that you wouldn't pay me the four pence you borrowed of me last week."

And the cruel penance was inflicted to the last inch. Near the end the Haddock groaned: "Here's Amelia Harringport—Oh! my God," and Dam quickly turned his face unto the South and gazed at the fair land of France. He remembered that General Harringport dwelt in these parts.

At the toll-gate Dam released the perspiration-soaked wretch, who had suffered the torments of the damned, and who seemed to have met every man and woman whom he knew in the world as he paraded the promenade hanging lovingly to the arm of a common soldier! He thought of suicide and shuddered at the bare idea.

"Well, I'm awf'ly sorry to have to run away and leave you now, dear Haddock. I might have taken you to all the pubs in Folkestone if I'd had time. I might have come to your hotel and dined with you. You *will* excuse me, won't you? I *must* go now. I've got to wash up the tea things and clean the Sergeant's boots," said Dam, cruelly wringing the Haddock's agonized soft hand, and, with a complete and disconcerting change, added, "And if you breathe a word about having seen me, at Monksmead, or tell Lucille, *I'll seek you out, my Haddock,* and—we will hold converse with thee". Then he strode away, cursing himself for a fool, a cad, and a deteriorated, demoralized ruffian. Anyhow, the Haddock would not mention the appalling incident and give him away.

Nemesis followed him.

Seeking a quiet shop in a back street where he could have the long-desired meal in private, he came to a small taxidermist's, glanced in as he passed, and beheld the pride and joy of the taxidermist's heart—a magnificent and really well-mounted boa-constrictor, and fell shrieking, struggling, and screaming in the gutter.

That night Damocles de Warrenne, ill, incoherent, and delirious, passed in a cell, on a charge of drunk and disorderly and disgracing the Queen's uniform.

Mr. Levi Solomonson had not disgraced it, of course.

"If we were not eating this excellent bread-and-dripping and drinking this vile tea, what would you like to be eating and drinking, Matthewson?" asked Trooper Nemo (formerly Aubrey Roussac d'Aubigny of Harrow and Trinity).

"Oh, ... a little real turtle," said Dam, "just a lamina of *sole frite*, a trifle of *vol an vent a la financiere*, a breast of partridge, a mite of *pate de fois gras*, a peach *a la Melba*, the roe of a bloater, and a few fat grapes—"

"'Twould do. 'Twould pass," sighed Trooper Burke, and added, "I would suggest a certain Moselle I used to get at the Byculla Club in Bombay, and a wondrous fine claret that spread a ruby haze of charm o'er my lunch at the Yacht Club of the same fair city. A *'Mouton Rothschild* something,' which was cheap at nine rupees a small bottle on the morrow of a good day on the Mahaluxmi Racecourse." (It was strongly suspected that Trooper Burke had worn a star on his shoulder-strap in those Indian days.)

"It's an awful shame we can't all emerge from the depths and run up to Town to breathe the sweet original atmosphere for just one night before we leave old England," put in Trooper Punch Peerson (son of a noble lord) who would at that moment have been in the Officers' Mess but for a congenital weakness in spelling and a dislike of mathematics. "Pity we can't get 'leaf,' and do ourselves glorious at the Carlton, and 'afterwards'. We could change at my Governor's place into borrowed, stolen, and hired evening-kit, paint the village as scarlet as Sin or a trooper's jacket, and then come home, like the Blackbird, to tea. I am going, and if I can't get 'leaf' I shall return under the bread in the rations-cart. Money's the root of all (successful) evil."

Trooper Punch Peerson was a born leader of men, a splendid horseman and soldier, and he had the Army in his ardent, gallant blood and bones; but how shall a man head a cavalry charge or win the love and enthusiastic obedience of men and horses when he is weak in spelling and has a dislike of mathematics?

However, he was determined to follow in the footsteps of his ancestors, to serve his country in spite of her, and his Commission was certain and near. Meanwhile he endeavoured to be a first-class trooper, had his uniform made of officers' materials in Bond Street by his father's famous tailor, and "got the stick" with ease and frequency.

"We're not all gilded popinjays (nor poppin' bottles)," observed a young giant who called himself Adam Goate, and had certainly been one in the days when he was Eugene Featherstonthwaite. "All very well for you to come to the surface and breathe, seeing that you'll be out of it soon. You're having nothing but a valuable experience and a hardening. You're going through the mill. We've got to *live* in it. What's the good of our stirring everything up again? Dam-silly of a skinned eel to grow another skin, to be skinned again.... No, 'my co-mates and brothers in exile,' what I say is—you can get just as drunk on 'four-'arf' as on champagne, and a lot cheaper. Ask my honourable friend, Bear."

(Trooper Bear gave a realistic, but musical hiccup.)

"Also, to the Philosopher, bread-and-dripping is as interesting and desirable prog as the voluble-varied heterogeny of the menu at the Carlton or the Ritz—'specially when you've no choice."

"Hear, hear," put in Dam.

"Goatey ol' Goate!" said Trooper Bear with impressive solemnity. "Give me your hand, Philossiler. I adore dripping. I'ss a (hic) mystery. (No, I don' want both hands," as Goate offered his right to Bear's warm embrace.) I'm a colliseur of Dripping. I understan' it. I write odes to it. Yesh. A basin of dripping is like a Woman. 'Strornarillily. You never know what's beneath fair surface.... Below a placid, level, unrevealing surface there may be—nothing ... and there may be a rich deposit of glorious, stimulating, piquant *essence*."

"Oh, shut up, Bear, and don't be an Ass," implored Trooper Burke (formerly Desmond Villiers FitzGerald) ... "but I admit, all the same, there's lots of worse prog in the Officers' Mess than a crisp crust generously bedaubed with the rich jellified gravy that (occasionally) lurks like rubies beneath the fatty soil of dripping."

"Sound plan to think so, anyway," agreed Trooper Little (*ci devant* Man About Town and the Honourable Bertie Le Grand). "Reminds me of a proverb I used to hear in Alt Heidelberg, *'What I have in my hand is best'*."

"Qui' sho," murmured Trooper Bear with a seraphic smile, "an' wha' I have in my 'place of departed *spirits*,' my tummy, is better. Glor'us mixshure. Earned an honest penny sheven sheparate times cleaning the 'coutrements of better men ... *'an look at me for shevenpence'* ..." and he slept happily on Dam's shoulder.

In liquor, Trooper Bear was, if possible, gentler, kinder, and of sweeter disposition than when sober; wittier, more hopelessly lovable and disarming. These eight men—the "gentlemen-rankers" of the Queen's Greys, made it a point of honour to out-Tommy "Tommy" as troopers, and, when in his company, to show a heavier cavalry-swagger, a broader accent, a quiffier "quiff," a cuttier cutty-pipe, a smarter smartness; to groom a horse better, to muck out a stall better, to scrub a floor better, to spring more smartly to attention or to a disagreeable "fatigue," and to set an example of Tomminess from turning out on an Inspection Parade to waxing a moustache.

Trooper Bear professed to specialize as a model in the carrying of liquor "like a man and a soldier". When by themselves, they made it a point of honour to behave and speak as though in the clubs to which they once belonged, to eat with washen hands and ordered attire, to behave at table and elsewhere with that truest of consideration that offends no man willingly by mannerism, appearance, word or act, and which is the whole Art of Gentility.

118

They carefully avoided any appearance of exclusiveness, but sought every legitimate opportunity of united companionship, and formed a "mess" of eight at a table which just held that number, and on a couple of benches each of which exactly fulfilled the slang expression "room for four Dragoons on a form".

It was their great ambition to avoid the reproach of earning the soubriquet "gentleman-ranker," a term that too often, and too justly, stinks in the nostrils of officer, non-commissioned officer, and man (for, as a rule, the "gentleman-ranker" is a complete failure as a gentleman and a completer one as a ranker).

To prove a rule by a remarkably fine exception, these eight were among the very smartest and best troopers of one of the smartest and best Corps in the world—and to Damocles de Warrenne, their "Society of the Knights of the dirty Square Table" was a Rock and a Salvation in the midst of a howling sea of misery—a cool pool in a searing branding Hell.

Trooper Bear's brief nap appeared to have revived him wonderfully.

"Let us, like the Hosts of Midian, prowl around this happy Sabbeth eve, my dear," quoth he to Dam, "and, like wise virgins, up and smite them, when we meet the Red-Caps.... No, I'm getting confused. It's they up and smite us, when we've nothing to tip them.... I feel I could be virtuous in your company—since you never offer beer to the (more or less) fatherless and widowed—and since I'm stony. How *did* you work that colossal drunk, Matty, when you came home on a stretcher and the Red-Caps said you *'was the first-classest delirious-trimmings as ever was, aseein' snakes somethink 'orrible,'* and in no wise to be persuaded *'as 'ow there wasn't one underyer bloomin' foot the 'ole time'.* Oh you teetotallers!"

Dam shuddered and paled. "Yes, let's go for as long a walk as we can manage, and get as far from this cursed place as time allows," he replied.

His hair was still short and horribly hacked from the prison-crop he had had as a preliminary to "168 hours cells," for "drunk and disorderly".

"I'll come too," announced the Honourable Bertie.

"Yes," chimed in Trooper Adam Goate, "let's go and gladden the eyes, if not the hearts of the nurse-maids of Folkestone."

"Bless their nurse-maidenly hearts," murmured Trooper Bear. "One made honourable proposals of marriage to me, quite recently, in return for my catching the runaway hat of her young charge.... Come on." And in due course the four derelicts set forth with a uniformity of step and action that corresponded with their uniformity of dress.

"Let's take the Lower Road," said Dam, as they reached the western limit of the front at Folkestone. "I fear we rather contaminate the pure social air of the Upper Road and the fashionable promenade."

"Where every prospect pleases and only man, in the Queen's uniform, is vile," observed Trooper Bear.

Dam remembered afterwards that it was he who sought the quiet Lower Road—and he had good reason to remember it. For suddenly, a fashionably dressed and beautiful young girl, sitting alone in a passing private victoria, stood up, called "Stop! Stop!" to the coachman, and ere the carriage well came to a standstill, sprang out, rushed up to the double file of soldiers, and flung her arms around the neck of the outside one of the front rank.

With a cry of "Oh, *Dam*! Oh, *Dammy*!"—a cry that mightily scandalized a serious-minded policeman who stood monumentally at the corner—she kissed him again and again!

Troopers Bear, Goate, and Little, halting not in their stride, glancing not unto the right hand nor unto the left hand, speaking no word, and giving no sign of surprise, marched on in perfect silence, until Trooper Bear observed to the world in general "The lady was *not* swearing. His *name* must be Dam—short for Damon or Pythias or Iphigenia or something which we may proceed to forget.... Poor old chappie—no wonder he's taking to secret drinking. *I* should drink, myself. *Poor* chap!" and Trooper Goate, heaving a sympathetic sigh, murmured also "Poor chap!"

But Trooper Little, once the Hon. Bertie Le Grand, thought "Poor *lady*!"

* * * * *

The heart of Damocles de Warrenne bounded within him, stood still, and then seemed like to burst.

"Oh, *Lucille*! Oh, darling!" he groaned, as he kissed her fiercely and then endeavoured to thrust her from him. "Jump into your carriage quickly. *Lucille*—Don't ... *Here* ...! Not *here*.... People are looking ... *You* ...! A common soldier.... Let me go. Quick.... Your carriage.... Some one may—"

"Let you *go*, darling ...! Now I have found you.... If you say another word I'll serve you as you served the Haddock. I'll hang on to your arm right along the Leas. I'll hang round your neck and scream if you try to run away. This is poetic justice, darling. Now you know how our Haddock felt. *No*—I *won't* leave go of your sleeve. Where shall we go, dearest darling Dammy. Dare you drive up and down the Front with me in Amelia Harringport's sister's young man's mother's victoria? oh, my *darling* Dam...." and Lucille burst into happy tears.

120

"Go up that winding path and I'll follow in a minute. There will be secluded seats."

"And you'll bolt directly I leave go of you?... I—"

"No, darling, God knows I should if I were a man, but I can't, *I can't*. Oh, Lucille!"

"Stay here," cried the utterly fearless, unashamed girl to the unspeakably astounded coachman of the mother of the minor Canon who had the felicity of being Amelia Harringport's sister's young man, and she strode up the pathway that wound, tree-shaded, along the front of the gently sloping cliff.

In the utter privacy of a small seat-enclosing, bush-hidden half-cave, Damocles de Warrenne crushed Lucille to his breast as she again flung her arms around his neck.

"Oh, Lucille, how *could* you expose yourself to scandal like that; I ought to be hung for not taking to my heels as you came, but I could not believe my eyes, I thought I was going mad again," and he shivered.

"What should I have cared if every soul in the world who knows me had arranged himself and herself in rows and ranks to get a good view? I'd have done the same if Grumper had been beside me in the carriage. What is the rest of the World to me, beside *you*, darling?... Oh, your *poor* hair, and what is that horrid scar, my dearest? And you are a '2 Q.G.' are you, and how soon may you marry? I'm going to disappear from Monksmead, now, just like you did, darling, and I'm coming here and I'm going to be a soldier's wife. Can I live with you in your house in barracks, Dammy, or must I live outside, and you come home directly your drill and things are finished?"

Dam groaned aloud in hopeless bitterness of soul.

"Lucille—listen," said he. "I earn one-and tuppence a day. I may not marry. If you were a factory-girl or a coster-woman I would not drag you down so. Apart from that, I am unfit to marry any decent woman. I am—what you know I am.... I have—fits. I am not—sound—normal—I may go m...."

"Don't be a pure priceless Ass, darling. You are my own splendid hero—and I am going to marry you, if I have to *be* a factory-girl or a coster-woman, and I am going to live either with you or near you. You want looking after, my own boy. I shall have some money, though, when I am of age. When may I run away from Monksmead, darling?"

"Lucille," groaned the miserable man. "Do you think that the sight of you in the mire in which I wallow would make me happier? Can't you realize that I'm ruined and done—disgraced and smashed? Lucille, I am not sane at times.... The SNAKE ... *Do* you love me, Lucille? Then if so, I beg and implore you to forget me, to leave me alone, to wait awhile and then marry Delorme or some sane, wholesome *man*—

who is neither a coward nor a lunatic nor an epileptic. Lucille, you double and treble my misery. I *can't* bear it if I see you. Oh, why didn't you forget me and do the right and proper thing? I am unfit to touch you! I am a damned scoundrel to be here now," and leaping up he fled like a maddened horse, bounded down the slope, sprang into the road, nor ceased to run till he fell exhausted, miles away from the spot whereon he had suffered as he believed few men had done before.

And thus and thus we women live!
With none to question, none to give
The Nay or Aye, the Aye or Nay
That might smoothe half our cares away.
O, strange indeed! And sad to know
We pitch too high and doing so,
Intent and eager not to fall,
We miss the low clear note of call.
Why is it so? Are we indeed
So like unto the shaken reed?
Of such poor clay? Such puny strength?
That e'en throughout the breadth and length
Of purer vision's stern domain
We bend to serve and serve in vain?
To some, indeed, strange power is lent
To stand content. Love, heaven-sent,
(For things or high or pure or rare)
Shows likest God, makes Life less bare.
And, ever and anon there stray
In faint far-reaching virelay
The songs of angels, Heav'nward-found,
Of little children, earthward-bound.

A. L. WREN.

CHAPTER X.

MUCH ADO ABOUT ALMOST NOTHING—A TROOPER.

Mr. Ormonde Delorme, Second Lieutenant of the 34th Lancers, sat in his quarters at Aldershot, reading and re-reading with mingled feelings a letter from the woman he loved.

It is one thing to extract a promise from The Woman that she will turn to you for help if ever your help should be needed (knowing that there could be no greater joy than to serve her at any cost whatsoever, though it led to death or ruin), but it is quite another thing when that help is invited for the benefit of the successful rival!

To go to the world's end for Lucille were a very small matter to Ormonde Delorme—but to go across the road for the man who had won her away, was not.

For Dam *had* won her away from him, Delorme considered, inasmuch as he had brought him to Monksmead, time after time, had seen him falling in love with Lucille, had received his confidences, and spoken no warning word. Had he said but "No poaching, Delorme," nothing more would have been necessary; he would have kept away thenceforth, and smothered the flame ere it became a raging and consuming fire. No, de Warrenne had served him badly in not telling him plainly that there was an understanding between him and his cousin, in letting him sink more and more deeply over head and ears in love, in letting him go on until he proposed to Lucille and learnt from her that while she liked him better than any man in the world but one—she did not love him, and that, frankly, yes, she *did* love somebody else, and it was hopeless for him to hope....

He read the letter again:—

"MY DEAR ORMONDE,

"This is a begging letter, and I should loathe to write it, under the circumstances, to any man but such a one as you. For I am going to ask a great deal of you and to appeal to that nobleness of character for which I have always admired you and which made you poor Dam's hero from Lower School days at Wellingborough until you left Sandhurst (and, alas! quarrelled with him—or rather with his memory—about me). That was a sad blow to me, and I tell you again as I told you before, Dam had not the faintest notion that *I* cared for *him* and would not have told me that he cared for me had I not shown it. Your belief that he didn't trouble to warn you because he had me safe is utterly wrong, absurd, and unjust.

"When you did me the great honour and paid me the undeserved and tremendous compliment of asking me to marry you, and I told you that I could not, and *why* I could not, I never dreamed that Dam could care for me in that way, and I knew that I should never marry any one at all unless he did.

"And on the same occasion, Ormonde, you begged me to promise that if ever you could serve me in any way, I would ask for your help. You were a dear romantic boy then, Ormonde, and I loved you in a different way, and cried all night that you and I could not be friends without thought of love, and I most solemnly promised that I would turn to you if I ever needed help that you could give. (Alas, I thought to myself then that nobody in the world could do anything for me that Dam could not do, and that I should never need help from others while he lived.)

"I want your help, Ormonde, and I want it for Dam—and me.

"You have, of course, heard some garbled scandal about his being driven away from home and cut off from Sandhurst by grandfather. I need not ask if you have believed ill of him and I need not say he is absolutely innocent of any wrong or failure whatever. He is *not* an effeminate coward, he is as brave as a lion. He is a splendid hero, Ormonde, and I want you to simply strangle and kill any man who says a word to the contrary.

"When he left home, he enlisted, and Haddon Berners saw him in uniform at Folkestone where he had gone from Canterbury (cricket week) to see Amelia Harringport's gang. Amelia whose sister is to be the Reverend Mrs. Canon Mellifle at Folkestone, you know, met the wretched Haddon being rushed along the front by a soldier and nearly died at the sight—she declares he was weeping!

"Directly she told me I guessed at once that he had met Dam and either insulted or cut him, and that poor Dam, in his bitter humour and self-loathing had used his own presence as a punishment and had made the Haddock walk with him! Imagine the company of Damocles de Warrenne being anything but an ennobling condescension! Fancy Dam's society a horrible injury and disgrace! To a thing like Haddon Berners!

"Well, I simply haunted Folkestone after that, and developed a love for Amelia Harringport and her brothers that surprised them—hypocrite that I am! (but I was punished when they talked slightingly of Dam and she sneered at the man whom she had shamelessly pursued when all was well with him. She 'admires' Haddon now.)

"At last I met him on one of my week-end visits—on a Sunday evening it was—and I simply flew at him in the sight of all respectable, prayer-book-displaying, before-Church-parading, well-behaved Folkestone, and kissed him nearly to death.... And can you believe a woman could be such a *fool*, Ormonde—while carefully noting the '2 Q.G.' on his shoulder-straps, I never thought to find out his *alias*—for of course he hides his identity, thinking as he does, poor darling boy, that he has brought eternal disgrace on an honoured name—a name that appears twice on the rolls of the V.C. records.

"Ormonde, were it not that it would *increase* his misery and agony of mind I would run away from Monksmead, take a room near the Queen's Greys barracks, and haunt the main gates until I saw him again. He should then tell me how to communicate with him, or I would hang about there till he did. I'd marry him 'off the strength' and live (till I am 'of age') by needlework if he would have me. But, of course, he'd *never* understand that I'd be happier, and a better woman, in a Shorncliffe lodging, as a soldier's wife, than ever I shall be here in this dreary Monksmead—until he is restored and re-habilitated (is that the word? I mean—comes into his own as a brave and noble gentleman who never did a mean or cowardly action in his life).

"And he is *so* thin and unhappy looking, Ormonde, and his poor hands are in such a state and his beautiful hair is all hacked about and done like a soldier's, all short except for a long piece brushed down his forehead and round to his cap—oh, dreadful ... and he has a scar on his face! No wonder Amelia never recognized him. Oh, *do* help me, Ormonde. I *must* find out how to address him. I dare not let them know there is a *D. de Warrenne* in the regiment—and he'd never get it either—he's probably Smith or Jones or Robinson now. If some horrid Sergeant called out 'Trooper D. de Warrenne,' when distributing letters, Dam would never answer to the name he thinks he has eternally disgraced, and disgrace it further by dragging it in the mire of the ranks. How *can* people be such snobs? Isn't a good private a better man than a bad officer? Why should there be any 'taint' about serving your country in any capacity?

"How *can* I find him, Ormonde, unless you help me? I could pay a servant to hang about the barracks until he recognized Dam—but that would be horrible for the poor boy. He'd deny it and say the man was mad, I expect—and it would be most unpleasant and unfair to Dam to set some one to find out from his comrades what he calls himself. If he chooses to hide from what he thinks is the chance of further disgracing his people, and suffers what he does in order to remain hidden, shall *I* be the one to do anything to show him up and cause him worse suffering—expose him to a servant?

"How *can* I get him a letter that shall not have his name on it? If I wrote to his Colonel or the Adjutant and enclosed a letter with just 'Dam' on it they'd not know for whom it was meant—and I dare not tell them his real name.

"Could you get a letter to him, Ormonde, without letting him know that you know he is a private soldier, and without letting a soul know his real name?

"I do apologize for the length of this interminable letter, but if you only knew the *relief* it is to me to be doing something that may help him, and to be talking, or rather writing about him, you would forgive me.

"His name must not be mentioned here. Think of it!

"Oh, if it only would not make him *more* unhappy, I would go to him this minute, and refuse ever to leave him again.

"Does that sound unmaidenly, Ormonde? I don't care whether it does or not, nor whether it *is* or not. I love him, and he loves me. I am his *friend*. Could I stay here in luxury if it would make him happier to marry me? Am I a terribly abandoned female? I told Auntie Yvette just what I had done, and though it simply saved her life to know he had not committed suicide (I believe she *worshipped* father)—she seemed mortally shocked at me for behaving so. I am not a bit ashamed though. Dam is more important than good form, and I had to show him in the strongest possible way that he was dearer to me than ever. If it *was* 'behaving like a servant-girl'—all honour to servant-girls, I think ... considering the circumstances. You should have seen his face before he caught sight of me. Yes—*and* after, too. Though really I think he suffered more from my kissing him—in uniform, in the street—than if I had cut him. It would be only for the minute though ... it *must* comfort him *now*, and always, to think that I love

126

him so (since he loves *me*—and always has done). But what I must know before I can sleep peacefully again is the name by which he goes in the '2 Q.G's.,' so that I can write and comfort him regularly, send him things, and make him buy himself out when he sees he has been foolish and wicked in supposing that he has publicly disgraced himself and his name and us. And I'm going to make Grandfather's life a misery, and go about skinny and ragged and weeping, and say: '*This* is how you treat the daughter of your dead friend, you wicked, cruel, unjust old man,' until he relents and sends for Dam and gets him into the Army properly.... But I am afraid Dam will think it his silly duty to flee from me and all my works, and hide himself where the names of de Warrenne and Stukeley are unknown and cannot be disgraced.

"I rely on you, Ormonde,

"Your ashamed grateful friend,

"LUCILLE GAVESTONE."

Second Lieutenant Delorme rang the bell.

"Bradshaw," he said, as his soldier-servant appeared. "And get me a telegraph form."

"Yussir," said Private Billings, and marched to the Mess ante-room purposefully, with hope in his heart that Mr. Delorme 'ad nothink less than a 'alf dollar for the telegram and would forgit to arx for the chainge, as was his occasional praiseworthy procedure.

Mr. Delorme, alas, proved to have a mean and vulgar shilling, the which he handed to Private Billings with a form containing the message:—

"Can do. So cheer up. Writing his adjutant, pal of mine. Coming over Saturday if get leave. Going Shorncliffe if necessary. Leave due. Dam all right. Will blow over. Thanks for letting me help."

"'Fraid they don' give no tick at the Telegraft Orfis, Sir," observed Private Billings, who, as quondam "trained observer" of his troop, had noted the length of the telegram and the shortness of the allowance therefor.

"What the deuce...?"

"This is more like a 'alf-dollar job, Sir," he groaned, waving the paper, "wot wiv' the haddress an' all."

"Oh—er—yes, bit thick for a bob, perhaps; here's half a sov...."

"*That's* more like ''*Eres to yer*,' Mr. D——" remarked the good man—outside the door. "And don't yer werry about trifles o' chainge. Be a gent!"

* * * * *

Lucille read and re-read the telegram in many ways.

"Can do so. Cheer up. Writing his adjutant. Pal of mine coming over Saturday. If get leave going Shorncliffe if necessary leave due Dam. All right will blow over thanks." No, *that* wouldn't do.

(What a pity people *would* not remember when writing telegrams that the stops and capitals they put are ignored by the operators.)

At last, the wish being father to the thought, she decided it to be "Can do" (she knew that to be a navy expression). "So cheer up. Writing. His adjutant a pal of mine. Coming over Saturday if I get leave. Going Shorncliffe if necessary. Leave due. Dam all right. Will blow over. Thanks for letting me help." Which was not far wrong.

Dear old Ormonde! She knew he would not fail her—although he had been terribly cut up by her rejection of his suit and by his belief that Dam had let him haunt her in the knowledge that she was his own private property, secured to him.

* * * * *

Having dispatched his telegram and interviewed his Adjutant, Captain, and Colonel, Mr. Delorme sat him down and wrote to Lieutenant the Honourable Reginald Montague Despencer, Adjutant of the Queen's Greys:—

"MY DEAR MONTY,

"At the Rag. the other day, respectfully dining with my respected parent, I encountered, respectfully dining with his respected parent, your embryo Strawberry Leaf, old 'Punch Peerson'. (Do you remember his standing on his head on the engine at Blackwater Station when he was too 'merry' to be able to stand steady on his feet?) I learnt that he is still with you and I want him to do something for me. He'll be serious about it if *you* speak to him about it—and I am writing

128

to him direct. I'm going to send you a letter (under my cover), and on it will be one word 'Dam' (on the envelope, of course). I want you to give this to Punch and order him to show it privately to the *gentlemenrankers* of the corps till one says he recognizes the force of the word (pretty forceful, too, what!) and the writing. To this chap he is to give it. Be good to your poor 'rankers,' Monty, I know one damned hard case among them. No fault of *his*, poor chap. I could say a lot—-surprise you—but I mustn't. It's awfully good of you, old chap. I know you'll see it through. It concerns as fine a gentleman as ever stepped and *the* finest woman!

"Ever thine,

"O. DELORME."

"Look here, my lambs—or rather, Black Sheep," quoth Trooper Punch Peerson one tea-time to Troopers Bear, Little, Goate, Nemo, Burke, Jones, and Matthewson, "I suppose none of you answers to the name of '*Dam*'?"

No man answered, and Trooper Peerson looked at the face of no man, nor any one at any other.

"No. I thought not. Well, I have a letter addressed in that objurgatory term, and I am going to place it beneath my pillow before I go out to-night. If it is there when I come in I'll destroy it unopened. 'Nuff said,' as the lady remarked when she put the mop in her husband's mouth. Origin of the phrase 'don't chew the mop,' I should think," and he babbled on, having let his unfortunate friends know that for one of them he had a letter which might be received by the addressed without the least loss of his anonymity.

Dam's heart beat hard and seemed to swell to bursting. He felt suffocated.

"Quaint superscription," he managed to observe. "How did you come by it?" and then wished he had not spoken.... Who but the recipient could be interested in its method of delivery? If anyone suspected him of being "Dam" would they not at once connect him with the notorious Damocles de Warrenne, ex-Sandhurst cadet, proclaimed coward and wretched neurotic decadent before the pained, disgusted eyes of his county, kicked out by his guardian ... a disgrace to two honoured names. ... "The Adjer handed it over. Thought *I* was the biggest Damn here, I suppose," Trooper Peerson replied without looking up from his plate. "Practical silly joke I should think. No one here with such a l_oath_some, name as *Dam*, of course," but Trooper Punch Peerson had his philosophic "doots". He, like others of that set, had heard of a big chap who was a marvel at Sandhurst with the gloves, sword, horse, and other things, and who had suddenly and marvellously disappeared into thin air

129

leaving no trace behind him, after some public scandal or other.... But that was no concern of Trooper Punch Peerson, gentleman....

With a wary eye on Peerson, Dam lay on his bed, affecting to read a stale and dirty news-sheet. He saw him slip something beneath his pillow and swagger out of the barrack-room. Anon no member of the little band of gentleman-rankers was left. Later, the room was empty, save for a heavily snoring drunkard and a busy polisher who, at the shelf-table at the far end of the room, laboured on his jack-boots, hissing the while, like a groom with a dandy-brush.

Going to Peerson's bed, Dam snatched the letter, returned to his own, and flung himself down again—his heart pumping as though he had just finished a mile race. *Lucille had got a letter to him somehow.* Lucille was not going to drop him yet—in spite of having seen him a red-handed, crop-haired, "quiff"-wearing, coarse-looking soldier.... Was there another woman in the world like Lucille? Would any other girl have so risen superior to her breeding, and the teachings of Miss Smellie, as to do what she thought right, regardless of public scandal...? But he must not give her the opportunity of being seen talking to a soldier again—much less kissing one. Not that she would want to kiss him again like that. That was the kiss of welcome, of encouragement, of proof that she was unchanged to him—her first sight of him after the *debacle*. It was the unchecked impulse of a noble heart—and the action showed that Miss Smellie had been unable to do it much harm with her miserable artificialities and stiflings of all that is natural and human and right.... Should he read the letter at once or treasure it up and keep it as a treat in store? He would hold it in his hand unopened and imagine its contents. He would spin out the glorious pleasure of possession of an unopened letter from Lucille. He could, of course, read it hundreds of times—but he would then soon know it by heart, and although its charm and value would be no less, it would merge with his other memories and become a memory itself. He did not want it to become a memory too soon.

The longer it remained an anticipation, the more distant the day when it became a memory....

With a groan of "Oh, my brain's softening and I'm becoming a sentimentalist," he opened the letter and read Lucille's loving, cheering—yet agonizing, maddening—-words:—

"MY OWN DARLING DAM,

"If this letter reaches you safely you are to sit down at once and write to me to tell me how to address you by post in the ordinary way. If you don't I shall come and haunt the entrance to the Lines and waylay you. People will think I am a poor soul whom you have married and deserted, or whom you won't marry. *I'll* show up your wicked cruelty to a poor girl! How would you like your comrades to say 'Look out,

Bill, your pore wife's 'anging about the gates' and to have to lie low—
and send out scouts to see if the coast was clear later on? Don't you
go playing fast and loose with *me*, master Dam, winning my young
affections, making love to me, kissing me—and then refusing to marry
me after it all! I don't want to be too hard on you (and I am reasonable
enough to admit that one-and-two a day puts things on a smaller scale
than I have been accustomed to in the home of my fathers—or rather
uncles, or perhaps uncles-in-law), and like the kind Tailor whom the
Haddock advertises (and like the unkind Judge before whom he'll
some day come for something) I will 'give you time'. But it's only a
respite, Mr. de Warrenne. You are not going to trifle with my young
feelings and escape altogether. I have my eye on you—and if I respect
your one-and-twopence a day *now*, it is on the clear understanding that
you share my Little All on the day I come of age. I will trust you once
more, although you *have* treated me so—bolting and hiding from your
confiding fiancee.

"So write and tell me what you call yourself, so that I can write to you
regularly and satisfy myself that you are not escaping me again. How
could you treat a poor trusting female so—and then when she had
found you again, and was showing her delight and begging to be
married and settled in life—to rush away from her, leaving her and her
modest matrimonial proposals scorned and rejected! For shame, Sir!
I've a good mind to come and complain to your Colonel and ask him
to make you keep your solemn promises and marry me....

"Now look here, darling, nonsense aside—I solemnly swear that if you
don't buy yourself out of the army on the day I come of age (or before,
if you will, and can) I will really come and make you marry me and I
will live with you as a soldier's wife. If you persist in your wrong-
headed notion of being a 'disgrace' (*you!*) then we'll just adopt the
army as a career, and we'll go through all the phases till you get a
Commission. I hope you won't take this course—but if you do, you'll
be a second Hector Macdonald and retire as Lieutenant-General Sir
Damocles de Warrenne (K.C.B., K.C.M.G., K.C.S.I., D.S.O., and, of
course, V.C.), having confessed to an *alias*. It will be a long time
before we should be in really congenial society, that way, darling, but
I'm sure I should enjoy every hour of it with you, so long as I felt I
was a comfort and happiness to you. And when you got your
Commission I should not be a social drag upon you as sometimes
happens. Nor before it should I be a nuisance and hindrance to you
and make you wish you were 'shut of the curse of a soldier'. I could

'rough it' as well as you and, besides, there would *be* no 'roughing it' where you were, for me. It is *here* that I am 'roughing it,' sitting impotent and wondering what is happening to you, and whether that terrible illness ever seizes you, and whether you are properly looked after when it does.

"Now, just realize, dearest Dam—I said I would wait twenty years for you, if necessary. I would and I will, but don't make me do it, darling. Realize how happy I should be if I could only come and sew and cook and scrub and work for you. Can you understand that life is only measurable in terms of happiness and that *my* happiness can only be where *you*, are? If you weren't liable to these seizures I could bear to wait, but as it is, I can't. I beg and beseech you not to make me wait till I am of age, Dam. There's no telling what may happen to you and I just can't bear it. *I'm coming*, if I don't hear from you, and I can easily do something to compel you to marry me, if I come. You are *not* going to bear this alone, darling, so don't imagine it. We're not going to keep separate shops after all these years, just because you're ill with a trouble of some kind that fools can't understand.

"Now write to me at once and put me in a position to write to you in the ordinary way—or look out for me! I'm all ready to run away, all sorts of useful things packed—ready to come and be a soldier's girl.

"You know that I *do* what I think I'll do—you spoke of my 'steel-straight directness and sweet brave will' in the poem you were making about me, you poor funny old boy, when you vanished, and which I found in your room when I went there to cry, (Oh, *how* I cried when I found your odds and ends of verse about me there—I really did think my heart was 'broken' in actual fact.) Don't make me suffer any more, darling. I'm sure your Colonel will be sweet about it and give us a nice little house all to ourselves, now he has seen what a splendid soldier you are. If you stick to your folly about 'disgrace' I need not tell him our names and Grumper couldn't take me away from you, even if he ever found out where we were.

"I could go on writing all night, darling, but I'll only just say again *I am going to marry you and take care of you, Dam, in the army or out of it.*

"Your fiancee and friend,

"LUCILLE GAVESTONE."

132

Dam groaned aloud.

"Four o' rum 'ot, is wot *you* want, mate, for that," said the industrious self-improver at the shelf-table. "Got a chill on yer stummick on sentry-go in the fog an' rine las' night.... I'd give a 'ogs'ead to see the bloke who wrote in the bloomin' Reggilashuns *'nor must bloomin' sentries stand in their blasted sentry-boxes in good or even in moderate-weather'* a doin' of it 'isself in 'is bloomin' 'moderate weather' with water a runnin' down 'is back, an' 'is feet froze into a puddle, an' the fog a chokin' of 'im, an' 'is blighted carbine feelin' like a yard o' bad ice—an' then find the bloomin' winder above 'is bed been opened by some kind bloke an' 'is bed a blasted swamp... Yus—you 'ave four o' rum 'ot and you'll feel like the bloomin' 'Ouse o' Lords. Then 'ave a Livin'stone Rouser." "Oh, shut up," said Dam, cursing the Bathos of Things and returning to the beginning of Lucille's letter.

* * * * *

In his somewhat incoherent reply, Dam assured Lucille that he was in the rudest health and spirits, and the particular pet of his Colonel who inquired after his health almost daily with tender solicitude; that he had exaggerated his feeling on That Evening when he had kissed Lucille as a lover, and begged forgiveness; that marriage would seriously hamper a most promising military career; that he had had no recurrence of the "fit" (a mere touch of sun); that it would be unkind and unfair of Lucille to bring scandal and disgrace upon a rising young soldier by hanging about the Lines and making inquiries about him with a view to forcing him into marriage, making him keep to a bargain made in a rash, unguarded moment of sentimentality; that, in any case, soldiers could not marry until they had a certain income and status, and, if they did so, it was no marriage and they were sent to jail; that his worst enemy would not do anything to drag him out once again into the light of publicity, and disgrace his family further, now that he had effectually disappeared and was being forgotten; and that he announced that he was known as Trooper Matthewson (E Troop, The Queen's Greys, Cavalry Lines, Shorncliffe) to prevent Lucille from keeping her most unladylike promise of persecuting him.

Lucille's next letter was shorter than the first.

"MY DARLING DAM,

"Don't be such a *priceless* Ass. Come off it.

"Your own

"LUCILLE.

"P.S.—Write to me properly at once—or expect me on Monday."

He obeyed, poured out his whole heart in love and thanks and blessings, and persuaded her that the one thing that could increase his misery would be her presence, and swore that he would strain every nerve to appear before her at the earliest possible moment a free man with redeemed name—provided he could persuade himself he was not *a congenital lunatic, an epileptic, a decadent—could cure himself of his mental disease....*

CHAPTER XI.

MORE MYRMIDONS.

The truly busy man cannot be actively and consciously unhappy. The truly miserable and despondent person is never continuously and actively employed. Fits of deep depression there may be for the worker when work is impossible, but, unless there be mental and physical illness, sleep is the other anæsthetic, refuge—and reward.

The Wise thank God for Work and for Sleep—and pay large premia of the former as Insurance in the latter.

To Damocles de Warrenne—to whom the name "Trooper Matthewson" now seemed the only one he had ever had—the craved necessity of life and sanity was *work*, occupation, mental and physical labour. He would have blessed the man who sentenced him to commence the digging of a trench ten miles long and a yard deep for morning and evening labour, and to take over all the accounts of each squadron, for employment in the heat of the day. There was no man in the regiment so indefatigable, so energetic, so persevering, so insatiable of "fatigues," so willing and anxious to do other people's duty as well as his own, so restless, so untiring as Trooper Matthewson of E Troop. For Damocles de Warrenne was in the Land of the Serpent and lived in fear. He lived in fear and feared to live; he thought of Fear and feared to think. He turned to work as, but for the memory of Lucille, he would have turned to drink: he laboured to earn deep dreamless sleep and he dreaded sleep. Awake, he could drug himself with work; asleep, he was the prey—the bound, gagged helpless, abject prey—of the Snake. The greediest glutton for work in the best working regiment in the world was Trooper Matthewson—but for him was no promotion. He was, alas, "unreliable"—apt to be "drunk and disorderly," drunk to the point of "seeing snakes" and becoming a weeping, screaming lunatic—a disgusting spectacle. And, when brought up for sentence, would solemnly assure the Colonel that he was *a total abstainer*, and stick to it when "told-off" for adding impudent lying to shameful indulgence and sickening behaviour. No promotion for that type of waster while Colonel the Earl of A—— commanded the Queen's Greys, nor while Captain Daunt commanded the squadron the trooper occasionally disgraced.

But he had his points, mark you, and it was a thousand pities that so fine a soldier was undeniably subject to attacks of *delirium tremens* and unmistakeably a secret drinker who might at any time have a violent outburst, finishing in screams, sobs, and tears. A *most* remarkable case! Who ever heard of a magnificent athlete—regimental champion boxer and swordsman, admittedly as fine and bold a horseman and horse-master as the Rough-Riding Sergeant-Major or the Riding-Master himself—being a sufficiently industrious secret-drinker to get "goes" of "d.t.," to drink till he behaved like some God-and-man-forsaken wretch that lives on cheap gin in a chronic state of alcoholism. He had his points, and if the Brigadier had ever happened to say to the Colonel: "Send me your smartest, most intelligent, and keenest man to gallop for me at the manoeuvres," or the Inspector of Army Gymnasia had asked for the regiment's finest specimen, or if one representative private soldier had to be sent somewhere to uphold the credit and honour of the Queen's Greys, undoubtedly Trooper Matthewson would have been chosen.

What a splendid squadron-sergeant major, regimental sergeant-major, yea, what a fine officer he would have made, had he been reliable. But there, you can't have an officer, nor a non-com., either, who lies shrieking and blubbering on the floor *coram publico*, and screams to God and man to save him from the snakes that exist only in his own drink-deranged mind. For of course it can only be Drink that produces "Snakes"! Yes, it is only through the ghastly alcohol-tinted glasses that you can "see snakes"—any fool knows *that*.

And the fools of the Queen's Greys knew it, and hoped to God that Matthewson would "keep off it" till after the Divisional Boxing Tournament and Assault-at-Arms, for, if he did, the Queen's Greys would certainly have the Best Man-at-Arms in the Division and have a mighty good shot at having the Heavy-Weight All-India Champion, since Matthewson had challenged the Holder and held an absolutely unbroken record of victories in the various regimental and inter-regimental boxing tournaments in which he had taken part since joining the regiment. And he had been "up against some useful lads" as Captain Chevalier, the president and Maecenas of the Queen's Greys' boxing-club, expressed it. Yes, Matthewson had his points and the man who brought the Regiment the kudos of having best Man-at-Arms and Heavy-Weight Champion of India would be forgiven a lot.

And Damocles de Warrenne blessed the Divisional Boxing Tournament, Assault-at-Arms, and, particularly, the All-India Heavy-Weight Championship.

Occupation, labour, anodyne.... Work and deep Sleep. Fighting to keep the Snake at bay. No, fighting to get away from it—there was no keeping it at bay—nothing but shrieking collapse when It came....

From parade ground to gymnasium, from gymnasium to swimming-bath, from swimming-bath to running-track, from running-track to boxing-ring, from boxing-ring to gymnasium again. Work, occupation, forgetfulness. Forget the Snake for a little while—even though it is surely lurking near—waiting, waiting, waiting; nay, even beneath his very foot and *moving*....

Well, a man can struggle with himself until the Thing actually appears in the concrete, and he goes mad—but Night! Oh, God grant deep sleep at night—or wide wakefulness *and a light*. Neither Nightmare nor wakefulness *in the dark*, oh, Merciful God.

Yes, things were getting worse. *He was going mad. MAD.* Desert—and get out of India somehow?

136

Never! No gentleman "deserts" anything or anybody.

Suicide—and face God unafraid and unashamed?

Never! The worst and meanest form of "deserting".

No. Stick it. And live to work—work to live. And strive and strive and strive to obliterate the image of Lucille—that sorrow's crown of sorrow.

And so Trooper Matthewson's course of training was a severe one and he appeared to fear rest and relaxation as some people fear work and employment.

His favourite occupation was to get the ten best boxers of the regiment to jointly engage in a ten-round contest with him, one round each. He would frequently finish fresher than the tenth man. Coming of notedly powerful stock on both sides, and having been physically *educated* from babyhood, Dam, with clean living and constant training, was a very uncommon specimen. There may have been one or two other men in the regiment as well developed, or nearly so; but when poise, rapidity, and skill were taken into account there was no one near him. Captain Chevalier said he was infinitely the quickest heavy-weight boxer he had ever seen—and Captain Chevalier was a pillar of the National Sporting Club and always knew the current professionals personally when he was in England. In fact, with the enormous strength of the best heavy-weight, Dam combined the lightning rapidity and mobility of the best feather-weight.

His own doubt as to the result of his contest with the heavy-weight Champion of India arose from the fact that the latter was a person of much lower nervous development, a creature far less sensitive to shock, a denser and more elementary organism altogether, and possessed of a far thicker skull, shorter jaw, and thicker neck. Dam summed him up thus with no sense of contemptuous superiority, but with a plain recognition of the facts that the Champion was a fighting machine, a dull, foreheadless, brutal gladiator who owed his championship very largely to the fact that he was barely sensible to pain, and impervious to padded blows. It was said that he had never been knocked out in all his boxing-career, that the kick of a horse on his chin would not knock him out, that his head was solid bone, and that the shortness of his jaw and thickness of his neck absolutely prevented sufficient leverage between the point of the jaw and the spinal cord for the administration of the shock to the *medulla oblongata* that causes the necessary ten-seconds' unconsciousness of the "knock-out".

He was known as the Gorilla by reason of his long arms, incredible strength, beauty, and pleasing habits, and he bore the reputation of a merciless and unchivalrous opponent and one who needed the strictest and most experienced refereeing. It would be a real terrific fight, and that was the main thing to Dam, though he would do his very utmost to win, for the credit of the Queen's Greys, and would leave no stone unturned to that end. He regretted that he could not get leave and go to Pultanpur to see the Champion box, and learn something of his style and methods when easily defending his title in the Pultanpur tournament. And when the Tournament and Assault-at-Arms were over he must find something else to occupy him by day and tire him before night. Meanwhile life was bearable, with the fight to come—except for sentry-go work. That was awful, unspeakable, and each time was worse than the last. Sitting up all night in the guard-room under the big lamp, and perhaps with some other wakeful wretch to talk to, was nothing. That was well enough—but to be on a lonely post on a dark night ... well—he couldn't do it much longer.

Darkness and the Snake that was always coming and never came! To prowl round and round some magazine, store, or boundary-stone with his carbine at the "support," or to tramp up and down by the horse-lines, armed only with his cutting-whip; to stand in a sentry-box while the rain fell in sheets and there was no telling what the next flash of lightning might reveal—that was what would send him to a lunatic's padded cell.

To see the Snake by day would give him a cruel, terrible fit—but to be aware of it in the dark would be final—and fatal to his reason (which was none too firmly enthroned). No, he had the dreadful feeling that his reason was none too solidly based and fixed. He had horrible experiences, apart from the snake-nightmares, nowadays. One night when he awoke and lay staring up at his mosquito-curtain in the blessed light of the big room-lamp (always provided in India on account of rifle thieves) he had suddenly felt an overwhelming surge of fear. He sat up. God!—he was in a marble box! These white walls and roof were not mosquito-netting, they were solid marble! He was in a tomb. He was buried alive. The air was growing foul. His screams would be absolutely inaudible. He screamed, and struck wildly at the cold cruel marble, and found it was soft, yielding netting after all. But it was a worse horror to find that he had thought it marble than if he had found it to be marble. He sprang from his cot.

"I am going mad," he cried.

"Goin'?... *Gorn*, more like," observed the disrobing room-corporal. "Why donchew keep orf the booze, Maffewson? You silly gapin' goat. Git inter bed and shut yer 'ead—or I'll get yew a night in clink, me lad—and wiv'out a light, see?"

Corporal Prag knew his victim's little weakness and grinned maliciously as Dam sprang into bed without a word.

The Stone Jug without a gleam of light! Could a man choke himself with his own fingers if the worst came to the worst? The Digger and Stygian darkness—now—- *when he was going mad*! Men could not be so cruel.... But they'd say he was drunk. He would lie still and cling with all his strength and heart and soul to sanity. He would think of That Evening with Lucille—and of her kisses. He would recite the Odes of Horace, the Aeneid, the Odyssey as far as he could remember them, and then fall back on Shakespeare and other English poets. Probably he knew a lot more Greek and Latin poetry (little as it was) than he did of English....

138

Corporal Prag improved the occasion as he unlaced his boots. "Bloomin' biby! Afraid o' the dark! See wot boozin' brings yer to. Look at yer! An' look at *me*. Non-c'misshn'd orficer in free an' a 'arf years from j'inin'. Never tasted alc'ol in me life, an' if any man offud me a glarse, d'ye know what I'd *dew*?"

"No, Corporal, I'd like to hear," replied Dam. (Must keep the animal talking as long as possible for the sake of human company. He'd go mad at once, perhaps, when the Corporal went to bed.)

"I'd frow it strite in 'is faice, I would," announced the virtuous youth. A big boot flopped heavily on the floor.

"I daresay you come of good old teetotal stock," observed Dam, to make conversation. Perhaps the fellow would pause in his assault upon the other boot and reply—so lengthening out the precious minutes of diversion. Every minute was a minute nearer dawn....

"*Do* yer? Well, you're bloomin' well wrong, Maffewson, me lad. My farver 'ad a bout every Saturday arternoon and kep' it up all day a Sund'y, 'e did—an' in the werry las' bout 'e ever 'ad 'e bashed 'is ole woman's 'ead in wiv' a bottle."

"And was hanged?" inquired Dam politely and innocently, but most tactlessly.

"Mind yer own b—— business," roared Corporal Prag. "Other people's farvers wasn't gallows-birds if yourn was. 'Ow'd you look if I come and punched you on the nose, eh? Wot 'ud you do if I come an' set abaht yer, eh?"

"Break your neck," replied Dam tersely.

"Ho, yus. *And* wot 'ud yew say when I calls the guard and they frows you into clink? Without no light, Trooper Maffewson!"

Dam shuddered.

Corporal Prag yet further improved the occasion, earning Dam's heartfelt blessing.

"Don't you fergit it, Trooper Maffewson. I'm yore sooperier orficer. You *may* be better'n me in the Ring, praps, or with the sword (Dam could have killed him in five minutes, with or without weapons), but if I 'olds up my little finger *you* comes to 'eel—or other'ow you goes ter clink. 'Ung indeed! You look after yer own farver an' don' pass remarks on yer betters. Why! You boozin' waster, I shall be Regimental Sargen' Majer when you're a bloomin' discharged private wiv an 'undred '*drunks*' in red on yer Defaulter's Sheet. Regimental Sarjen' Majer! I shall be an Orficer more like, and walk acrost the crossin' wot *you're* asweepin', to me Club in bloomin' well Pickerdilly! Yus. This is the days o' _? Demockerycy_, me lad. 'Good Lloyd George's golden days' as they sing—and steady fellers like me is goin' to ave C'missh'ns—an' don' you fergit it! Farver 'ung indeed!"

"I'm awf'ly sorry, Corporal, really," apologized Dam. "I didn't think...."

"No, me lad," returned the unmollified superior, as he stooped to the other boot, "if you was to think more an' booze less you'd do better.... 'Ow an' where you gets 'old of it, beats me. I've seed you in delirium trimmings but I ain't never seed you drinkin' nor yet smelt it on yer. You're a cunnin' 'ound in yer way. One o' them beastly secret-drinkin' swine wots never suspected till they falls down 'owlin' blue 'orrors an' seem' pink toadses. Leastways it's snakes *you* sees. See 'em oncte too orfen, you will.... See 'em on p'rade one day in front o' the Colonel. Fall orf yer long-face an get trampled—an' serve yer glad.... An' now shut yer silly 'ed an' don't chew the mop so much. Let me get some sleep. *I* 'as respontsibillaties *I* do...."

A crossing outside a Club! More likely a padded cell in a troopship and hospital until an asylum claimed him.

In the finals, "Sword versus Sword Dismounted," Dam had a foeman worthy of his steel.

A glorious chilly morning, sunrise on a wide high open *maidan*, rows of tents for the spectators at the great evening final, and crowds of officers and men in uniform or gymnasium kit. On a group of chairs sat the Divisional General, his Colonel on the Staff, and Aide-de-Camp; the Brigadier-General, his Brigade-Major, and a few ladies, wives of regimental colonels, officers, and leading Civilians.

Semi-finals of Tent-pegging, Sword v. Sword Mounted, Bayonet-fighting, Tug-of-War, Fencing, and other officers' and men's events had been, or were being, contested.

The finals of the British Troops' Sword *v.* Sword Dismounted, was being reserved for the last, as of supreme interest to the experts present, but not sufficiently spectacular to be kept for the evening final "show," when the whole of Society would assemble to be thrilled by the final Jumping, Driving, Tent-pegging, Sword *v.* Sword Mounted, Bayonet-fighting, Sword *v.* Lance, Tug-of-War, and other events for British and Indian officers and men of all arms.

It was rumoured that there was a Sergeant of Hussars who would give Trooper Matthewson a warm time with the sabre. As the crowd of competitors and spectators gathered round the sabres-ring, and chairs were carried up for the Generals, ladies, and staff, to witness the last and most exciting contest of the morning's meeting, a Corporal-official of the Assault-at-Arms Executive Committee called aloud, "Sergeant O'Malley, 14th Hussars, get ready," and another fastened a red band to the Sergeant's arm as he stepped forward, clad in leather jacket and leg-guards and carrying the heavy iron-and-leather head-guard necessary in sabre combats, and the blunt-edged, blunt-pointed sabre.

Dam approached him.

"Don't let my point rest on your hilt, Sergeant," he said.

"What's the game?" inquired the surprised and suspicious Sergeant.

"My little trick. I thrust rather than cut, you know," said Dam.

"I'll watch it, me lad," returned Sergeant O'Malley, wondering whether Dam were fool or knave.

"Trooper Matthewson, get ready," called the Corporal, and Dam stepped into the ring, saluted, and faced the Sergeant.

A brief direction and caution, the usual preliminary, and the word—

"On guard—*Play*" and Dam was parrying a series of the quickest cuts he had ever met. The Sergeant's sword flickered like the tongue of a—*Snake*. Yes—of a *Snake*! and even as Dam's hand dropped limp and nerveless, the Sergeant's sword fell with a dull heavy thud on his head-guard. The stroke would have split Dam's head right neatly, in actual fighting.

"Stop," shouted the referee. "Point to Red."

"On guard—*Play*"

But if the Sergeant's sword flickered like the tongue of a snake—why then Dam must be fighting the Snake. *Fighting the Snake* and in another second the referee again cried "Stop!" And added, "Don't fight savage, White, or I'll disqualify you".

"I'm awf'ly sorry," said Dam, "I thought I was fighting the Sn——"

"Hold your tongue, and don't argue," replied the referee sternly.

"On Guard—*Play*."

Ere the Sergeant could move his sword from its upward-inclined position Dam's blade dropped to its hilt, shot in over it, and as the Sergeant raised his forearm in guard, flashed beneath it and bent on his breast.

"Stop," cried the referee. "Point to White. Double"—two marks being then awarded for the thrust hit, and one for the cut.

"On guard—*Play*."

Absolutely the same thing happened again within the next half-second, and Dam had won the British Troops' Sword *v.* Sword Dismounted, in addition to being in for the finals in Tent-pegging, Sword *v.* Sword Mounted, Jumping (Individual and By Sections), Sword *v.* Lance, and Tug-of-War.

"Now jest keep orf it, Matthewson, and sweep the bloomin' board," urged Troop-Sergeant-Major Scoles as Dam removed his fencing-jacket, preparatory to returning to barracks. "You be Best Man-at-arms in the Division and win everythink that's open to British Troops Mounted, and git the 'Eavy-Weight Championship from the Gorilla—an' there'll be some talk about promotion for yer, me lad."

"Thank you, Sergeant," replied Dam. "I am a total abstainer."

"Yah! *Chuck* it," observed the Sergeant-Major.

Of no interest to Women nor modern civilized Men.

The long-anticipated hour had struck, the great moment had arrived, and (literally) thousands of British soldiers sat in a state of expectant thrill and excited interest, awaiting the appearance of the Gorilla (Corporal Dowdall of the 111th Battery, Royal Garrison Artillery—fourteen stone twelve) and Trooper Matthewson (Queen's Greys—fourteen stone) who were to fight for the Elliott Belt, the Motipur Cup, and the Heavy-Weight Championship of India.

The Boxing Tournament had lasted for a week and had been a huge success. Now came the *piece de resistance, the* fight of the Meeting, the event for which special trains had brought hundreds of civilians and soldiers from neighbouring and distant cantonments. Bombay herself sent a crowded train-load, and it was said that a, by no means small, contingent had come from Madras. Certainly more than one sporting patron of the Great Sport, the Noble Art, the Manly Game, had travelled from far Calcutta. So well-established was the fame of the great Gorilla, and so widely published the rumour that the Queen's Greys had a prodigy who'd lower his flag in ten rounds—or less.

A great square of the grassy plain above Motipur had been enclosed by a high canvas wall, and around a twenty-four foot raised "ring" (which was square) seating accommodation for four thousand spectators had been provided. The front rows consisted of arm-chairs, sofas, and drawing-room settees (from the wonderful stock of Mr. Dadabhoy Pochajee Furniturewallah of the Sudder Bazaar) for the officers and leading civilians of Motipur, and such other visitors as chose to purchase the highly priced reserved-seat tickets.

Not only was every seat in the vast enclosure occupied, but every square inch of standing-room, by the time the combatants entered the arena.

142

A few dark faces were to be seen (Native Officers of the pultans[23] and rissal[24] of the Motipur Brigade), and the idea occurred to not a few that it was a pity the proceedings could not be witnessed by every Indian in India. It would do them good in more ways than one.

Although a large number of the enormously preponderating military spectators were in the khaki kit so admirable for work (and so depressing, unswanksome and anti-enlistment for play, or rather for walking-out and leisure), the experienced eye could see that almost every corps in India furnished contingents to the gathering. Lancers, dragoons, hussars, artillery, riflemen, Highlanders, supply and transport, infantry of a score of regiments, and, rare sight away from the Ports, a small party of Man-o'-War's-men in white duck, blue collars, and straw hats (huge, solemn-faced men who jested with grimmest seriousness of mien and insulted each other outrageously). Officers in scarlet, in dark blue, in black and cherry colour, in fawn and cherry colour, in pale blue and silver, in almost every combination of colours, showed that the commissioned ranks of the British and Indian Services were well represented, horse, foot, guns, engineers, doctors, and veterinary surgeons—every rank and every branch. On two sides of the roped ring, with its padded posts, sat the judges, boxing Captains both, who had won distinction at Aldershot and in many a local tournament. On another side sat the referee, *ex*-Public-Schools Champion, Aldershot Light-Weight Champion, and, admittedly, the best boxer of his weight among the officers of the British Army. Beside him sat the time-keeper. Overhead a circle of large incandescent lamps made the scene as bright as day.

"Well, d'you take it?" asked Seaman Jones of Seaman Smith. "Better strike while the grog's 'ot. A double-prick o' baccy and a gallon o' four-'arf, evens, on the Griller. I ain't never 'eard o' the Griller till we come 'ere, and I never 'eard o' t'other bloke neether—but I 'olds by the Griller, cos of 'is name and I backs me fancy afore I sees 'em.—Loser to 'elp the winner with the gallon."

"Done, Bill," replied the challenged promptly, on hearing the last condition. (He could drink as fast as Bill if he lost, and he could borrer on the baccy till it was wore out.) "Got that bloomin' 'igh-falutin' lar-de-dar giddy baccy-pouch and yaller baccy you inwested in at Bombay?" he asked. "Yus, 'Enery," replied William, diving deeply for it.

"Then push it 'ere, an' likewise them bloomin' 'igh-falutin' lar-de-dar giddy fag-papers you fumble wiv'. Blimey! ain't a honest clay good enough for yer now? I knows wots the matter wiv *you*, Billy Jones! You've got a weather-heye on the Quarter Deck you 'ave. You fink you're agoin' to be a blighted perishin' orficer you do! Yus, you flat-footed matlot—not even a blasted tiffy you ain't, and you buys a blighted baccy-pouch and yaller baccy and fag-pipers, like a Snottie, an' reckons you's on the 'igh road to be a bloomin' Winnie Lloyd Gorgeous Orficer. 'And 'em 'ere—fore I'm sick. Lootenant,—Gunnery Jack,—Number One,—Commerdore!"

"Parding me, 'Enery Smiff," returned William Jones with quiet dignity. "In consequents o' wot you said, an' more in consequents o' yore clumsy fat fingers not been used to 'andlin' dellikit objex, and most in consequents o' yore been a most ontrustable thief, I will perceed to roll you a fag meself, me been 'ighly competent so fer to do. Not but wot a fag'll look most outer place in *your* silly great ugly faice."

The other sailor watched the speaker in cold contempt as he prepared a distinctly exiguous, ill-fed cigarette.

"Harthur Handrews," he said, turning to his other neighbour, "'Ave yew 'appened to see the Master Sail-maker or any of 'is mermydiuns 'ere-abahts, by any chawnst?"

"Nope. 'An don' want. Don' wan' see nothink to remind me o'

Ther blue, ther fresh, ther *hever* free,
Ther blarsted, beastly, boundin' sea.

Not even your distressin' face and dirty norticle apparile. Why do you arksk sich silly questchings?"

"Willyerm Jones is amakin' a needle for 'im."

"As 'ow?"

"Wiv a fag-paper an' a thread o' yaller baccy. 'E's makin' a bloomin' needle," and with a sudden grab he possessed himself of the pouch, papers, and finished product of Seaman Jones's labours and generosity.

Having pricked himself severely and painfully with the alleged cigarette, he howled with pain, cast it from him, proceeded to stick two papers together and to make an uncommonly stout, well-nourished, and bounteous cigarette.

"I 'fought I offered you to make yourself a cigarette, 'Enery," observed the astounded owner of the *materia nicotina.*

"I grabbed for to make myself a cigarette, Willyerm," was the pedantically correct restatement of Henry.

"Then why go for to try an' mannyfacter a bloomin' banana?" asked the indignant victim, whose further remarks were drowned in the roars of applause which greeted the appearance from the dressing-tents of the Champion and the Challenger.

Dam and Corporal Dowdall entered the ring from opposite corners, seated themselves in the chairs provided for them, and submitted themselves to the ministrations of their respective seconds.

144

Trooper Herbert Hawker violently chafed Dam's legs, Trooper Bear his arms and chest, while Trooper Goate struggled to force a pair of new boxing-gloves upon his hands, which were scientifically bandaged around knuckles, back, and wrist, against untimely dislocations and sprains.

Clean water was poured into the bowls which stood behind each chair, and fresh resin was sprinkled over the canvas-covered boards of the Ring.

Men whose favourite "carried their money" (and each carried a good deal) anxiously studied that favourite's opponent.

The Queen's Greys beheld a gorilla indeed, a vast, square, long-armed hairy monster, with the true pugilist face and head.

"Wot a werry ugly bloke," observed Seaman Arthur Andrews to Seaman Henry Smith. "'E reminds me o' Hadmiral Sir Percy 'Opkinton, so 'e do. P'raps 'e's a pore relation."

"Yus," agreed Seaman Smith. "A crost between our beloved 'Oppy an' ole Bill Jones 'ere. Bill was reported to 'ave 'ad a twin brother—but it was allus serposed Bill ate 'im when 'e wasn' lookin'."

The backers of Corporal Dowdall were encouraged at seeing a man who looked like a gentleman and bore none of the traditional marks of the prize-fighter. His head was not cropped to the point of bristly baldness, his nose was unbroken, his eyes well opened and unblackened, his ears unthickened, his body untattooed. He had the white skin, small trim moustache, high-bred features, small extremities, and general appearance and bearing of an officer.

Ho, G'rilla Dowdall would make short work of *that* tippy young toff. Why, look at him!

And indeed it made you shudder to think of that enormous ferocity, that dynamic truculence, doing its best to destroy you in a space twenty-four feet square.

Let the challenger wait till G'rilla put his fighting face on—fair terrifyin'.

Not an Artilleryman but felt sure that the garrison-gunner would successfully defend the title and "give the swankin' Queen's Greys something to keep them *choop*[25] for a bit. Gettin' above 'emselves they was, becos' this bloke of theirs had won Best Man-at-Arms and had the nerve to challenge G'rilla Dowdall, R.G.A."

Even the R.H.A. admitted the R.G.A. to terms of perfect equality on that great occasion.

But a few observant and experienced officers, gymnasium instructors, and ancient followers of the Noble Art were not so sure.

"Put steel-and-whalebone against granite and I back the former," said Major Decoulis to Colonel Hanking; "other things being equal of course—skill and ring-craft. And I hear that No. 2—the Queen's Greys' man—is unusually fast for a heavy-weight."

"I'd like to see him win," admitted the Colonel. "The man looks a gentleman. *Doesn't* the other look a Bill Sykes, by Jove!"

The Staff Sergeant Instructor of the Motipur Gymnasium stepped into the ring.

"Silence, please," he bawled. "Fifteen-round contest between Corporal Dowdall, 111th Battery, Royal Garrison Artillery, Heavy-Weight Champion of Hindia, fourteen twelve (Number 1—on my right 'and) and Trooper Matthewson, Queen's Greys, fourteen stun (Number 2—on my left 'and). Please keep silence durin' the rounds. The winner is Heavy-Weight Champion of Hindia, winner of the Motipur Cup and 'older of the Elliott Belt. All ready there?"

Both combatants were ready.

"Come here, both of you," said the referee.

As he arose to obey, Dam was irresistibly reminded of his fight with Bully Harberth and smiled.

"Nervous sort o' grin on the figger-'ead o' the smaller wessel, don't it," observed Seaman Smith.

"There wouldn't be no grin on *your* fat face at all," returned Seaman Jones. "It wouldn't be there. You'd be full-steam-ahead, bearings 'eated, and showin' no lights, for them tents—when you see wot you was up against."

The referee felt Dam's gloves to see that they contained no foreign bodies in the shape of plummets of lead or other illegal gratifications. (He had known a man fill the stuffing-compartments of his gloves with plaster of Paris, that by the third or fourth round he might be striking with a kind of stone cestus as the plaster moulded with sweat and water, and hardened to the shape of the fist.)

As he stepped back, Dam looked for the first time at his opponent, conned his bruiser face and Herculean body, and, with a gasp and shudder, was aware that a huge tattooed serpent reared its head in the centre of his vast chest while smaller ones encircled the mighty biceps of his arms. He clutched the rope and leant trembling against the post as the referee satisfied himself (with very great care in this case) of the innocence of the Gorilla's gloves.

146

"I know you of old, Dowdall," he said, "and I shall only caution you once mind. Second offence—and out you go."

Corporal Dowdall grinned sheepishly. He appeared to think that a delicate and gentlemanly compliment had been paid to his general downiness, flyness, and ring-craft,—the last of which, for Corporal Dowdall, included every form of foul that a weak referee would pass, an inexperienced one misunderstand, or a lazy one miss. Major O'Halloran, first-class bruiser himself, was in the habit of doing his refereeing inside the ring and within a foot or two of the principals, where he expected foul play.

As the Major cautioned the Gorilla, Dam passed his hand wearily across his face, swallowed once or twice and groaned aloud.

It was *not* fair. Why should the Snake be allowed to humiliate him before thousands of spectators? Why should It be brought here to shame him in the utmost publicity, to make him fail his comrades, disgrace his regiment, make the Queen's Greys a laughing-stock?

But—he had fought an emissary of the Snake before—and he had won. This villainous-looking pugilist was perhaps *the Snake Itself in human form*—and, see, he was free, he was in God's open air, no chains bound him, he was not gagged, this place was not a pit dug beneath the Pit itself! This was all tangible and real. He would have fair play and be able to defend himself. This was not a blue room with a mud floor. Nay, he would be able to attack—to fight, fight like a wounded pantheress for her cubs. This accursed Snake in Human Form would only be able to use puny fists. Mere trivial human fists and human strength. Everything would be on the human plane. It would be unable to wrap him in its awful coils and crush and crush the soul and life and manhood out of him, as it did at night before burrowing its way ten million miles below the floor of Hell with him, and immuring him in a molten incandescent tomb where he could not even scream or writhe.

"Get to your corners," said the referee, and Dam returned to his place with a cruel smile upon his compressed lips. By the Merciful Living God he had the Snake Itself delivered unto him in human form—to do with as he could. Oh, that It might last out the fifteen times of facing him in his wrath, his pent-up vengeful wrath at a ruined life, a dishonoured name and *a lost Lucille!*

When would they give the word for him to spring upon it and batter it lifeless to the ground?

"Don't grind yer silly teeth like that," whispered Hawker, his grim ugly face white with anxiety and suspense (for he loved Damocles de Warrenne as the faithfullest of hounds loves the best of masters). "You're awastin' henergy all the time."

"God! if they don't give the word in a minute I shall be unable to hold off It," replied Dam wildly.

"That's the sperrit, Cocky," approved Hawker, "but donchew fergit you gotter larst fifteen bloomin' rahnds. 'Taint no kindergarters. '*E*'ll stick it orlrite, an' you'll avter win on *points*——"

"Seconds out of the Ring," cried the time-keeper, staring at his watch.

"Don't get knocked out, dear boy," implored Trooper Bear. "Fight to win on points. You *can't* knock him out. I'm going to pray like hell through the rounds——"

"Time" barked the time-keeper, and, catching up the chair as Dam rose, Trooper Bear dropped down from the boards of the ring to the turf, where already crouched Hawker and Goate, looking like men about to be hanged.

The large assembly drew a deep breath as the combatants approached each other with extended right hands—Dam clad in a pair of blue silk shorts, silk socks and high, thin, rubber-soled boots, the Gorilla in an exiguous bathing-garment and a pair of gymnasium shoes.

Dam a picture of the Perfect Man, was the taller, and the Gorilla, a perfect Caliban, was the broader and had the longer reach. Their right hands touched in perfunctory shake, Dam drew back to allow the Snake to assume sparring attitude, and, as he saw the huge shoulders hunch, the great biceps rise, and the clenched gloves come to position, he assumed the American "crouch" attitude and sprang like a tiger upon the incarnation of the utter Damnation and Ruin that had cursed his life to living death.

The Gorilla was shocked and pained! The tippy pink-and-white blasted rookie was "all over him" and he was sent staggering with such a rain of smashing blows as he had never, never felt, nor seen others receive. The whole assembly of soldiers, saving the Garrison Artillerymen, raised a wild yell, regardless of the referee's ferocious expostulations (in dumb-show) and even the ranks of the Horse-Gunners could scarce forbear to cheer. The Queen's Greys howled like fiends and Hawker, unknown to himself, punched the boards before him with terrific violence. Never had anything like it been seen. Matthewson was a human whirlwind, and Dowdall had not had a chance to return a blow. More than half the tremendous punches, hooks and in-fighting jabs delivered by his opponent had got home, and he was "rattled". A fair hook to the chin might send him down and out at any moment.

Surely never had human being aimed such an unceasing, unending, rain of blows in the space of two minutes as had Trooper Matthewson. His arms had worked like the piston rods of an express engine—as fast and as untiringly. He had taken the Gorilla by surprise, had rushed him, and had never given him a fraction of time in which to attack. Beneath the rain of sledge-hammer blows the Gorilla had shrunk, guarding for dear life. Driven into a corner, he cowered down, crouched beneath his raised arms, and allowed his face to sink forward. Like a whirling piece of machinery Dam's arm flew round to administer the *coup-de-grace*, the upper cut, that would lay the Snake twitching and unconscious on the boards.

The Gorilla was expecting it.

As it came, his bullet head was jerked aside, and as the first swung harmlessly up, he arose like a flash, and, as he did so, his mighty right shot up, took Darn on the chin and laid him flat and senseless in the middle of the ring.

The Gorilla breathed heavily and made the most of the respite. He knew it must be about "Time," and that he had not won. If it wasn't "Time," and the cub arose he'd knock him to glory as he did so. Yes, the moment the most liberal-minded critic could say he was just about on his feet, he'd give him a finisher that he'd bear the mark of. The bloomin' young swine had nearly "had" him—him, the great G'rilla Dowdall, about to buy himself out with his prize-money, and take to pugilism as a profession.

"*One—two—three—four,*" counted the timekeeper amid the most deathly silence, and, as he added, "*five—six—Time,*" a shout arose that was heard for miles.

Trooper Matthewson was saved—if his seconds could pull him round in time.

At sound of the word "Time," the seconds leapt into the ring. Hawker and Bear rushed to the prostrate Dam, hauled him to his feet, and dragged him to the chair which Goate had placed ready. As he was dropped into it, a spongeful of icy water from Goate's big sponge brought Dam to consciousness.

"Breave for all y'r worf," grunted Hawker, as he mightily swung a big bath-towel in swift eddies, to drive refreshing air upon the heaving, panting body of his principal.

Bear and Goate applied massaging hands with skilled violence.

"By Jove, I thought you had him," panted Goate as he kneaded triceps and biceps. "And then I thought he had you. It's anybody's fight, Matty—but *don't* try and knock him out. You couldn't do it with an axe."

"No," agreed Bear. "You've got to keep on your feet and win on points."

"I've got to kill *the Snake*," hissed Dam, and his seconds glanced at each other anxiously.

He felt that nothing could keep him from victory. He was regaining his faith in a just Heaven, now that the Snake had been compelled to face him in the puny form of a wretched pugilist. Some one had said something about an axe. It would be but fair if he had an axe, seeing that hitherto the Snake had had him utterly defenceless while exercising its own immeasurable and supernatural powers, when torturing him to its heart's content for endless aeons. But—no—since it was here in human form and without weapons, *he* would use none, and would observe the strictest fairness in fight, just as he would to a real human enemy.

"Abaht that there little bet, 'Enery," observed Seaman Jones, "I fink we'll alter of it. I don't wish to give no moral support to this 'ere Griller. T'other bloke's only jus' fresh from the Novice Class, I reckon, jedgin' by 'is innercent young faice, an' e's aputtin' up the werry best fight as ever I see. We'll chainge it like this 'ere. We backs the 'orse-soldier to win, and, if he *do*, we drinks a gallon between us. If 'e don't, we drinks *two* fer to console 'im, an' drahn sorrer, wot?"

"So it are, Will'm," agreed Henery. "Then we wins *either* way! *You* got a 'ead fer logger-rhythms. Oughter been a bloomin' bookie. They 'as to be big an' ugly——"

"Seconds out of the Ring," called the referee, and a hush fell upon the excited throng.

Bear and Goate dropped to the ground, Hawker splashed water all over Dam's body and, as he rose on the word "*Time*" snatched away the chair and joined his colleagues, who crouched with faces on a level with the boards.

"Oh, buck him up, good Lord, and put ginger in his short-arm work, and O Lord, take care of his chin and mark," prayed Trooper Bear, with deep and serious devoutness.

No need to shake hands this bout—not again till the fifteenth, noted Dam, as he arose and literally leapt at his opponent with a smashing drive of his right and a feint of his left which drew the Gorilla's guard and left his face exposed. The Gorilla received Dam's full weight and full strength, and, but for the ropes, would have been knocked among the spectators.

A tremendous yell went up, led by the Queen's Greys.

As the tautening of the ropes swayed the Gorilla inward again, Dam delivered a brace of lightning strokes that, though they did not find the chin, staggered and partly stunned him, and, ere he could pull himself together, Dam was inside his guard, almost breast to breast with him, and raining terrific blows, just above the belt. Left, right, left, right, and no chance for the Gorilla to get his own hands up for a couple of seconds, and, when he could, and drove an appalling blow at Dam's chin, it was dodged and he received a cross-counter that shook him. He must sham weariness and demoralization, lead the tippy rookie on to over-confidence and then land him clean over the ropes. A sullen rage grew in the Gorilla's heart. He wasn't doing himself justice. He wasn't having a fair show. This blasted half-set pink and white recruit hadn't given him time to settle down. A fifteen-round contest shouldn't be bustled like *this!* The bloke was more like a wild-cat than a sober heavyweight boxer.

He received a heavy blow in the face and, as he shook his head with an evil grin, according to his custom when well struck, he found it followed practically instantaneously by another. The swab was about the quickest thing that ever got into a ring. He was like one of these bloomin', tricky, jack-in-the-box featherweights, instead of a steady lumbering "heavy". And the Gorilla allowed himself to be driven to a corner again, and let his head sink forward, that the incautious youth might again put all his strength into an upper-cut, miss as the other dodged, and be at the mercy of the Gorilla as the errant fist completed its over-driven swing.

But Damocles de Warrenne fought with his brain as well as his strength and skill. He had learnt a lesson, and no dull-witted oaf of a Gorilla was going to have him like that twice. As the Gorilla cowered and crouched in simulated defeat and placed his face to tempt the *coup de grace* which he would see swinging up, and easily dodge, Dam swiftly side-stepped and summoning every ounce of strength, rage, and mad protesting frenzy against the life-long torturing tyrant, he delivered a Homeric blow at the champion's head, beside and behind the ear. (Since he was indestructible by the ordinary point-of-the-chin knock-out, let him make the best of that fearful blow upon the base of the brain and spinal cord, direct.)

Experienced men said it was the heaviest blow they had ever seen struck with the human fist. It was delivered slightly downward, coolly, at measured distance, with change from left foot to right in the act of delivery, and with the uttermost strength of a most powerful athlete in perfect training—and Hate Incarnate lent the strength of madness to the strength of training and skill.

THUD!—and the Gorilla dropped like a log.

"One—two—three—four—five—six—seven—" counted the time-keeper, as men scarcely breathed in the dead silence into which the voice cut sharply—*"eight—"* and, in perfect silence, every man of those thousands slowly rose to his feet—- *"nine—OUT!"* and such a roar arose as bade fair to rend the skies. *"Outed" in two rounds!* Men howled like lunatics, and the Queen's Greys behaved like very dangerous lunatics. Hawker flung his arms round Dam and endeavoured to raise him on his shoulders and chair him unaided. Bear and Goate got each a hand and proceeded to do their best to crush it.

Seamen Jones and Smith exchanged a chaste kiss.

Damocles de Warrenne was the hero of the Queen's Greys. Best Man-at-Arms in the Division, winner in Sword v. Sword Mounted and Dismounted, Tent-pegging, Sword v. Lance, and Individual Jumping, and in the winning teams for Tug-of-War, Section Jumping, and Section Tent-pegging!

"Give him a trial as Corporal then, from the first of next month, sir, if there's no sign of anything wrong during the week," agreed Captain Daunt, talking him over with the Colonel, after receiving through Troop-Sergeant-Major Scoles a petition to promote the man.

Within twenty-four hours of his fight with the Gorilla, Dam found himself on sentry-go over what was known in the Regiment as "the Dead 'Ole"—which was the mortuary, situated in a lonely, isolated spot beyond a nullah some half-furlong from the Hospital, and cut off from view of human habitation by a belt of trees.

On mounting guard that evening, the Sergeant of the Guard had been informed that a corpse lay in the mortuary, a young soldier having been taken ill and having died within a few hours, of some disease of a distinctly choleraic nature.

"I'll tell *you* orf for that post, Matthewson," said the Sergeant. "P'raps you'll see ghosties there, for a change," for it was customary to mount a sentry over "the Dead 'Ole" when it contained an occupant, and one of the sentry's pleasing duties was to rap loudly and frequently upon the door throughout the night to scare away those vermin which are no respecters of persons when the persons happen to be dead and the vermin ravenous.

"I'm not afraid of ghosts, Sergeant," replied Dam—though his heart sank within him at the thought of the long lonely vigil in the dark, when he would be so utterly at the mercy of the Snake—the Snake over whom he had just won a signal victory, and who would be all the more vindictive and terrible in consequence. Could he keep sane through the lonely darkness of those dreadful hours? Perhaps—if he kept himself in some severe physical agony. He would put a spur beneath his tight-drawn belt and next to his skin, he would strike his knee frequently with the "toe of the butt" of his carbine, he would put pebbles in his boots, and he would cause cramp in his limbs, one after the other. Any kind of pain would help.

* * * * *

It must be quarter of an hour since he had rapped on the mortuary door and sent his messages of prohibition to mouse, rat, bandicoot, civet-cat, wild-cat or other vermin intruder through the roof-ventilation holes. He would knock again. A strange thing this—knocking at a dead man's door in the middle of the night. Suppose the dead man called "Come in!" It would be intensely interesting, but in no wise terrifying or horrible. Presumably poor young Trooper Priddell was no more dangerous or dreadful in the spirit than he had been in the flesh.... Fortunate young man! Were he only on sentry-go outside the peaceful mortuary and Damocles de Warrenne stretched on the bier within, to await the morrow and its pomp and ceremony, when the carcass of the dead soldier would receive honours never paid to the living, sentient man, be he never so worthy, heroic, virtuous and deserving. Oh, to be lying in there at rest, to be on the other side of that closed door at peace!...

152

To-morrow that poor dead yokel's body would receive a "Present Arms" (as though he were an armed party commanded by an Officer) from the Guard, which the sentry would turn out as the coffin passed the Guard-room. For the first and last time in his life, he would get a *"Present Arms"*. It wouldn't be in his *life* though. For the first and last time in his death? That didn't sound right either. Anyhow he would get it, and lots of strange, inexplicable, origin-forgotten rites would be observed over this piece of clay—hitherto so cheaply held and roughly treated.

Queer! As "Trooper Priddell" he was of no account. As a piece of fast-decaying carrion he would be the centre of a piece of elaborate ceremonial! His troop would parade in full dress and (save for a firing-party of twelve who would carry carbines) without arms. A special black horse would be decked out with a pall of black velvet and black plumes. Across this horse the spurred jackboots of the dead man would be slung with toes pointing to the rear. Two men, wearing black cloaks, would lead the horse by means of new handkerchiefs passed through the bridoon rings of its bridle, handkerchiefs which would become their perquisites and *memento mori*.

With crape-draped drums, the band, in silence, would lead the troop to the mortuary where would await it a gun-carriage with its six horses and coffin-supporting attachment. Here the troop would break ranks, file into the mortuary and bare-headed take, each man, his last look at the face of the dead as he lay in his coffin. The lid would then be screwed on, the troop would form a double line, facing inward, the firing-party would "present arms," and six of the dead man's more particular pals, or of his "townies," would bear the coffin out and place it upon the gun-carriage. It would then be covered with a Union Jack and on it would be placed the helmet, sword, and carbine of the deceased trooper, the firing-party standing meanwhile, leaning on their reversed carbines, with bowed heads.

As the melancholy procession formed up for its march to the graveyard, the smallest and junior men would take front place, the bigger and senior men behind them, non-commissioned officers would follow, and subalterns and captain last of all. In stepping off from the halt, all would step off with the right foot instead of with the left. Apparently the object was to reverse ordinary procedure to the uttermost—which would but be in keeping with the great reversal of showing honour to such an unhonoured thing as a private soldier—one of the despised and rejected band that enable the respectable, wealthy, and smug to remain so; one of the "licentious soldiery" that have made, and that keep, the Empire of which the respectable wealthy and smug are so proud.

At the "slow march," and in perfect silence until beyond hearing by the inmates of the Hospital, the cortege would proceed. Anon the band would call heaven and earth to mourn with the sonorous dreadful strains of the Dead March; whereafter the ordinary "quick march" would bring the funeral party to the cemetery, in sight of which the "slow march" would be resumed, and the Chaplain, surpliced, book-bearing, come forth to put himself at its head, leading the way to the grave-side where, with uncovered heads, the mourners would listen to the impressive words with feelings varying as their education, religion, temperament, and—digestion—- impelled.

At the close of the service, the firing-party in their places, six on either side of the grave, would fire three volleys into the air, while the band breathed a solemn dirge.

And—perhaps most impressively tragic touch of all—the party would march briskly off to the strains of the liveliest air in the whole repertoire of the band.

Why should John Humphreyville Priddell—doubtless scion of the great Norman houses of Humphreyville and Paradelle, who shared much of Dorsetshire between them from Domesday Book to Stuart downfall—have been born in a tiny village of the Vale of Froom in "Dorset Dear," to die of cholera in vile Motipur? Was some maid, in barton, byre, or dairy, thinking of him but now—with an ill-writ letter in her bosom, a letter beginning with *"I now take up my pen to right you these few lines hopping they find you the same which they now leave me at present"* according to right tradition and proper custom, and continuing to speak of homesick longings, dreams of furlough, promotion, marrying "on the strength," and retirement to green fair Dorset Dear on a Sergeant-Major's pension?

What was the meaning of it all? Was it pure chance and accident—or had a Living, Scheming, Purposeful Deity a great wise object in this that John Humphreyville Priddell should have been born and bred and nurtured in the Vale of Froom to be struck from lusty life to a death of agony in a few hours at Motipur in the cruel accursed blighted land of Ind?

Well, well!—high time to rap again upon the door, the last door, of John Humphreyville Priddell, Trooper, ex-dairyhand, decaying carrion,—and scare from his carcass such over-early visitants as anticipated....

How hollowly the blows re-echoed. Did they strike muffled but murderous upon the heart of the thousand-league distant dairymaid, or of the old cottage-mother whose evenings were spent in spelling out her boy's loving letters—that so oft covered a portion of his exiguous pay?...

Was that a scuttling within? Quite probably. It might be—rats, it might be a bandicoot; it could hardly be a jackal; it might be a SNAKE,—and Trooper Matthewson's carbine clattered to the ground and his knees smote together as he thought the word. Pulling himself together he hastily snatched up his carbine with a flush of shame at the slovenly unsoldierly "crime" of dropping it. He'd be dropping his arms on parade next! But it *might be a snake*—for he had certainly heard the sound of a movement of some sort. The strong man felt faint and leant against the mortuary wall for a moment.

Oh, that the wretched carbine were a sword! A man could feel a *man* with a sword in his hand. He could almost face the Snake, even in Snake form, if he had a sword

... but what is a carbine, even a loaded Martini-Henry carbine with its good soft man-stopping slug? There are no traditions to a carbine—nothing of the Spirit of one's Ancestors in one—a vile mechanic thing of villainous saltpetre. How should the Snake fear that? Now a sword was different. It stood for human war and human courage and human deeds from the mistiest past, and behind it must be a weight of human wrath, feats, and tradition that must make even the Snake pause. Oh, for his sword—if the Snake came upon him when he had but this wretched carbine he would probably desert his post, fling the useless toy from him, and flee till he fell blind and fainting on the ground.... And what would the Trooper of the Queen get who deserted his sentry-post, threw away his arms and fled—and explained in defence that he had seen a snake? Probably a court-martial would give him a spell of Military Prison. Yes—*Jail*.... What proportion of truth could there be in the firmly-held belief of the men that "crimes" are made so numerous and so inevitable, to the best-meaning and most careful, because there exist a great Military Prison System and a great Military Prison personnel—and that "criminals" are essential to the respective proper inhabitation and *raison d'etre* thereof—that unless a good supply of military "criminals" were forthcoming there might have to be reductions and curtailments—loss of snug billets.... Certainly soldiers got years of imprisonment for "crimes" for which civilians would get reprimands or nominal fines, and, moreover, when a man became a soldier he certainly lost the elementary fundamental rights guaranteed to Englishmen by Magna Charta—among them the right of trial by his peers....

Would poor Priddell mind if he did not knock again? If it were the Snake it could do Priddell no harm now—he being happily dead—whereas, if disturbed, it might emerge to the utter undoing—mind, body, and soul—of Trooper Matthewson. It would certainly send him to Jail or Lunatic Asylum—probably to both in due succession, for he was daily getting worse in the matter of the Snake.

No—it was part of his orders, on this sentry-post, to knock at the door, and he would do his duty, Snake or not. He had always tried to do his duty faithfully and he would continue....

Once more to knock at a dead man's door....

Bump, Bump: Bump, Bump: Bump, Bump.

"You'll soon be at rest, Priddell, old chap—and I wish I could join you," called Dam, and it seemed to his excited brain that *a deep hollow groan replied.*

"By Jove! He's not dead," coolly remarked the man who would have fled shrieking from a harmless blind-worm, and, going round to the back of the building, he placed his carbine against the wall and sprang up at a kind of window-ledge that formed the base of a grated aperture made for purposes of ventilation. Slowly raising his body till his face was above the ledge, he peered into the dimly moonlit cell and then dropped to the ground and, catching up his carbine, sprinted in the direction of the Hospital Guard-room.

There arrived, he shouted for the Corporal of the Guard and was quickly confronted by Corporal Prag.

"Wot the devil you deserted yore".... he began.

"Get the key of the mortuary, send for the Surgeon, and come at once," gasped Dam as soon as he could speak. "*Priddell's not dead.* Must be some kind of catalepsy. Quick, man"....

"Catter wot? You drunken 'og," drawled the Corporal. "Catter_waulin'_ more like it. Under arrest you goes, my lad. Now you *'ave* done it. 'Ere, 'Awker, run down an' call up the Sergeant o' the Guard an' tell 'im Maffewson's left 'is post. 'E'll 'ave to plant annuvver sentry. Maffewson goes ter clink."

"Yes—but send for the Surgeon and the key of the mortuary too," begged Dam. "I give you fair warning that Priddell is alive and groaning and off the bier—"

"Pity *you* ain't 'off the beer' too," said the Corporal with a yawn.

"Well—there are witnesses that I brought the report to you. If Priddell is found dead on the ground to-morrow you'll have to answer for manslaughter."

"'Ere, *chuck* it you snaike-seeing delirying trimmer, *will* yer! Give anyone the 'orrers to listen to yer! When Priddell is wrote off as 'Dead' 'e *is* dead, whether 'e likes it or no," and he turned to give orders to the listening guard to arrest Trooper Matthewson.

The Sergeant of the Guard arrived at the "double," followed by Trooper Bear carrying a hurricane-lamp.

"What's the row?" panted the Sergeant. "Matthewson on the booze agin?"

"I report that there is a living man in the mortuary, Sergeant," replied Dam. "Priddell is not dead. I heard him groan, and I scrambled up to the grating and saw him lying on the ground by the door."

"Well, you'll see yerself groanin' an' lyin' on the ground in the Digger, now," replied the Sergeant, and, as much in sorrow as in anger, he added, "An' *you*'re the bloke I signed a petition for his permotion are yer? At it agin a'ready!"

"But, good Heavens, man, can't you see I'm as sober as you are, and much less excited? Can't you send for the key of the mortuary and call the doctor? The poor chap may die for your stupidity."

156

"You call *me* a 'man' again, my lad, an' I'll show you what a Sergeant can do fer them as 'e don't like! As fer 'sober'—I've 'ad enough o' you 'sober'. W'y, in two ticks you may be on the ground 'owlin' and bellerin' and squealin' like a Berkshire pig over the blood-tub. *Sober!* Yus—I seen you at it."

"Why on earth can't you come and *prove* I'm drunk or mad," besought Dam. "Open the mortuary and prove I'm wrong—and then put me under arrest. Call the Surgeon and say the sentry over the mortuary reports the inmate to be alive—*he* has heard of catalepsy and comatose collapse simulating death if *you* haven't."

"Don' use sech 'orrible languidge," besought the respectable Corporal Prag.

"Ho, yus! *I'*m agoin' to see meself whipt on the peg fer turnin' out the Surgin from 'is little bed in the middle o' the night—to come an' 'ave a look at the dead corpse 'e put in orders fer the Dead 'Ole, ain't I? Jest becos the champion snaike-seer o' E Troop's got 'em agin, wot?"

Corporal Prag laughed merrily at the wit of his superior.

Turning to Bear, whom he knew to be as well educated as himself, Dam remarked:—

"Poor chap has rallied from the cholera collapse and could probably be saved by stimulants and warmth. This suspended animation is common enough in cholera. Why, the Brahmins have a regular ritual for dealing with cases of recovery on the funeral pyre—purification after defilement by the corpse-washers or something of the sort. These stupid oafs are letting poor Priddell die—"

"What! you drunken talkin' parrot," roared the incensed Sergeant. "'Ere, sling 'is drunken rotten carkis—"

"What's the row here?" cut in a quiet curt voice. "Noise enough for a gang of crows——"

Surgeon-Captain Blake of the Royal Army Medical Corps had just left the Hospital, having been sent for by the night Nursing Sister. The men sprang to attention and the Sergeant saluted.

"Drunk sentry left 'is post, Sir," he gabbled. "'Spose the Dead 'Ole—er—Morshuerry, that is, Sir, got on 'is nerves. 'E's given to secret boozin', Sir——"

"Excuse me, Sir," broke in Dam, daring to address an Officer unbidden, since a life was at stake, "I am a total abstainer and Trooper Priddell is not dead. It must have been cataleptic trance. I heard him groan and I climbed up and saw him lying on the ground."

157

"This man's not drunk," said Captain Blake, and added to himself, "and he's an educated man, and a cultured, poor devil."

"Oh, that's how 'e goes on, Sir, sober as a judge you'd say, an' then nex' minnit 'e's on the floor aseein' blue devils an' pink serpients——"

"The man's dying while we talk, Sir," put in Dam, whose wrath was rising. (If these dull-witted ignorant louts could not tell a drunken man from a sober, nor realize that a certified dead man may *not* be dead, surely the doctor could.)

The Sergeant and the Corporal ventured on a respectful snigger.

"Bring me that lamp," said Captain Blake, and Trooper Bear raised it to his extended hand. Lifting it so that its light shone straight in Dam's face the doctor scanned the latter and examined his eyes. This was not the face of a drunkard nor was the man in any way under the influence of liquor now. Absurd! Had he fever? Was he of deranged intellect? But, alas, the light that shone upon Dam's face also shone upon Captain Blake's collar and upon the badge of his Corps which adorned it—and that badge is a serpent entwining a rod.

It was the last straw! Dam had passed through a most disturbing night; he had kept guard in the lonely Snake-haunted darkness, guard over a mortuary in which lay a corpse; he had had to keep knocking at the corpse's door, his mind had run on funerals, he had thought he heard the dead man groan, he believed he had seen the dead man moving, he had wrestled with thick intelligences who held him drunk or mad while precious moments passed, and he had had the Snake before his mental vision throughout this terrible time—and here was another of its emissaries *wearing its badge*, an emissary of high rank, an Officer-Emissary!... Well, he was in the open air, thank God, and could put up a fight as before.

Like a panther he sprang upon the unfortunate officer and bore him to the ground, with his powerful hands enclosing the astounded gentleman's neck, and upon the couple sprang the Sergeant, the Corporal, and the Hospital Guard, all save the sentry, who (disciplined, well-drilled man!) brought his carbine to the "order" and stood stiffly at "attention" in a position favourable for a good view of the proceedings though strictly on his beat.

Trooper Bear, ejaculating "Why do the heathen rage furiously together," took a running jump and landed in sitting posture on the heap, rolled off, and proceeded to seize every opportunity of violently smiting his superior officers, in his apparent zeal to help to secure the dangerous criminal-lunatic. Thoughts of having just *one* punch at a real Officer (if only a non-combatant still a genuine Commissioned Officer) flashed across his depraved mind.

It was a Homeric struggle. Captain Blake was himself an old Guy's Rugger three-quarter and no mean boxer, and the Sergeant, Corporal, and Guard, were all powerful men, while Dam was a Samson further endowed with the strength of undeniable madness. When at length he was dragged from Captain Blake's recumbent form, his hands torn from that officer's throat, and the group stood for a second panting, Dam suddenly felled Corporal Prag with such a blow as had been the undoing of the Gorilla, sent Sergeant Wotting head over heels and, ere the Guard could again close with him, drove his fist into the face of the supposed myrmidon of the Snake and sprang upon his body once more....

It was some time before seven strong men could pinion him and carry him on a stretcher to the Guard-room, and, of those seven strong men, only Trooper Bear bore no mark of serious damage. (Trooper Bear had struck two non-commissioned officers with great violence, in his misdirected zeal, and one Commissioned Officer—though only playfully and for the satisfaction of being able to say that he had done so.) That night, half dead, wholly mad, bruised and bleeding, Damocles de Warrenne lay in the dark cell awaiting trial on a charge of assaulting an Officer, striking his superior officers, resisting the Guard, deserting his sentry-post, and being drunk and disorderly.

* * * * *

"What'll he get, d'you think?" sadly asked Trooper Goate of Trooper Hawker.

"Two stretch 'ard laiber and discharged from the Army wiv' iggernerminny," groaned Trooper Hawker. "Lucky fer 'im floggin's erbolished in the British Army."

* * * * *

When the mortuary door was unlocked next morning a little force was required to open it, some obstacle apparently retarding its inward movement. The obstacle proved to be the body, now certainly the dead body, of Trooper Priddell who had died with his fingers thrust under the said door.[26]

159

PART III.

THE SAVING OF A SOUL

CHAPTER XII.

VULTURES AND LUCK—GOOD AND BAD.

To the strongest and sanest mind there is something a small trifle disturbing, perhaps, in riding silently hour after hour on a soft-footed camel over soft sand in a silent empty land through the moonlit silent night, beside an overland-telegraph wire on every individual post of which sits a huge vulture!... Just as the sun set, a fiery red ball, behind the distant mountains, Damocles de Warrenne, gentleman-at-large, had caught sight of what he had sought in the desert for some days, the said overland telegraph, and thereby saved himself from the highly unpleasant death that follows prolonged deprivation of water. He had also saved his camel from a little earlier death, inasmuch as he had decided to probe for the faithful creature's jugular vein and carotid artery during the torturing heats of the morrow and prolong his life at its expense. (Had he not promised Lucille to do his best for himself?)

The overland telegraph pointed absolutely straight to the border city of Kot Ghazi and, better still, to a river-bed which would contain pools of water, thirty miles this side of it, at a spot a few miles from which stood a lost lone dak-bungalow on Indian soil—a dak-bungalow whereat would be waiting a *shikarri* retainer, and such things as tea, fuel, potted foods, possibly fresh meat, and luxury of luxuries, a hot bath....

And, with a sigh of relief, he had wheeled his camel under the telegraph wires after a glance at the stars and brief calculation as to whether he should turn to left or right. (He did not want to proceed until he collapsed under the realization that he was making for the troubled land of Persia.)

Anyhow, without knowing where he was, he knew he was on the road to water, food, human companionship (imagine Abdul Ghani a human companion!—but he had not seen a human face for three weeks, nor heard nor uttered a word), and safety, after suffering the unpleasant experience of wandering in circles, lost in the most inhospitable desert on the earth. Vultures! He had not realized there were so many in the world. Hour after hour, a post at every few yards, and on every post a vulture—a vulture that opened its eyes as he approached, regarded him from its own point of view—that of the Eater whose life is an unending search for Meat—calculatingly, and closed them again with a sigh at his remaining vigorousness.

He must have passed hundreds, thousands,—had he died of thirst in actual fact and was he doomed to follow this line through this desert for evermore as a punishment for his sins? No—much too mild a punishment for the God of Love to inflict, according to the Chaplain. This would be Eternal Bliss compared with the Eternal Fire. He must be still alive ... Was he mad, then, and *imagining* these unending bird-capped posts? If not mad, he soon would be. Why couldn't they say something—mannerless brutes! Should he swerve off and leave the telegraph line? No, he had starved and suffered the agonies of thirst for nearly a week—and, if he could hang on all night, he might reach water tomorrow and be saved. Food was a minor consideration and if he could drink a few gallons of water, soak his clothes in it, lie in it,—he could carry on for another day or two. Nearly as easy to sprawl face-downward on a camel-saddle as on the ground—and he had tied himself on. The camel would rub along all right for days with camel-thorn and similar dainties.... No, better not leave the line. Halt and camp within sight of it till the morning, when the brutes would fly away in search of food? No ... might find it impossible to get going again, if once man and beast lay down now ... Ride as far as possible from the line, keeping it in sight? No ... if he fell asleep the camel would go round in a circle again, and he'd wake up a dozen miles from the line, with no idea of direction and position. Best to carry straight on. The camel would stick to the line so long as he was left exactly on it ... think it a road ... He could sleep without danger thus. He would shut his eyes and not see the vultures, for if he saw a dozen more he knew that he would go raving mad, halt the camel and address an impassioned appeal to them to *say* something—for God's sake to *say something*. Didn't they know that he had been in solitary confinement in a desert for three weeks or three centuries (what is time?) without hearing a sound or seeing a living thing—expecting the SNAKE night and day, and, moreover, that he was starving, dying of thirst, and light-headed, and that he was in the awful position of choosing between murdering the camel that had stood by him—no, under him—all that fearful time, and breaking his word to Lucille—cheating and deceiving Lucille. Then why couldn't they *say* something instead of sitting there in their endless millions, mile after billions of miles, post after billions of trillions of posts—menacing, watchful, silent, silent as the awful desert, silent as the SNAKE.... This would not do ... he must think hard of Lucille, of the Sword, of his Dream, his Dream that came so seldom now. He would repeat Lucille's last letter, word for word:—

"MY DARLING,

"It is over, thank God—Oh, thank God—and you can leave the army at once and become a 'gentleman' in position as well as in fact. Poor old Grumper died on Saturday (as I cabled) and before he died he became quite another man—weak, gentle and anxious to make any amends he could to anybody. For nearly a week he was like this, and it was a most wonderful and pathetic thing. He spent most of the time in telling me, General Harringport, Auntie Yvette or the Vicar, about wicked things he had done, cruelties, meannesses, follies—it was most distressing, for really he has been simply a strong character with all the faults of one—including, as we know too well, lack of sympathy, hardness, and sometimes savage cruelty, which, after all, was only the natural result of the lack of sympathy and understanding.

"As he grew weaker he grew more sympathetic with illness and suffering, I suppose, for he sent for me in the middle of the night to say that he had suddenly remembered Major Decies' story about your probably being subject to fits and seizures in certain circumstances, and that he was coming to the conclusion that he had been hasty and unjust and had unmercifully punished you for no fault whatever. He said 'I have punished him for being punished. I have added my injustice to that of Fate. Write to him that I ask his pardon and confess my fault. Tell him I'll make such reparation as I can,' and oh, Dam—-he leaves *you* Monksmead, and *me* his money, on the understanding that we marry as soon as any physician, now living in Harley Street, says that you are fit to marry (I must write it I suppose) without fear of our children being epileptic, insane, or in any way tainted. If none of them will do this, I am to inherit Monksmead and part of the money and you are to have a part of the money. If we marry *then*, we lose everything and it goes to Haddon Berners. Mr. Wyllis, who has been his lawyer and agent for thirty years, is to take you to Harley Street (presumably to prevent your bribing and corrupting the whole of the profession there residing).

"Come at once, Darling. If the silly old physicians won't certify, why—what *does* it matter? I am going to let lodgings at Monksmead to a Respectable Single Man (with board) and Auntie Yvette will see that he behaves himself.

"Cable what boat you start by and I'll meet you at Port Said. I don't know how I keep myself sitting in this chair. I could turn head over heels for joy! (And poor Grumper only just buried and his Will read!) He didn't lose quite all his grim humour in that wonderful week of softening, relenting and humanizing. What do you think he solemnly gave and bequeathed to the poor Haddock? His *wardrobe*!!! And nothing else, but if the Haddock wears only Grumper's clothes, including his boots, shirts, ties, collars and everything else, for one full and complete year, and wears absolutely nothing else, he is to have five thousand pounds at the end of it—and he is to begin on the day after the funeral! And even at the last poor Grumper was a foot taller and a foot broader (not to mention *thicker*) than the Haddock! It appears that he systematically tried to poison Grumper's mind against you—presumably with an eye on this same last Will and Testament. He hasn't been seen since the funeral. I wonder if he is going to try to win the money by remaining in bed for a year in Grumper's pyjamas! "Am I not developing 'self-control and balance'? Here I sit writing news to you while my heart is screaming aloud with joy, crying 'Dam is coming home. Dam's troubles are over. Dam is saved!' Because if you are ever so 'ill,' Darling, there is nothing on earth to prevent your coming to your old home at once—and if we can't marry we can be pals for evermore in the dear old place of our childhood. But of *course* we can marry. Hurry home, and if any Harley Street doctor gives you even a doubtful look, throw him up his own stairs to show how feeble you are, or tie his poker round his neck in a neat bow, and refuse to undo it until he apologizes. I'm sure you could! '*Ill*' indeed! If you can't have a little fit, on the rare occasions when you see a snake, without fools saying you are ill or dotty or something, it is a pity! Anyhow there is one small woman who understands, and if she can't marry you she can at any rate be your inseparable pal—and if the Piffling Little World likes to talk scandal, in spite of Auntie Yvette's presence—why it will be amusing. Cable, Darling! I am just bursting with excitement and joy—and fear (that something may go wrong at the last moment). If it saved a single day I should start for Motipur myself at once. If we passed in mid-ocean I should jump overboard and swim to your ship. Then you'd do the same, and we should 'get left,' and look silly.... Oh, what nonsense I am talking—but I don't think I shall talk anything else again—for sheer joy!

"You can't write me a lot of bosh *now* about 'spoiling my life' and how you'd be ten times more miserable if I were your wife. Fancy—a soldier to-day and a 'landed proprietor' to-morrow! How I wish you were a *landed* traveller, and were in the train from Plymouth—no, from Dover and London, because of course you'd come the quickest way. Did my cable surprise you very much?

"I enclose fifty ten-pound notes, as I suppose they will be quicker and easier for you to cash than those 'draft' things, and they'll be quite safe in the insured packet. Send a cable at once, Darling. If you don't I shall imagine awful things and perhaps die of a broken heart or some other silly trifle.

"Mind then:—Cable to-day; Start to-morrow; Get here in a fortnight— and keep a beady eye open at Port Said and Brindisi and places—in case there has been time for me to get there. Au revoir. Darling Dam,

"Your

"LUCILLE.

"Three cheers! And a million more!"

* * * * *

Yes, a long letter, but he could almost say it backwards. He couldn't be anything like mad while he could do that?... How had she received his answer—in which he

164

tried to show her the impossibility of any decent man compromising a girl in the way she proposed in her sweet innocence and ignorance. Of course *he*, a half-mad, epileptic, fiend-ridden monomaniac—nay, dangerous lunatic,—could not *marry*. Why, he might murder his own wife under some such circumstances as those under which he attacked Captain Blake. (Splendid fellow Blake! Not every man after such a handling as that would make it his business to prove that his assailant was neither drunk, mad, nor criminal—merely under a hallucination. But for Blake he would now be in jail, or lunatic asylum, to a certainty. The Colonel would have had him court-martialled as a criminal, or else have had him out of the regiment as a lunatic. Nor, as a dangerous lunatic, would he have been allowed to buy himself out when Lucille's letter and his money arrived. Blake had got him into the position of a perfectly sober and sane person whose mind had been temporarily upset by a night of horror—in which a coffin-quitting corpse had figured, and so he had been able to steer between the cruel rocks of Jail and Asylum to the blessed harbour of Freedom.)

Yes—in spite of Blake's noble goodness and help, Dam knew that he was *not* normal, that he *was* dangerous, that he spent long periods on the very border-line of insanity, that he stood fascinated on that border-line and gazed far into the awful country beyond—the Realms of the Mad....

Marry! Not Lucille, while he had the sanity left to say "No"!

As for going to live at Monksmead with her and Auntie Yvette—it would be an even bigger crime. Was it for *him* to make *Lucille* a "problem" girl, a girl who was "talked about," a by-word for those vile old women of both sexes whose favourite pastime is the invention and dissemination of lies where they dare, and of even more damaging head-shakes, lip-pursings, gasps and innuendoes where they do not?

Was it for *him* to get *Lucille* called "The Woman Who Did," by those scum of the leisured classes, and "That peculiar young woman," by the better sort of matron, dowager and chaperone,—make her the kind of person from whose company careful mothers keep their innocent daughters (that their market price may never be in danger of the faintest depreciation when they are for sale in the matrimonial market), the kind of woman for whom men have a slightly and subtly different manner at meet, hunt-ball, dinner or theatre-box? Get Lucille "talked about"?

No—setting aside the question of the possibility of living under the same roof with her and conquering the longing to marry.

No—he had some decency left, tainted as he doubtless was by his barrack-room life.

Tainted of course.... What was it he had heard the senior soldierly-looking man, whom the other addressed as "General," say concerning some mutual acquaintance, at breakfast in the dining-car going up to Kot Ghazi?

165

"Yes, poor chap, was in the ranks—and no man can escape the barrack-room taint when he has once lived in it. Take me into any Officers' Mess you like—say 'There is a promoted gentleman-ranker here,' and I'll lay a thousand to one I spot him. Don't care if he's the son of a Dook—nor yet if he's Royal, you can spot him alright...."

Pleasant hearing for the "landed proprietor," whom a beautiful, wealthy and high-bred girl proposed to marry!

Tainted or not, in that way—he was *mentally* tainted, a fact beside which the other, if as true as Truth, paled into utterest insignificance.

No—he had taken the right line in replying to Lucille that he was getting worse mentally, that no doctor would dream of "vetting" him "sound," that he was not scoundrel enough to come and cause scandal and "talk" at Monksmead, and that he was going to disappear completely from the ken of man, wrestle with himself, and come to her and beg her to marry him directly he was better—sufficiently better to "pass the doctor," that is. If, meanwhile, she met and loved a man worthy of her, such a man as Ormonde Delorme, he implored her to marry him and to forget the wholly unworthy and undesirable person who had merely loomed large upon her horizon through the accident of propinquity ...

(He could always disappear again and blow out such brains as he possessed, if that came to pass, he told himself.)

Meanwhile letters to the Bank of Bombay would be sent for, at least once a year—but she was not to write—she was to forget him. As to searching for him—he had not quite decided whether he would walk from Rangoon to Pekin or from Quetta to Constantinople—perhaps neither, but from Peshawur to Irkutsk. Anyhow, he was going to hide himself pretty effectually, and put himself beyond the temptation of coming and spoiling her life. Sooner or later he would be mad, dead, or cured. If the last—why he would make for the nearest place where he could get news of her—and if she were then happily married to somebody else—why—why—she *would* be happy, and that would make him quite happy ...

Had the letter been quite sane and coherent—or had he been in a queer mental state when he wrote it?...

He opened his eyes, saw a vulture within a few yards of him, closed them again, and, soon after, fell into an uneasy slumber as the camel padded on at a steady seven miles an hour unurged—save by the *smell* of pure clear water which was still a score of miles distant....

When Damocles de Warrenne awoke, he was within a few hundred yards of the nearly dry River Helnuddi, where, failing occasional pools, the traveller can always procure water by digging and patiently awaiting the slow formation of a little puddle at the bottom of the hole.

For a minute he halted. Should he dig while he had strength, or should he turn to the left and follow the river-bed until he came to a pool—or could go no farther? Perhaps he would be too weak to dig, though, by that time.... Remarkable how eager to turn to the left and get on, the camel was—considering how tired he must be—-perhaps he could smell distant water or knew of a permanent pool hereabouts. Well, let that decide it....

An hour later, as the camel topped a rise in the river-bank, a considerable pool came into view, tree-shaded, heron-haunted, too incredibly beautiful and alluring for belief. Was it a mirage?...

A few minutes later, Damocles de Warrenne and his camel were drinking, and a few hours later entered the dreary featureless compound of a wretched hovel, which, to the man at least, was a palatial and magnificent asylum (no, not *asylum*—of all words)—refuge and home—the more so that a camel knelt chewing in the shade of the building, and a man, Abdul Ghani himself, lay slumbering in the verandah....

"You understand, then," said Dam in the vernacular, to the malodorous, hideous, avaricious Abdul who reappeared from Kot Ghazi a few days later, "you return here again, one week from to-day, bringing the things written down on this paper, from the shop of Rustomji at Kot Ghazi. Here you wait until I come. If I find there is truth in your *khubbar*[27] of ibex you will be rewarded ... Why don't I take you? Because I want to be alone. Set out now for Kot Ghazi. I may return." A stone fell and clattered. Dam shrank, cringed, and shut his eyes—as one expecting a heavy blow. *Ah-h-h-h-h*—had the beast bolted? With the slowness of an hour-hand he raised his head above the bank of the watercourse until his eye cleared the edge. *No*—still there. After a painful crawl that seemed to last for hours, he reached the point where the low ridge ran off at right-angles, crept behind it, and lay flat on his face, to rest and recover breath. He was soaked in perspiration from head to foot, giddy with sun and unnatural posture, very sore as to elbows and knees, out of breath, trembling—and entirely happy. The half-mile crawl, with the greater part of his body on the burning ground, and the rifle to shuffle steadily along without noise or damage, was the equivalent of a hard day's work to a strong man. At the end of it he lay gasping and sick, aching in every limb, almost blind with glare and over-exertion, weary to death—and entirely happy. Thank God he would be able to stand up in a moment and rest behind a big cactus. Then he would have a spell of foot-work for a change, and, though crouching double, would not be doing any crawling until he had crossed the plateau and reached the bushes.

The upward climb was successfully accomplished with frequent halts for breath, behind boulders. On the plateau all that was required was silence. The ibex could not see him up there. In his rubber-soled khaki-coloured shoes he could almost run, but it was a question whether a drink of cold water would not be worth more than all the ibexes in the world.

He tip-toed rapidly across the level hill-top, reached the belt of low bushes, dropped, and lay to recover breath before resuming the painful and laborious crawling part of his journey. Was it possible to tap one's tongue against one's teeth and hear the noise of it as though it were made of wood? It seemed so. Was this giddiness and dimness of vision sunstroke? What would he give to have that fly (that had followed him for hundreds of thousands of miles that morning) between his fingers?

Last lap! There was the rock, and below it must be the quarry—if it had not fled. He must keep that rock between himself and his prey and he must get to it without a sound. It would be easy enough without the rifle. Could he stick it through his belt and along his back, or trail it behind him? What nonsense! He must be getting a touch of sun. Would these stones leave marks of burns on his clothes? Surely he could smell himself singeing. Enough to explode the rifle ... The big rock at last! A rest and then a peep, with infinite precaution. Dam held his breath and edged his face to the corner of the great boulder. Moving imperceptibly, he peeped ... *No ibex!* ... He was about to spring up with a hearty malediction on his luck when he perceived a peculiar projection on a large stone some distance down the hill. It moved—and Dam dropped back. It must be the top of the curve of one of the horns of the ibex and the animal must be lying down.... What to do? It might lie for hours and he himself might go to sleep. It might get up and depart at any moment without coming into the line of fire—without being seen indeed. Better continue the stalk and hope to get a standing shot, or, failing that, a running one.

It looked a nasty descent, since silence was essential—steep, slippery, and strewn with round stones. Anyhow, he could go down on his feet, which was something to be thankful for, as it was agony to put a knee or elbow to the ground. He crept on.

Surely his luck was changing, for here he was, within fifty yards of a stone behind which lay an unsuspecting ibex with a world's-record head. Hullo! a nasty little precipice! With a nastily sloping shelf at the bottom too, eight feet away—and then another little precipice and another sloping shelf at its base.

Better lay the rifle on the edge, slip over, hang by the hands, grab it with one, and then drop the intervening few inches. Rubber soles would play their part here! Damn this giddiness—touch of sun, no doubt. Damocles de Warrenne knelt on the edge of the eight-foot drop, turned round, swayed, fell, struck the sloping ledge, rolled off it, fell, struck the next sloping ledge, fell thirty feet—arousing an astounded ibex *en route*—and landed in a queer heap on a third shelf, with a few broken ribs, a dislocated shoulder, broken ankles, and a fractured thigh.

A vulture, who had been interested in his proceedings for some time, dropped a few thousand feet and had a look. What he saw decided him to come to earth. He perched on a rock and waited patiently. He knew the symptoms and he knew the folly of taking risks. A friend or two joined him—each, as he left his place in the sky, being observed and followed by a brother who was himself in turn observed and followed by another who brought others....

One of the hideous band had drawn quite near and was meditating rewarding his own boldness with a succulent eye, when Dam groaned and moved. The pretty birds also moved and probably groaned in spirit—but they didn't move far.

What was that Miss Smellie had been so fond of saying? "There is no such thing as 'luck,' Damocles. All is ordered for the best by an all-seeing and merciful Providence." Yes. No doubt.

What was that remark of his old friend, "Holy Bill"?

"What do you mean by 'luck,' Damocles? All that happens is ordained by God in His infinite mercy." Yes.

Holy Bill had never done a day's work in his life nor missed a meal—save when bilious from overeating....

A pity the infinite mercy didn't run to a little water! It would have been easy for the all-seeing and merciful Providence to move him to retain his water-bottle when starting the stalk—if it were necessary to the schemes of the Deity to have him smashed like a dropped egg.... What agony a human being could endure!...

Not even his rifle at hand with its means of speedy death. He might live for days and then be torn alive by those accursed vultures. One mighty effort to turn on his back and he would breathe easier—but that would bring his eyes to the sun—and the vultures.... Had he slept or fainted? How long had he lain there?... Chance of being found? Absolutely none. Shikarri would have visited the dak-bungalow a week ago. Camel left below on the plain—and it would wander miles from where he left it when it grew hungry. Even if Abdul and an organized search-party were after him *now* they might as well be searching for a needle in a hay-stack. No one knew which of the thousand gullies he had ascended and no one could track camel-pads or flat rubber soles over bare solid rock, even if given the starting-point. No—he had got to die of thirst, starvation, and vultures, barring miracles of luck—and he had *never* had any good luck—for luck existed, undoubtedly, in spite of mealy-mouthed platitude-makers and twaddle about everything being pre-arranged and ordained with care and deliberation by a kind paternal Providence.

And what luck he had had—all his life! Born fated!

Had he fainted again or slept? And could he hear the tinkle of ice against the sides of a tall thin tumbler of lemonade, or was it the sound of a waterfall of clear, cold water close by? Were the servants asleep, or was the drink he had ordered being prepared?... No—he was dying in agony on a red-hot rock, surrounded by vultures and probably watched by foxes, jackals and hyenas. And a few yards away were the rifle that would have put him out of his misery, and the water-bottle that would have alleviated his pain—to the extent, at any rate, of enabling him to think clearly and perhaps scribble a few words in blood or something, somehow, for Lucille ...

169

Lucille! Would the All-Merciful let him see her once again for a moment in return for an extra thousand years of Hell or whatever it was that unhappy mortals got as a continuation of the joys of this gay world? Could he possibly induce the vultures to carry him home—if he pledged himself to feed them and support their progeny? They could each have a house in the compound. It would pay them far better than eating him now. Did they understand Pushtoo or was it Persian? Certainly not Hindustani and Urdu. People who came shooting alone in the desert and mountains, where vultures abounded, should learn to talk Vulture and pass the Higher Standard in that tongue. But even if they understood him they might be unwilling to serve a coward. *Was* he a coward? Anyhow he lay glued with his own blood to the spot he would never leave—unless the vultures could be bribed. Useless to hope anything of the jackals. He had hunted too many foxes to begin now to ask favours. Besides they could only drag, and he had been dragged once by a horse. Quite enough for one lifetime. But he had never injured a vulture. Pity he had no copy of Grimm or Anderson with him—they contained much useful information about talking foxes, obliging birds, and other matters germane to the occasion. If he could only get them to apply it, a working-party of vultures and jackals certainly had the strength to transport him a considerable distance—alternately carrying and dragging him. The big bird, stalking nearer, was probably the *macuddam* or foreman. Would it be at all possible for vultures to bring water? He would be very willing to offer his right hand in return for a little water. The bird would be welcome to eat it off his body if it would give him a drink first. Did not ravens bring meat to the prophet Elijah? Intelligent and obliging birds. Probably cooked it, too. But water was more difficult to carry, if easier to procure.

How close they were coming and how they watched with their horrible eyes—and pretended not to watch!...

Oh, the awful, unspeakable agony! Why was he alive again? Was his chest full of terribly rusty machinery that would go on when it ought to stop for want of oil?... If pain is punishment for sin, as placid stall-fed Holy Bill held (never having suffered any), then Damocles de Warrenne must have been the prince of sinners. Oh God! a little drop of water! Rivers of it flowing not many miles away!

Monsoons of it falling recently! A water-bottle full a few yards distant—and he must die for want of a drop ... What a complete circle the vultures made on the rocks and stunted trees of the sloping hill-side. Oh, for a revolver! A man ought to carry one on shikar expeditions. One would give him a chance of life when under a tiger or panther—and a chance of decent death in a position such as this. Where had he read that vultures begin on the eyes of their prey? Without awaiting its death either, so long as it could not defend itself. There were other depraved gustatory preferences, too, if he remembered rightly-He would have an opportunity of testing the accuracy of the statement—though not of assuring its author as to its correctness.

Water ... Water ... Water ...

170

Had he fainted again, that the vultures were so much nearer?... Why should he be a second Prometheus? Had he not had suffering enough in his life, without having more in his death?... If the sending of a little water were too obvious a miracle, was it too much to ask that his next fainting and collapse might last long enough for the vultures to get to work, make a beginning, and an end?

Surely that would not be too great a miracle, since he had lain for years on a red-hot rock with blood in his mouth and his body wrecked like a smashed egg. He must be practically dead. Perhaps if he held his laboured breath and closed his eyes they *would* begin, and he would have the strength to keep still when they did so. That would be the quickest way. Once they started, it would not be long before his bones were cleaned. No possible ghost of a chance of being saved. Probably no human foot had been on these particular rocks since human feet existed. Nor would he ever again have the strength to drag his shattered body to where the rifle lay. Only a few yards away lay speedy happy release.

"No such thing as luck, Damocles."

Perhaps the vultures thought otherwise.

Colonel John Decies, still of Bimariabad, but long retired on pension from the Indian Medical Service, was showing his mental and physical unfitness for the service of the Government that had ordered his retirement, by devoting himself at the age of fifty-nine to aviation—aviation in the interests of the wounded on the battlefield. What he wanted to live to see was a flying stretcher-service of the Royal Army Medical Corps that should flash to and fro at the rate of a hundred miles an hour between the rear of the firing-line and the field hospital and base hospital in aeroplanes built especially for the accommodation of wounded men—an officer of the Corps accompanying each in the dual capacity of surgeon and potential pilot. When he allowed his practical mind to wander among the vast possibilities of the distant future, he dreamed of bigger and bigger aeroplanes until they became fully equipped flying hospitals themselves, and removed the wounded from the danger zone to the nearest salubrious spot for their convalescence. Meanwhile, he saw no reason why the more powerful biplanes should not carry an operating-table and all surgical accessories, a surgeon, and two or three wounded men who could not be made sitting-up cases.

To Colonel John Decies it seemed that if soldiers schemed to adapt the flying-machine to purposes of death and destruction, doctors might do the same to purposes of life and salvation. Think of the difference between being jolted for hours in a bullock-cart in the dust and heat and being borne through the air without jerk or jar. Think of the hundreds of men who, in the course of one campaign, would be saved from the ghastly fate of lying unfound, unseen by the stretcher-bearers, to starve to death, to lie weltering in their blood, to live through days of agony....

He was making quite a name for himself by his experiments at the Kot Ghazi flying-school and by his articles and speeches on the formation and training of a R.A.M.C.

flying branch. Small beginnings would content him (provided they were intended to lead to great developments)—an aeroplane at first, that could carry one or two special cases to which the ordinary means of transport would be fatal, and that could scour the ground, especially in the case of very broken terrain and hill-country, for overlooked cases, wounded men unable to move or call, and undiscovered by the searchers.

He was hard at work on the invention of a strong collapsible operating-table (that could readily be brought into use in the field and also be used in aerial transport) and a case for the concentration of equipment—operation instruments, rubber gloves, surgical gauntlets, saline infusion apparatus, sterilizer, aseptic towels, chloroform, bandages, gauze, wool, sponges, drainage-tubing, inhaler, silk skeins, syringes, field tourniquets, waterproof cloth, stethoscope—everything, and the whole outfit, table and all, weighing forty pounds. This would be an improvement on the system of having to open half a dozen medical and surgical cases when operating on the line of march, cases requiring the most expert repacking after use ...

* * * * *

Perhaps it was a sign of advancing years and weakening mind that this fine specimen of a fine service felt that, when flying some thousands of feet above the earth, he was nearer to Lenore in Heaven. All his science and sad experience had failed to deprive him of a sub-conscious belief in an actual place "above," a material Hereafter beyond the sky, and, when clouds cut him off from sight of the earth, he had a quaint, half-realized feeling of being in the ante-room of the Great House of many mansions, wherein dwelt Lenore.

Yes, when flying, Colonel John Decies felt that he was nearer to the woman he had lost nearly a quarter of a century before. In one sense he may have been so, for he was a very reckless airman, and never in greater danger than when engaged in what he called "ground-scouring" among the air-current haunted, mist-haunted mountains of the Border. He anticipated an early Border-war and realized that here would be a great opportunity for a keen-sighted and iron-nerved medical airman to locate, if not to pick up, overlooked wounded. Here, too, would be a double need of such service in a country where "the women come out to cut up what remains"! Imagine, too, cavalry reconnaissances and bad casualties a score of miles from medical help ...

Whether it brought him nearer in any sense to Lenore de Warrenne, it brought him nearer to her son, on one of those hundred-mile circular "scours" which he practised when opportunity offered, generally accompanied by a like-minded officer of the R.A.M.C., to which Corps he had become a kind of unofficial and honorary instructor in "First-Aid Flying" at the Kot Ghazi flying-school, situate in the plains at the foot of the "Roof of the World".

"Hullo!" said Colonel John Decies to himself—"vultures! I suppose they might be referred to in my manual as a likely guide to the wounded. Good idea. 'The flying casualty-scout should always take note of the conduct of vultures, noting the direction of flight if any are seen dropping to earth. These birds may prove invaluable guides. A collection of them on the ground may indicate a wounded man who may be alive.' ..."

The Colonel was thinking of his *magnum opus*, "The Aeroplane and the Surgeon, in War," wherewith he lived laborious days at Bimariabad in the intervals of testing, developing, and demonstrating his theories at Kot Ghazi.

Turning his head, he shouted to Surgeon-Captain Digby-Soames, R.A.M.C., his passenger and pupil:—

"Vultures on the left-front or starboard bow. 'Invariable battle-field sign of wounded man. Note spot if unable to land and rescue. Call up stretcher-party by signal—*Vide* page 100 of Decies' great work,' what?"

"By Jove, it is a wounded man," replied Captain Digby-Soames, who was using field-glasses. "Damned if it isn't a Sahib, too! Out shikarring and sprained his ankle, I suppose. Dead, I'm afraid. Poor devil!"

"Vultures aren't *at work*, anyhow," commented Colonel Decies. "Can't land anywhere hereabouts, and I'm afraid 'calling up the stretcher party' isn't in the game here."

"Nothing nearer than Kot Ghazi and that's a good thirty miles," replied Captain Digby-Soames as the aeroplane hovered and slowly sank.

"Let's see all we can and then find the nearest landing-place. Search all round for any sign of a tent or encampment. There may be a dak-bungalow somewhere down in the plains, too. The river-bed down on the right there, marks the border."

Captain Digby-Soames "scoured" earnestly with his glasses.

"Camel on the port-bow, at the foot of the hills," he announced. "What may be a dak-bungalow several miles away ... a white square dot, anyhow ... Camel saddled up, kneeling ... His, no doubt. Wonder where his shikarri is—"

As the aeroplane approached, the disappointed vultures departed, misliking the size, shape and sounds of the strange fowl. As it passed over him, and the Major shouted, Dam opened his eyes.

This must be pretty well the end—when he heard the voice of some one he knew well, and saw a flying-machine just above him. He would see blocks of ice and cascades of cold water in a moment, doubtless, and hear Lucille calling.

A flying-machine in Ghazistan! The voice of an old, old friend to whom he could not, for the moment, give a name ... Why couldn't the cowardly brutes of vultures begin their business, and end his? What was that familiar voice calling:—

"Hold on a bit, we'll soon be with you! Don't give up. We can't land just here. If we drop anything can you crawl and get it?"

"He opened his eyes," said Captain Digby-Soames, "but I doubt if he's conscious. He must have come a frightful cropper. You can see there's a compound fracture of the right femur from here, and one of his feet is fairly pointing backwards. Blood from the mouth, too. Anyhow he's alive. Better shoot him if we can't shift him——"

"We'll *get* him all right. This is a Heaven-sent 'problem' and we'll solve it—and I'll quote it in my 'manual'. Quite war-conditions. Very badly wounded man—-inaccessible position—stretcher-parties all out of sight—aeroplane can't land for any first-aid nor to pick up the casualty—*excellent* problem and demonstration. That oont[28] will simplify it, though. Look here—I'll drop down and land you by it, and then come here again and hover. You bring the beast up—you'll be able to ride most of the way if you zig-zag, and lead him most of the rest. Then you'll have to carry the casualty to the oont and bring him down."

The aeroplane swooped down and grounded gently within a hundred yards of the kneeling camel, who eyed it with the cold and supercilious disdain of his kind.

"Tell you what," said Colonel Decies, "when I get up there again, have a good squint and see if you think you can locate the spot for yourself from below. If you can, I'll come down again and we'll both go up on the oont. Bring the poor beggar down much better if one of us can hold him while the other drives the camel. It's no Grand Trunk Road, by Jove."

"Right-O," acquiesced Captain Digby-Soames. "If I can get a clear bearing to a point immediately below where you hover, I'll lie flat on the ground as an affirmative signal. If there's no good landmark I'll stay perpendicular, what?"

"That's it," said Colonel Decies, and, with a swift run and throbbing whirr, the aeroplane soared from the ground and rose to where, a thousand feet from the plain, lay the mangled "problem". As it came to a halt and hovered[29] (like a gigantic dragon-fly poised on its invisibly-rapid wings above a pool), the junior officer's practised eye noted a practicable gully that debouched on a level with, and not far from, the ledge over which the aeroplane hung, and that a stunted thorn-tree stood below the shelf and two large cactus bushes on its immediate left. Having taken careful note of other landmarks and glanced at the sun, he lay on the ground at full length for a minute and then arose and approached the camel, who greeted him with a bubbling snarl. On its great double saddle were a gun-cover and a long cane, while from it dangled a haversack, camera, cartridge-case, satchel, canvas water-bag, and a cord-net holdall of odds and ends.

174

Obviously the "problem's" shikar-camel. Apparently he was out without any shikarri, orderly, or servant—a foolish thing to do when stalking in country in which a sprained ankle is more than a possibility, and a long-range bullet in the back a probability anywhere on that side of the border.

The aeroplane returned to earth and grounded near by. Stopping the engine Colonel Decies climbed out and swung himself into the rear seat of the camel saddle. Captain Digby-Soames sprang into the front one and the camel lurched to its feet, and was driven to the mouth of the gully which the Captain had noted as running up to the scene of the tragedy.

To and fro, in and out of the gully, winding, zig-zagging, often travelling a hundred yards to make a dozen, the sure-footed and well-trained beast made its way upward.

"Coming down will be joy," observed the Colonel. "I'd sooner be on a broken aeroplane in a cyclone."

"Better hop off here, I should think," said Captain Digby-Soames anon. "We can lead him a good way yet, though. Case of divided we stand, united we fall. Let him fall by himself if he wants to," and at the next reasonably level spot the camel was made to kneel, that his riders might descend. Slithering down from a standing camel is not a sport to practise on a steep hillside, if indulged in at all.

Another winding, scrambling climb and the head of the nullah was reached.

"Have to get the beast kneeling when we climb down to him with the casualty," opined the Colonel. "Better get him down here, I think. Doesn't seem any decent place farther on," and the camel was brought to an anchor and left to his own devices.

"By Jove, the poor beggar *has* come a purler," said Captain Digby-Soames, as the two bent over the apparently unconscious man.

"Ever seen him at Kot Ghazi or Bimariabad?" inquired Colonel Decies.

"No," said the Captain, "never seen him anywhere. Why—have you?"

"Certainly seen him somewhere—trying to remember where. I thought perhaps it might have been at the flying-school or at one of the messes. Can't place him at all, but I'll swear I've met him."

"Manoeuvres, perhaps," suggested the other, "or 'board ship."

"Extraordinary thing is that I feel I *ought* to know him well. Something most familiar about the face. I'm afraid it's a bit too late to—Broken ribs—fractured thigh—broken ankles—broken arm—perforated lungs—not much good trying to get him down, I'm afraid. He might linger for days, though, if we decided to stand by, up here. A really first-class problem for solution—we're in luck," mused Colonel Decies, making his rapid and skilful examination. "Yes, we must get him down, of course—after a bit of splinting."

"And then the real 'problem' will commence, I suppose," observed Captain Digby-Soames. "You couldn't put him into my seat and fly him to Kot Ghazi while I dossed down with the camel and waited for you to come for me. And it wouldn't do to camel him to that building which looks like a dak-bungalow."

"No. I think you'll have to stand by while I fly to Kot Ghazi and bring the necessary things for a temporary job, and then return and try to guide an ambulance waggon here. Oh, for an aeroplane-ambulance! This job brings it home to you pretty clearly, doesn't it? Or I might first go and have a look at the alleged dak-bungalow and see if we could possibly run him over there on a charpoy[30] or an improvised camel-stretcher. It'll be a ghastly job getting down. I don't know that you hadn't better stick to him up here while I go straight back for proper splints and bandages and so forth, and bring another chap too ... Where the devil have I seen him before? I shall forget my own name next."

The Colonel pondered a moment.

"Look here," he decided. "This case is urgent enough to justify a risky experiment. He's been here a devil of a time and if he's not in a *pukka* hospital within the next few hours it's all up with him. He's going to have the distinction of being the first casualty removed to hospital by flying-machine. I'll tie him on somewhere. We'll splint him up as well as possible, and then make him into a blooming cocoon with the cord, and whisk him away."

"Pity we haven't a few planks," observed Captain Digby-Soames. "We could make one big splint of his whole body and sling him, planks and all, underneath the aeroplane."

"Well, you start splinting that right leg on to the left and stiffen the knees with something (you'll probably be able to get a decent stick or two off that small tree), and shove the arm inside his leather legging. We've two pairs of putties you can bandage with, and there are *puggries* on all three *topis*. Probably his gun's somewhere about, for another leg-splint, too. I'll get down to the machine for the cord and then I'll skirmish around for anything in the nature of poles or planks. I can get over to that hut and back before you've done. It'll be the camelling that'll kill him."

At the distant building the Colonel found an abandoned broken-wheeled bullock-cart, from which he looted the bottom-boards, which were planks six feet long, laid upon, but not fastened to, the framework of the body of the cart. From the compound of the place (an ancient and rarely-visited dak-bungalow, probably the

176

most outlying and deserted in India) he procured a bamboo pole that had once supported a lamp, the long leg-rests of an old chair, and two or three sticks, more or less serviceable for his purpose.

Returning to the camel, he ascended to where his passenger and pupil awaited him. Over his shoulder he bore the planks, pole and sticks that the contemptuous but invaluable camel had borne to a point a few yards below the scene of the tragedy.

"Good egg," observed the younger man. "We'll do him up in those like a mummy."

"Yes," returned the Colonel, "then carry him to the oont and bind him along one side of the saddle, and then lead the beast down. Easily sling him on to the machine, and there we are. Lucky we've got the coil of cord. Fine demonstration for the Kot Ghazi fellers! Show that the thing can be done, even without the proper kind of 'plane and surgical outfit. What luck we spotted him—or that he fell just in our return track!"

"Doubtless he was born to that end," observed the Captain, who was apt to get a little peevish when hungry and tired.

And when the Army Aeroplane *Hawk* returned from its "ground-scouring for casualties" trip, lo, it bore, beneath and beside the pilot and passenger, a real casualty slung in a kind of crude coffin-cradle of planks and poles, a casualty in whose recovery the Colonel took the very deepest interest, for was he not a heaven-sent case, born to the end that he might be smashed to demonstrate the Colonel's theories? But no credit was given to the vultures, without whom the "casualty" would never have been found.

CHAPTER XIII.

FOUND.

Colonel John Decies, I.M.S. (retired), visiting the Kot Ghazi Station Hospital, whereof his friend and pupil, Captain Digby-Soames, was Commandant, scanned the temperature chart of the unknown, the desperately injured "case," retrieved by his beloved flying-machine, who, judging by his utterances in delirium, appeared to be even worse damaged in spirit than he was in body.

"Very high again last night," he observed to Miss Norah O'Neill of the Queen Alexandra Military Nursing Sisterhood.

"Yes, and very violent," replied Miss O'Neill. "I had to call two orderlies and they could hardly hold him. He appeared to think he was fighting a huge snake or fleeing from one. He also repeatedly screamed: 'It is under my foot! It is moving, moving, moving *out*.'"

"*Got it*, by God!" cried the Colonel, suddenly smiting his forehead with violence. "*Of course!* Fool! Fool that I am! Merciful God in Heaven—*it's her boy*—and *I* have saved him! *Her boy!* And I've been cudgelling my failing addled brains for months, wondering where I had seen his face before. He's my godson, Sister, and I haven't set eyes on him for the last—nearly twenty years!"

Miss Norah O'Neill had never before seen an excited doctor in a hospital ward, but she now beheld one nearly beside himself with excitement, joy, surprise, and incredulity. (It is sad to have to relate that she also heard one murmuring over and over again to himself, "Well, I am damned".)

At last Colonel John Decies announced that the world was a tiny, small place and a very rum one, that it was just like *The Hawk* to be the means of saving *her* boy of all people, and then took the patient's hand in his, and sat studying his face, in wondering, pondering silence.

To Miss Norah O'Neill this seemed extraordinarily powerful affection for a mere *godson*, and one lost to sight for twenty years at that. Yet Colonel Decies was a bachelor and, no, the patient certainly resembled him in no way whatsoever. The tiny new-born germ of a romance died at once in Miss O'Neill's romantic heart—- and yet, had she but known, here was a romance such as her soul loved above all things—the son of the adored dead mistress discovered *in extremis*, and saved, by the devout platonic lover, the life-long lover, and revealed to him by the utterance of the pre-natally learnt words of the dead woman herself!

Yes—how many times through those awful days had Decies heard that heart-rending cry! How cruelly the words had tortured him! And here, they were repeated twenty years on—for the identification of the son by the friend!

178

That afternoon Colonel Decies dispatched a cablegram addressed to a Miss Gavestone, Monksmead, Southshire, England, and containing the words, "Have found him, Kot Ghazi, bad accident, doing well, Decies," and by the next mail Lucille, with Aunt Yvette and a maid, left Port Said, having travelled overland to Brindisi and taken passage to Egypt by the *Osiris* to overtake the liner that had left Tilbury several days before the cable reached Monksmead. And in Lucille's largest trunk was an article the like of which is rarely to be found in the baggage of a young lady—nothing more nor less than an ancient rapier of Italian pattern!...

To Lucille, who knew her lover so well, it seemed that the sight and feel of the worshipped Sword of his Ancestors must bring him comfort, self-respect, memories, thoughts of the joint youth and happiness of himself and her.

She knew what the Sword had been to him, how he had felt a different person when he held its inspiring hilt, how it had moved him to the telling of his wondrous dream and stories of its stirring past, how he had revered and loved it ...surely it must do him good to have it? If he were stretched upon a bed of sickness, and it were hung where he could see it, it *must* help him. It would bring diversion of thought, cheer him, suggest bright memories—perhaps give him brave dreams that would usurp the place of bad ones.

If he were well or convalescent it might be even more needful as a tonic to self-respect, a reminder of high tradition, a message from dead sires. Yes, surely it must do him good where she could not. If there were any really insurmountable obstacle to their—their —union—the Sword could still be with him always, and say unceasingly: "Do not be world-beaten, son of the de Warrennes and Stukeleys. Do not despair. Do not be fate-conquered. Fight! Fight! Look upon me not as merely the symbol of struggle but as the actual Sword of your actual Fathers. Fight Fate! Die fighting—but do not live defeated"—but of course her hero Dam needed no such exhortations. Still—the Sword must be a comfort, a pleasure, a hope, an inspiration, a symbol. When she brought it him he would understand. Swords were to sever, but *the* Sword should be a link—a visible bond between them, and between them again and their common past.

To her fellow-passengers Lucille was a puzzling enigma. What could be the story of the beautiful, and obviously wealthy, girl with the anxious, preoccupied look, whose thoughts were always far away, who took no interest in the pursuits and pastimes usual to her sex and age on a long sea voyage; who gave no glance at the wares of local vendors that came aboard at Port Said and Aden; who occupied her leisure with no book, no writing, no conversation, no deck-games; and who constantly consulted her watch as though impatient of the slow flight of time or the slow progress of the ship?

Many leading questions were put to Auntie Yvette, but, dearly as she would have liked to talk about her charge's romantic trouble, her tongue was tied and she dreaded to let slip any information that might possibly lead to a train of thought connecting Lucille, Dam, and the old half-forgotten scandal of the outcast from

Monksmead and Sandhurst. If her beloved nephew foolishly chose to hide his head in shame when there was no shame, it was not for those who loved him best to say anything which might possibly lead to his discovery and identification.

While cordially polite to all men (including women) Lucille was found to be surrounded by an impenetrable wall of what was either glass or ice according to the nature of the investigator. Those who would fain extend relationship beyond that of merest ephemeral ship-board acquaintanceship (and the inevitabilities of close, though temporary, daily contact), while admitting that her manner and manners were beautiful, had to admit also that she was an extremely difficult young person "to get to know". A gilt-edged, bumptious young subalternknut, who commenced the voyage apoplectically full of self-admiration, self-confidence, and admiring wonder at his enormous attractiveness, importance, and value, finished the same in a ludicrously deflated condition—and a quiet civilian, to whom the cub had been shamefully insolent, was moved to present him with a little poem of his composition commencing "There was a puppy caught a wasp," which gave him the transient though salutary gift of sight of himself as certain others saw him....

Even the Great Mrs. "Justice" Spywell (her husband was a wee meek joint-sessions-judge) was foiled in her diligent endeavours, and those who know the Great Mrs. "Justice" Spywell will appreciate the defensive abilities of Lucille. To those poor souls, throughout the world, who stand lorn and cold without the charmed and charming circle of Anglo-Indiandom, it may be explained that the Great Mrs. "Justice" Spywell was far too Great to be hampered by silly scruples of diffidence when on the track of information concerning the private affairs of lesser folk—which is to say other folk.

When travelling abroad she is THE Judge's Wife; when staying at Hill Stations she is The JUDGE'S Wife, and when adorning her proper sphere, her native heath of Chota Pagalabad, she is The Judge's WIFE. As she is the Senior Lady of all Chota Pagalabad she, of course, always (like Mary) Goes In First at the solemn and superior dinner parties of that important place, and is feared, flattered, and fawned upon by the other ladies of the station, since she can socially put down the mighty from their seat and exalt the humble and meek and them of low degree (though she would not be likely to touch the last-named with a pair of tongs, socially speaking, of course). And yet, such is this queer world, the said lesser ladies of the famous mofussil station of Chota Pagalabad are, among themselves, agreed *nemine contradicente* that the Great Mrs. "Justice" Spywell is a vulgar old frump ("country-bred to say the least of it"), and call her The First Seven Sister. This curious and unsyntactically expressed epithet alludes to the fact that she and six other "ladies" of like instincts meet daily for tea and scandal at the Gymkhana and, for three solid hours, pull to pieces the reputations of all and sundry their acquaintances, reminding the amused on-looker, by their voices, manner, and appearance, of those strange birds the *Sat Bai* or Seven Sisters, who in gangs of seven make day hideous in their neighbourhood ...

180

"Are you going to India to be married, my dear child?" she asked Lucille, before she knew her name.

"I really don't know," replied Lucille.

"You are not actually engaged, then?"

"I really don't know."

"Oh, of course, if you'd rather keep your own counsel, pray do so," snapped the Great Lady, bridling.

"Yes," replied Lucille, and Mrs. Spywell informed her circle of stereotypes that Lucille was a stupid chit without a word to say for herself, and an artful designing hussy who was probably an adventuress of the "fishing-fleet".

To Auntie Yvette it appeared matter of marvel that earth and sky and sea were much as when she last passed that way. In quarter of a century or so there appeared to be but little change in the Egyptian and Arabian deserts, in the mountains of the African and Arabian coasts, of the Gulf of Suez, in the contours of the islands of the Red Sea, and of Aden, whilst, in mid-ocean, there was absolutely no observable difference between then and now. Wonderful indeed!

This theme, that of what was going on at Monksmead, and that of what to do when Dam was recaptured, formed the bulk of her conversation with her young companion.

"What will you *do*, dear, when we *have* found the poor darling boy?" she would ask.

"Take him by the ear to the nearest church and marry him," Lucille would reply; or—"Stick to him like a leech for evermore, Auntie"; or—"Marry him when he isn't looking, or while he's asleep, if he's ill—or by the scruff of his neck if he's well...."

(What a pity the Great Mrs. "Justice" Spywell could not hear these terrible and unmaidenly sentiments! An adventuress of the "fishing-fleet" in very truth!)

And with reproving smile the gentle spinster would reply:—

"My *dear!* Suppose anyone overheard you, what *would* they think?" Whereunto the naughty girl would answer:—

"The truth, Auntie—that I'm going to pursue some poor young man to his doom. If Dam were a leper in the gutter, begging his bread, I would marry him in spite of himself—or share the gutter and bread in—er—guilty splendour. If he were a criminal in jail I would sit on the doorstep till he came out, and do the same dreadful

181

thing. I'm just going to marry Dam at the first possible moment—like the Wild West 'shoot on sight' idea. I'm going to seize him and marry him and take care of him for the rest of his life. If he never had another grief, ache, or pain in the whole of his life, he must have had more than ten times his share already. Anyhow whether he'll marry me or whether he won't—in his stupid quixotic ideas of his 'fitness' to do so—I'm never going to part from him again."

And Auntie Yvette would endeavour to be less shocked than a right-minded spinster aunt should be at such wild un-Early-Victorian sentiments.

* * * * *

Come, this was a better sort of dream! This was better than dreaming of prison-cells, lunatic asylums, tortures by the Snake, lying smashed on rocks, being eaten alive by vultures, wandering for aeons in red-hot waterless deserts, and other horrors. However illusory and tantalizing, this was at least a glorious dream, a delirium to welcome, a wondrous change indeed—to seem to be holding the hand of Lucille while she gazed into his eyes and, from time to time, pressed her lips to his forehead. A good job most of the bandages were gone or she could hardly have done that, even in a dream. And how wondrously *real!* Her hand felt quite solid, there were tears trickling down her cheeks, tears that sometimes dropped on to his own hand with an incredible effect of actuality. It was even more vivid than his Sword-dream which was always so extraordinarily realistic and clear. And there, yes, by Jove, was dear old Auntie Yvette, smiling and weeping simultaneously. Such a dream was the next best thing to reality—save that it brought home to one too vividly what one had lost. Pain of that kind was nevertheless a magnificent change from the other ghastly nightmares, of the wholly maleficent kind. This was a kindly, helpful pain....It is so rare to see the faces of our best-beloved in dreams ... Sleep was going to be something other than a procession of hideous nightmares then ...

"I believe he knew me, Auntie," whispered Lucille. "Oh, when will Colonel Decies come back. I want him to be here when he opens his eyes again. He would know at a glance whether he were in his right mind and knew me."

"I am certain he did, dear," replied Auntie Yvette. "I am positive he smiled at you, and I believe he knew me too."

"I *won't* believe I have found him too late. It *couldn't* be true," wept the girl, overstrained and unstrung by long vigils, heart-sick with hope deferred, as she turned to her companion.

"Lucille! Is it real?" came a feeble whisper from the bed—and Lucille, in the next moments, wondered if it be true that joy cannot kill ...

* * * * *

182

A few weeks later, Damocles de Warrenne sat on the verandah of the Grand Imperial Hotel Royal of Kot Ghazi, which has five rooms and five million cockroaches, and stared blankly into the moonlit compound, beyond which stretched the bare rocky plain that was bounded on the north and west by mighty mountains, on the east by a mighty river, and on the south by the more mighty ocean, many hundreds of miles away.

He had just parted from Auntie Yvette and Lucille—Lucille whose last words as she turned to go to her room had been:—

"Now, understand, Dammy, what you want now is a sea-voyage, a sea-voyage to England and Monksmead. When we have got you absolutely right, Mr. Wyllis shall show you as a specimen of the Perfect Man in Harley Street—and *then*, Dammy ..." and his burning kisses had closed her mouth.

Was he scoundrel enough to do it? Had he deteriorated to such a depth of villainy? Could he let that noblest and finest flower of womanhood marry a—dangerous lunatic, a homicidal maniac who had nearly killed the man who proved to be almost his greatest benefactor? Could he? Would the noble-hearted Decies frankly say that he was normal and had a right to marry? He would not, and no living man was better qualified to give an opinion on the case of Damocles de Warrenne than the man who was a foster-father to him in childhood, and who brought him into the world in such tragic circumstances. Decies had loved his mother, Lenore de Warrenne. Would he have married *her* in such circumstances? Would he have lived under the same roof with her permanently—knowing how overpowering would be the temptation to give way and marry her, knowing how scandal would inevitably arise? A thousand times No. Was there *no* gentlemanliness left in Damocles de Warrenne that he should even contemplate the doing of a deed at which his old comrades-in-arms, Bear, Burke, Jones, Little, Goate, Nemo and Peerson would stand aghast, would be ready to kick him out of a decent barrack-room—and the poor demented creature called for a "boy," and ordered him to send, at once, for one Abdul Ghani who would, as usual, be found sleeping beside his camels in the market-place ...

Anon the gentle Abdul came, received certain instructions, and departed smiling till his great yellow fangs gleamed in the moonlight beneath the bristling moustache, cut back from the lips as that of a righteous Mussulman *shikarri* and *oont-wallah* should be.

Damocles de Warrenne's brain became active with plots and plans for escape—-escape from himself and the temptation which he must avoid by flight, since he felt he could not conquer it in fight.

He must disappear. He must die—die in such a way that Lucille would never suppose he had committed suicide. It was the only way to save himself from so awful a crime and to save her from himself.

He would start just before dawn on Abdul's shikar camel, be well away from Kot Ghazi by daylight and reach the old deserted dak-bungalow, that no one ever used, by evening. There Abdul would come to him with his *bhoja-oont*[31] bringing the usual supplies, and on receipt of them he would dismiss Abdul altogether and disappear again into the desert, this time for good. Criminal lunatics and homicidal maniacs are better dead, especially when they are tempted beyond their strength to marry innocent, beautiful girls who do not understand the position.

CHAPTER XIV.

THE SNAKE AND THE SWORD.

The dak-bungalow again at last! But how terribly dreary, depressing, and horrible it looked *now*—the hut that had once seemed a kind of heaven on earth to the starving wanderer. Then, Lucille was thousands of miles away (geographically, and millions of miles away in imagination). Now, she was but thirty miles away—and it was almost more than human endurance could bear.... Should he turn back even now, ride straight to Kot Ghazi, fall at her feet and say: "I can struggle no longer. Come back to Monksmead—and let what will be, be. I have no more courage."

And go mad, one day, and kill her? Keep sane, and sully her fair name? On to the hovel. Rest for the night, and, at dawn, strike into the desert and there let what will be, be.

Making the camel kneel, Damocles de Warrenne removed its saddle, fastened its rein-cord tightly to a post, fed it, and then detached the saddle-bags that hung flatly on either side of the saddle frame, as well as a patent-leather sword-cover which contained a sword of very different pattern from that for which it had been made.

Entering the hut, of which the doors and windows were bolted on the outside, he flung open the shutters of the glassless windows, lit a candle, and prepared to eat a frugal meal. From the saddlebags he took bread, eggs, chocolate, sardines, biscuits and apples. With a mixture of permanganate of potash, tea and cold water from the well, if the puddle at the bottom of a deep hole could be so termed, he made a drink that, while drinkable by one who has known worse, was unlikely to cause an attack upon an enfeebled constitution, of cholera, enteric, dysentery or any other of India's specialities. What would he not have given for a clean whisky-and-soda in the place of the nauseating muck—but what should be the end of a man who, in his position, turned to *alcohol* for help and comfort? "The last state of that man ..."

After striking a judicious balance between what he should eat for dinner and what he should reserve for breakfast, he fell to, ate sparingly, lit his pipe, and gazed around the wretched room, of which the walls were blue-washed with a most offensive shade of blue, the bare floor was frankly dry mud and dust, the roof was bare cob-webbed thatch and rafter, and the furniture a rickety table, a dangerous-looking cane-bottomed settee and a leg-rest arm-chair from which some one had removed the leg-rests. Had some scoundrelly *oont-wallah* pinched them for fuel? (No, Damocles, an ex-Colonel of the Indian Medical Service "pinched" them for splints.) A most depressing human habitation even for the most cheerful and care-free of souls, a terrible place for a man in a dangerous mental state of unstable equilibrium and cruel agony.... Only thirty miles away—and a camel at the door. *Lucille* still within a night's ride. Lucille and absolute joy.... The desert and certain death—a death of which she must be assured, that in time she might marry Ormonde Delorme or some such sound, fine man. Abdul must find his body—and it must be the body not of an obvious suicide, but of a man who, lost in the desert, had evidently travelled in

circles, trying to find his way to the hut he had left, on a shooting expedition. Yes—
he knew all about travelling in circles—and what he had done in ignorance (as well
as in agony and horror), he would now do intentionally and with grim purpose. Hard
on the poor camel!... Perhaps he could manage so that it was set free in time to find
its way back somehow. It would if it were loosed within smell of water.... He must
die fairly and squarely of hunger and thirst—no blowing out of brains or throat-
cutting, no trace of suicide; just lost, poor chap, and no more to be said.... Death of
thirst—in that awful desert—*again*—No! God in Heaven he had faced the actual
pangs of it once, and escaped—he could *not* face it again—he wasn't strong enough
... and the unhappy man sprang to his feet to rush from the room and saddle-up the
camel for—Life and Lucille—and then his eye fell on the Sword, the Sword of his
Fathers, brought to him by Lucille, who had said, "Have it with you always,
Dearest. It can *talk* to you, as even I can not...."

He sat down and drew it from the incongruous modern case and from its scabbard.
Ha! What did it say but "*Honour!*" What was its message but "Do the right thing.
Death is nothing—Honour is everything. Be worthy of your Name, your Traditions,
your Ancestors—"

He would die.

Let him die that Lucille's honour, Lucille's happiness, Lucille's welfare, might
live—and he kissed the hilt of the Sword as he had so often done in childhood.
Having removed boots, leggings and socks, he lay down on the settee—innocent of
bedding and pillows, pulled over him the coat that had been rolled and strapped
trooper-fashion behind the saddle and fell asleep....

And dreamed that he was shut naked in a tiny cell with a gigantic python upon
whose yard-long fangs he was about to be impaled and, as usual, awoke trembling
and bathed in perspiration, with dry mouth and throbbing head, sickness, and tingling
extremities.

The wind had got up and had blown out the candle which should have lasted till
dawn!...

As he lay shaking, terrified (uncertain as to whether he were a soul in torment or a
human being still alive), and debating as to whether he could get off the couch,
relight the candle, and close the windward window, he heard a sound that caused his
heart to miss a beat and his hair to rise on end. A strange, dry rustle merged in the
sound of paper being dragged across the floor, and he knew that he *was* shut in with
a snake, shut up in a *blue room*, cut off from the matches on the table, and doomed to
lie and await the Death he dreaded more than ten thousand others—or, going mad, to
rush upon that Death.

He was shut in with the SNAKE. At last it had come for him in its own concrete
form and had him bound and gagged by fascination and fear—in the Dark, the awful
cruel Dark. No more mere myrmidons. *The SNAKE ITSELF.*

186

He tried to scream and could not. He tried to strike out at an imaginary serpent-head, huge as an elephant, that reared itself above him—and could not.

He could not even draw his bare foot in under the overcoat. And steadily the paper dragged across the floor ... Was it approaching? Was it progressing round and round by the walls? Would the Snake find the bed and climb on to it? Would it coil round his throat and gaze with-luminescent eyes into his, and torture him thus for hours ere thrusting its fangs into his brain? Would it coil up and sleep upon his body for hours before doing so, knowing that he could not move? Here were his Snake-Dreams realized, and in the actual flesh he lay awake and conscious, and could neither move nor cry aloud!

In the Dark he lay bound and gagged, in a blue-walled room, and the Snake enveloped him with its Presence, and he could in no wise save himself.

Oh, God, why let a sentient creature suffer thus? He himself would have shot any human being guilty of inflicting a tithe of the agony on a pariah dog. There could *be* no God!... and then the beams of the rising moon fell upon the blade of the Sword, making it shine like a lamp, and, with a roar as of a charging lion, Damocles de Warrenne sprang from the bed, seized it by the hilt, and was aware, without a tremor, of a cobra that reared itself before him in the moonlight, swaying in the Dance of Death.

With a mere flick of the sword he laid the reptile twitching on the floor—and for a few minutes was madder with Joy than ever in his life he had been with Fear.

For Fear was gone. The World of Woe had fallen from his shoulders. The Snake was to him but a wretched reptile whose head he would crush ere it bruised his heel. He was sane—he was safe—he was a Man again, and ere many days were past he would be the husband of Lucille and the master of Monksmead.

"Oh, God forgive me for a blind, rebellious worm," he prayed. "Forgive me, and strike not this cup from my lips. You would not punish the blasphemy of a madman? I *cannot* pray in ordered forms, but I beg forgiveness for my hasty cry 'There is on God' ..." and then pressed the Sword to his lips—the Sword that, under God, had overthrown the *"Darling, I am cured! I have not the slightest fear of snakes. The Sword has saved me. I am a Man again."*

He told her all as she sat laughing and sobbing for joy and the dying snake lay at their feet.

In her heart of hearts Lucille determined that the wedding should take place immediately, so that if this were but a temporary respite, the result of the flash of daring inspired by the Sword, she would have the right to care for him for the rest of his life ... She would——

187

"Look!" she suddenly shrieked, and pointed to where, in the doorway, cutting them off from escape, was the mate of the cobra that lay mangled before them. Had the injured reptile in some way called its mate—or were they regular inhabitants of this deserted hut?

It was Lucille's first experience of cobras and she shuddered to see the second—evidently comprehending, aggressive, vengeful—would it spring from there ... and the Sword lay on the bed, out of reach.

Dam arose with a laugh, picked up his heavy boot as he did so, and, all in one swift movement, hurled it at the half-coiled swaying creature, with the true aim of the first-class cricketer and trained athlete; then, following his boot with a leap, he snatched at the tail of the coiling, thrashing reptile and "cracked" the snake as a carter cracks a whip—whereafter it dangled limp and dead from his hand! Lucille shrieked, paled, and sprang towards him.

"Oh, Dam!" she cried, "how *could* you!"

"Pooh, Kiddy," he replied. "I'm going to invite the Harley Street cove to have a match at that—and I'm going to give a little exhibition of it on the lawn at Monksmead—to all the good folk who witnessed my disgrace.... What's a snake after all? It's *my* turn now;" and Lucille's heart was at rest and very thankful. This was not a temporary "cure". Oh, thank God for her inspiration anent the Sword ... Thank God, thank God!...

SEVEN YEARS AFTER.

A beautiful woman, whose face is that of one whose soul is full of peace and joy, passes up the great staircase of the stately mansion of Monksmead. Slowly, because her hand holds that of a chubby youth of five, a picture of sturdy health, strength and happiness. They pass beneath an ancient Sword and the boy wheels to the right, stiffens himself, brings his heels together, and raises a fat little hand to his forehead in solemn salute. The journey is continued without remark until they reach the day nursery, a big, bright room of which a striking feature is the mural decoration in a conventional pattern of entwined serpents, the number of brilliant pictures of snakes, framed and hung upon the walls, and two glass cases, the one containing a pair of stuffed cobras and the other a finely-mounted specimen of a boa-constrictor (which had once been the pride of the heart of a Folkestone taxidermist).

"Go away, Mitthis Beaton," says the small boy to a white-haired but fresh-looking and comely old dame; "I'se not going to bed till Mummy hath tolded me about ve bwacelet again."

"But I've told you a *thousand* times, Dammykins," says the lady.

"Well, now tell me ten hundred times," replies the young man coolly, and attempts to draw from the lady's wrist a huge and remarkable bracelet.

This uncommon ornament consists of a great ruby-eyed gold snake which coils around the lady's arm and which is pierced through every coil by a platinum, diamond-hilted sword, an exact model of the Sword which hangs on the staircase.

"You tell *me*, Sonny, for a change," suggests the lady.

"Velly well," replies the boy.... "Vere was once a Daddy and a hobberell gweat Thnake always bovvered him and followed him about and wouldn't let him gone to thleep and made him be ill like he had eaten too much sweets, and the doctor came and gave him lotths of meddisnin. Then he had to wun away from the Thnake, but it wunned after him, and it wath jutht going to kill him when Mummy bwoughted the Thword and Daddy killed the Thnake all dead. And I am going to have the Thword when I gwow up, but vere aren't any more bad Thnakes. They is all good now and Daddy likes vem and I likes vem. Amen."

"*I* never said *Amen*, when I told you the story, Sonny," remarks the lady.

"Well you can, now I have tolded you it," permits her son. "It means *bus*[32]—all finished. Mitthis Beaton thaid tho. And when I am as big as Daddy I'm going to be the Generwal of the Queenth Gweyth and thay '*Charge!*' and wear the Thword."

189

Lucille de Warrenne here smothers conversation in the manner common to worshipping mothers whose prodigies make remarks indicative of marvellous precocity, in fact absolutely unique intelligence.

EPILOGUE.

Is it well, O my Soul, is it well?

In silent aisles of sombre tone
Where phantoms roam, thou dwell'st apart
In drear alone.
Where serpents coil and night-birds dart
Thou liest prone, O Heart, my Heart,
In dread unknown.
O Soul of Night, surpassing fair,
Guide this poor spirit through the air,
And thus atone ...

This sad Soul, searching for the light....

O Soul of Night, enstarred bright,
Shine over all.
Enforce thy right to fend for us
Extend thy power to fight for us
Raise thou night's pall.
Ensteep our minds in loveliness
In all sweet hope and godliness
Give guard o'er all ...
This brave Soul striving in stern fight....

Thou soul of Night, thou spirit-elf,
Rise up and bless.
Help us to cleanse in holiness
Show how to dress in saintliness
Our weary selves,
Expurge our deeds of earthiness
Expunge desires of selfliness
Rise up and bless ...
This strong Soul dying in such plight....

* * * * *

Night gently spreads her wings and flies
Star-laden, wide across the skies.
My Soul, new strong,
So late enstained with earthly dust
So long estranged in wander-lust
Gives praise and song,
Strives to create in morning light

191

The starry wonders of the night
In praise and song ...

This strong Soul praising in new right.
It is well, O my Soul, it is well....

A. L. WREN.

[Footnote 1: Store-room.]

[Footnote 2: Footman and male "housemaid".]

[Footnote 3: Gardener.]

[Footnote 4: Groom.]

[Footnote 5: Real, solid, permanent, proper, ripe, genuine.]

[Footnote 6: Anna = a penny.]

[Footnote 7: Strong, powerful chief.]

[Footnote 8: Grass-man.]

[Footnote 9: Carriage.]

[Footnote 10: Bullock-carts.]

[Footnote 11: A kind of starling.]

[Footnote 12: Water-carriers.]

[Footnote 13: Servant.]

[Footnote 14: Camel-man.]

[Footnote 15: Confined to barracks.]

[Footnote 16: A famous Hussar regiment.]

[Footnote 17: Teetotal.]

[Footnote 18: Cigarettes.]

[Footnote 19: When a non-commissioned officer does anything to risk losing his stripes he says he "chances his arm".]

[Footnote 20: Permanent Military Police.]

[Footnote 21: Summons before the Commanding Officer in Orderly Room.]

[Footnote 22: Guard-room.]

[Footnote 23: Infantry Regiments.]

[Footnote 24: Cavalry Regiment.]

[Footnote 25: Silent.]

[Footnote 26: This actually happened some years ago at Bangalore.—AUTHOR.]

[Footnote 27: News, information.]

[Footnote 28: Camel.]

[Footnote 29: By means of its "Decies Horizontal Screw Stabilizer," which enabled it to "hover" with only a very slight rise and fall.]

[Footnote 30: Native bed-frame.]

[Footnote 31: Baggage-camel.]

[Footnote 32: Hindustani—enough, finished, complete.]

12467807R00112

Made in the USA
Lexington, KY
11 December 2011